# Additional Praise for *The New Know*

Thornton May has his finger on a key mantra of the future: Mastery of information will differentiate world class enterprises from those that will flounder in the uncharted waters ahead. And the future masters of this universe will be those that excel at analytics—knowing not just that things are related, but why, and how. Seems simple, doesn't it? As anyone knows who has lived through the past year, it's just not that simple. This book shows you why.

**—J. Pari Sabety**
Director, Office of Budget and Management, State of Ohio

This book is nothing more than the usual from Thornton May. Brilliantly reasoned and insightful thinking, presented in a rational and eccentrically entertaining way as only Thornton can do. This book could not have come along at a better time. Analyze this!

**—Jerry Gregoire**
Former CIO of Pepsi Cola and Dell Computer Company, Chairman, Redbird Flight Simulations, Inc.

As the tub was to Archimedes and the apple to Newton, so is Thornton May to the CIO community. Thornton's unique style and insights create eureka moments on a regular basis. Known as much for his scathing wit and delivery as he is for his intellect, what truly sets Thornton apart is his intimate understanding of the CIO habitat and his ability to anticipate the future in a way few others can. In his new book Thornton takes a lifetime of observation and research and creates his magnum opus, a true Eureka for all of us.

**—Tom Murphy**
Senior Vice President and CIO, Amerisourceberge

It's not what you know, nor who you know it's HOW you know! *The New Know* unlocks the secrets of how to think for success in the Information Age 2.0 and best of all it's vintage Thornton . . . professionally provocative and endlessly entertaining.

**—Maria A. Cirino**
Entrepreneur and Venture Capitalist, Managing Director, 406 Ventures

Thornton May is one of those rare individuals whose line of sight always extends far beyond the horizon. In *The New Know* Thornton shares a thoughtful vision of the impact that unlocking the treasure trove of digital information being amassed will have on every aspect of our lives in the years to come. Fasten your seatbelt and discover how knowledge analytics is becoming the new alchemy transforming bits into insight.

> **—Dennis Devlin**
> CISO, Brandeis University

Everyone is on a transformational journey, rapid, glacial or somewhere between. This body of knowledge will help you speed your journey up tremendously. Whether your world is retail, services, hospitality, finance IT or …….. you will realize quickly upon picking up this work that you will gain significant advantage by reading and absorbing.

> **—Shannon Stowell**
> President, Adventure Travel Trade Association

# The
# New
# Know

# Wiley & SAS Business Series

The Wiley & SAS Business Series presents books that help senior-level managers with their critical management decisions.

Titles in the Wiley and SAS Business Series include:

For more information on any of the above titles, please visit www.wiley.com.

# The
# New
# Know

## Innovation Powered
## by Analytics

## Thornton May

WILEY

John Wiley & Sons, Inc.

For general information on our other products and services or for technical support, please contact our Customer Care Department within the United States at (800) 762-2974, outside the United States at (317) 572-3993 or fax (317) 572-4002.

Wiley also publishes its books in a variety of electronic formats. Some content that appears in print may not be available in electronic books. For more information about Wiley products, visit our web site at www.wiley.com.

**Library of Congress Cataloging-in-Publication Data**

May, Thornton A.
   The new know: innovation powered by analytics / Thornton May.
      p. cm.–(Wiley and SAS business series; 23)
   Includes index.
   Summary: "Learn to manage and grow successful analytical teams within your business Examining analytics–one of the hottest business topics today–The New KNOW argues that analytics is needed by all enterprises in order to be successful. Until now, enterprises have been required to know what happened in the past, but in today's environment, your organization is expected to have a good knowledge of what happens next. This innovative book covers Where analytics live in the enterprise The value of analytics Relationships betwixt and between Technologies of analytics Markets and marketers of analytics. The New KNOW is a timely, essential resource to staying competitive in your field"–Provided by publisher.
      ISBN 978-0-470-46171-6
         1. Business intelligence.   2. Technological innovations.   I. Title.
   HD38.7.M383 2009
   658.4'038--dc22

                                                                    2009024942

Printed in the United States of America
10  9  8  7  6  5  4  3  2

# Contents

# Foreword

## *The Blending of Insight and Technology*

### By Jean E. Engle

T hornton, in this book, has provided one of the most comprehensive perspectives on a truly unsung hero, the analyst. These are the go-to guys who seamlessly cut through the organizational bureaucracy and technical mumbo jumbo to succinctly turn data into a point of view that makes sense for decision makers.

One of the aspects that I enjoyed most is this book is not all about information technology or all about people, but that natural blend of human intellect with enabling technologies to produce insight out of chaos. It is refreshing to see the value of human intelligence highlighted in this enlightening discussion; it is far too easy to rely on technology to provide the "right" answers.

---

The views expressed are not necessarily those of the National Aeronautics and Space Administration or the United States Government.

I have had the fortune of working in an environment where analytics is critical to the success of human exploration. Every day at the Johnson Space Center, thousands of men and women work in one of the most complex organizations in the world making the almost impossible look easy. These dedicated personnel spend years devoted to the discipline of human spaceflight—a complete system of systems that requires in-depth analysis expertise in the definition, design, development, verification and validation, systems integration, science integration, testing, astronaut training, and operations tied to a strong safety culture and effective risk management to ensure mission success at every turn.

Where are the analysts located within the space center? They can be found at every level of the organization—are depended on at every level of the organization. The tools and technologies have certainly evolved over the decades; however, each successive mission has been built on the lessons and expertise gained from those preceding: the knowledge and wisdom passed from generation to generation. As we celebrate the fortieth anniversary of man's first steps on the moon, it is interesting to note that the computing capability in most hand-held devices is far more powerful than what was used in the Mission Control Center during that era.

The future of analytics is one certainly open for further debate, and Thornton has provided an excellent framework to shape the discussion. However, one cannot beat Yogi Berra for stating the obvious: "The future ain't what it used to be."

**Jean E. Engle** is the chief knowledge office for the Johnson Space Center. In this capacity, Ms. Engle is responsible for the development of an integrated knowledge management plan across the entire center as well as collaborating with other NASA Centers and industry to identify and utilize best practices. At Johnson Space Center, Ms. Engle has also held the positions of chief information officer, where she was named to the senior executive service of the federal government, and director of information resources.

Ms. Engle earned a BA in Mathematics and an MBA from the University of Houston—Clear Lake. She has been the recipient of numerous awards including the astronaut's personal award, the Silver Snoopy; two NASA Exceptional Service Medals; the JSC Certificate of Commendation; and the Goddard Space Flight Center Group Achievement Award.

# Foreword

## *Are We at the Advent of Something Big?*

### By John E. Chickering, CRM

Like it or not, the way we manage information today is not much different from how we, as a "superior" species, have done for millennia. Let's start with a very early form of recorded information: prehistoric cave drawings. The information is there, it's in an analog graphic format, and the rock on which it's written has proven to be more stable than anything sold by any technology vendor ever. Depending on your religious views, you may even regard the manufacturer as still "in business." Somebody decided to create this record, which means that we now have something more enduring than oral tradition.

So storing the data has been something we've been able to do for a long time. Where we've had trouble has been in access and meaning. The cave drawings required the user to be physically colocated (and with a light source) in order to support retrieval. That's an access issue. Once you get there with your torch, you then must ponder the two-dimensional characters that appear to illustrate people, animals, and weapons. That's when meaning comes in. Is the picture a menu? Is it perhaps a census record or an instruction manual? Or is it just art? Oh, and whose meaning is most important? Does it matter why the picture was created in the first place? Say it's art. If we can look at it today and infer something about the society, the picture in and of itself conveys information the artist may never have meant to record in the first place.

Over the next several centuries, we can see a thread of information management evolution that really doesn't go very far. We change technologies along the way, but information management doesn't go all that far. We became pretty good at creating paper, which allows for transportability far beyond what granite could provide, meaning we could bring the medium bearing information to the beholder. That was a step forward, but it did come at a cost, because we became so efficient at paper that we created another problem: too much to search through when seeking to know. We became so efficient that our ability to discern the fleeting imperative of what needs to be known at any particular instant requires the same basic set of skills: finding and understanding in a world of incredible volume growth.

Computers have only begun to make their mark. During the early automation years, we started a decades-long movement from simply keeping the computer running to getting it to do something useful in much less space. Individual applications came along, forming the infamous islands of automation and spawning a natural desire to link them together. As networks evolved, the connectivity helped exchange data, but meaning was something altogether different. Simply linking the computers together has proven much easier than connecting the information.

At the same time, two other trends were unfolding:

1. Storage media were getting cheaper and faster. Viewing the art had gone from "you had to be there," to "we'll bring you a copy," to a point where you could see it without anything being physically delivered. The "friction" of physicality that had both hampered and helped (think security issues here) us was melting away.
2. The ability to create a record was getting easier. What must have been a very arduous task in a cave was turned into mass production with the printing press and became so easy that we create huge

volumes today without consciously trying to create anything at all. No wonder some industry experts believe that data storage doubles in fewer than three years.

Based on my own survey of senior information technology (IT) professionals, we're pretty good at managing the data, but we have a way to go in managing the information. We know how to build networks, operate data centers, and set up multisite high-availability computing complexes resilient in the event of even significant disasters. We don't always do so, typically when the economics don't justify the investment, but we know how and the technology keeps getting cheaper. But the age-old twin challenges of finding and understanding remain today.

Once we make the technology cheap and reliable, the next frontier is for us to make it useful. Actually, we need to make it more useful for both ourselves and our customers than our competitors do. We make these investments so that we can deliver to our doorstep the information that will let us have the understanding we really need. We need understanding to take action and get rewards. And those rewards can range from finding a terrorist, to being first to market with the latest hot selling electronic gadget, to prescribing the right medical treatment the first time consistently.

I believe that conquering the next frontier will require more than simple technology savvy. It will require something more like a cultural shift. While a manufacturer doesn't have to know celestial navigation to ship parts and product overseas, understanding both the art and the science of supply chain logistics can create a competitive advantage. Knowledge as a competitive advantage comes when we have the ability to consistently work the interface between business (art) and technology (science) to know what we need to know, when we need to know it, where we didn't know what we needed to know when we first started. To raise the bar even higher, the competitive factor of copycat flattery means we can't expect our innovations to be unique competitive advantages for very long. We can't expect a one-trick pony to command the stage for more than a few moments.

Recognize that once we started making marks on rocks or paper or optical disks, information made a great leap from a transient asset (e.g., someone's memory) to a retained asset. Evolution in technology has helped with the ability to record and retrieve information, but the ability to apply understanding, to filter through the irrelevant to the critical nuggets of knowledge, has had trouble keeping pace. With volumes growing at rates unimaginable just a few years ago, we have data, data everywhere, but nary a drop to think. The data is all out there, stored several times over—but what does it all mean?

We're at a point where we need to move beyond simply getting the computers to run. We need to get the appropriate meanings to be as usable and sharable as the bits and bytes that we can push across networks today. Economic Darwinism tells us that the best among us—those who find the innovative ways to exploit technology and do it consistently better than our competitors and to the delight of our customers—will survive. This is about moving beyond having the data to knowing what we need to know when we need to know it. This is way more than a new project. It's a new business ecosystem to create a New Know.

**John E. Chickering** is a director at AIIM International (Association for Information and Image Management) and a vice president at a leading financial services provider. Mr. Chickering is an experienced consultant, software vendor, end user, and lecturer. He has also served as chief information officer at two human resource services companies and was a pioneer in the enterprise content management industry.
Mr. Chickering holds an MBA in operations research from the University of Maryland and a BS in marine engineering from the United States Merchant Marine Academy. He is the author of articles in the trade press and in peer-reviewed journals as well as an occasional speaker at both industry conferences and continuing education seminars hosted in academia.

# Introduction

# Standing at a Hinge of History

imelines and chronologies are a big part of knowing. We *know*
from physicists that 13 billion years ago, our universe started
expanding. We *know* from cosmologists that 4.6 billion years ago,
our planet, the rotating rock we call home, was formed. We *know* from
paleo-anthropologists that it was approximately 250,000 years ago that
our hominid ancestors first developed the capability of language, which
enabled the all-important and species-preserving trait: collective learning.
I knew from friends, colleagues, and thought leaders[1] that the time had
come to write a book[2] about a phenomenon and set of practices I came
to call *The New Know. The New Know* encompasses and celebrates the
tools, processes, people, and practices of business analytics (statistics, forecasting, operations research, and data mining).

Most readers are semi-aware (i.e., *they do not know*) that every
day—*every day*—there is more to know, more ways to know, and heightened expectations on the parts of customers, citizens, investors, and
regulators that you will do something efficacious with what you know.

The intersection of more to know, more tools to help us know, and expectations that we do something with what we know provides the environmental backdrop for *The New Know.* The New Know is a book, a time period, and a societal reality.

As we move forward from this point in time, unaugmented human cognition (the *old know*) is not sufficient. In every vertical market and just about every field of human endeavor, the magical carbon-chemo-electro processes known as thinking and the heretofore unaudited mysterious arts of decision making have to be linked with the tools, processes, and practices of business analytics if we are to expeditiously understand and then efficaciously act on the physical and virtual worlds we simultaneously inhabit. The mantra of the New Know age is to expeditiously understand and then efficaciously act.

The days of showing up, of attendance-based compensation, are *over.* The backlash associated with the bonuses paid to financial service executives involved in destabilizing the global financial infrastructure have created an atmosphere of measurement vigilantism. The desire to know will define the next quarter century. In the not-so-distant future, guessing/making things up, not having the right data, or employing the wrong algorithms to data will come to be viewed as termination offenses and egregious social taboos.[3] Your success—personal and professional—will increasingly come to depend on your ability to collect, organize, analyze, and act on the exponentially increasing mass of information that defines the first moments of the twenty-first century.

The global media, business school professors, and your children agree that most organizations are but passively engaged in managing the information swirling around and through them. A phrase increasingly heard in common parlance is "clueless." Many organizations don't even know what they know. Historically, plausible deniability (i.e., statements to the effect of "I didn't know") has been viewed as an acceptable excuse for poor performance. No more.

The big contemporary headline-grabbing news today is the after-the-fact shock and postmeltdown anguish regarding what senior executives did not know—about their employees, about their risk, about their cash flow, about their carbon footprint, and about their customers. The next big story, the headlines you and your team will be writing after reading *The New Know,* focuses on what can be known, what must be known, and most important what actions you will take because you know. This is the power of business analytics.

The new law of the new jungle stated simply is: Know and prosper; not know: Whither and die. You are standing at a hinge of history. The choice is yours.

Chapter 1 documents what can be known, what must be known, and how you come to know what (the various people, processes, and technologies whereby an enterprise migrates data to information, information to knowledge, knowledge to insight, and insight to action) has changed.

Chapter 2 documents how the rapid rise in data, the rapid expansion of tools, and maturation of information management processes are changing various vertical markets. I examine the advertising, agriculture, finance, government, grocery, healthcare, logistics, media, military, politics, retailing, science, technology, and transportation industries.

The New Know is changing how we do science, how we design and sell products, how we diagnose and medicate illnesses, how we run businesses, how we govern ourselves, how we fight, and how we relate to one another. What is "not knowable" and the permissible time frame for not knowing are undergoing a fundamental transformation.

Chapter 3 shines a much-needed spotlight on the professionals at the beating heart of business analytics. Analysts, you will soon discover, are very smart, interesting, and engaging people, doing very important things. These are people you should know and know about. I hope this book will serve as a wake-up call, similar to Rachel Carson's *Silent Spring* or Upton Sinclair's *The Jungle*.

The driving reason behind why I decided to write *The New Know* is because I really like analysts: the professionals who collect and organize the data; create the models and conduct the analysis that creates the insight that stimulates the action that leads to value. Over the course of the last year, I have immersed myself in the world of the analyst. This is a world little covered by the business or trade press and virtually unknown to many of the key decision makers at the top of the world's organizations—despite the fact that "statistics" and "analysis" surround us constantly.

Americans today are accustomed to a seemingly endless stream of questions from survey researchers, political pollsters, marketers, and census takers. They are equally familiar with the battery of results flowing from scientific investigation, of knowing that the majority of the nation supports the death penalty or that half of all marriages end in divorce. Public life is awash in statistics documenting phenomena as diverse as consumer confidence and religious faith.[4]

What is a bit surprising is that the people who crunch the numbers, create the models, and do the analysis have never really turned a social science or analytical lens on themselves. Socrates spoke of the power of the "examined life." The lives of analysts, for the most part, have never been systematically examined. *The New Know* is a humble attempt to at least partially fill that void. *The New Know* provides a map to the universe of analytics. No business book has really examined or celebrated these folks. This book will be the first vernacular ethnographic and anthropological study of the analytic community (patterned on anthropologist Ruth Benedict's *Chrysanthemum and the Sword*).

Being studied, and being privy to the results, is increasingly an understood and unexceptional feature of modern life. This book analyzes the analyzers. *The New Know* hopes to remove ignorance of the substantive and courageous work analysts do to make our world a better place. When possible, I attempted to use the tools of new journalism to bring the realities of *The New Know* front of mind.[5]

Most of the very fine books written to date about analytics or business intelligence tend to focus on ideas, methodologies, or technologies. This is a book about the people who conduct the analysis that makes life in these complex times possible. Business analytics is a critically important discipline that is tragically underfunded in most enterprises today.

Chapter 4 examines the habitat of the analyst. My research probed where analysts have been, where they are now, and where they are going. How do analysts live their lives? How do their minds work? What are some broadly held misconceptions about this very important subset of the working population? The data on analyst ethnographics is based on fieldwork—semistructured and conversational interviewing, individual and group observation, and the collection of documentation.

Every age has its heroes. During the mid-Industrial Age, Harvard scholar Joseph Schumpeter favored the word "entrepreneur"—the person who is willing and able to convert a new idea or invention into a successful innovation. Peter Drucker celebrated "knowledge workers." During the Internet boom, Bob Reich, Clinton's first-term secretary of labor, thought "symbol manipulators" would come to dominate society. I have no doubt that the new hero of the next age will be the analyst. This forecast is subject to one major contingency. Will the analytic community be able to master relationship management? Chapter 5 examines the day-to-day work of the analyst in context of the portfolio of relationships they manage and/or are managed by. What is working and what is not working, relationship-wise is highlighted.

Technology choice is an important success driver. Business history is full of stories of organizations that, upon making the right technology choice, moved on to greatness. The commercial fossil record also showcases the skeletal remains of entities guilty of "technological oversight"—of strategic missteps resulting from failure to notice or act on a technological opportunity. I believe that not stepping up to the value opportunities inherent to business analytics is a error similar in severity to choosing not to use fire. Chapter 6 utilizes three important frameworks to assess where business analytics sits in its life cycle and in its ability to add value to your enterprise.

Decision making has changed. Information systems used to be designed to move information to the top of the house. Senior managers were the ones who made decisions. In that world, technology tools for assisting decision making were designed for senior executives and managers. This is no longer the case. If you are not a decision maker, you probably won't have your job for long. The business analytics industry will continue to make tools for rocket scientist brainiacs. However, the market has expanded to include the rest of us mortals.

Chapter 7 examines how business analytics creates measurable value. I think evangelical enthusiasm is warranted in support of analytics. This surprisingly affordable, accessible, and powerful set of tools and practices is available to all and yet—inexplicably—many are still living in the analytical dark ages. Research surfaced that some organizations, although fully aware just how powerful analytics is and what a source of sustainable competitive advantage it can be, actively seek to keep it a secret. An executive at a prominent financial services firm in charge of customer analytics for one of the business groups told me:

> What we did was so critical I was not allowed to go out. I was asked many times to go out and talk about how we built this customer information management platform that joined U.S. consumer behavior and [our] business marketplace behavior. They found that so valuable that I was not allowed to talk about it outside because they didn't want competitors knowing what we had. It transformed [our] ability to look at share of wallet.

Organizations getting full value from their investments in business analytics ask themselves: Do we know stuff that nobody else knows? Do we see how the pieces fit together? Can we make connections nobody else can make?

This chapter also examines the facts of how innovation happens in complex organizations today. Most of the stories you read about innovation are false. James G. March, emeritus professor at Stanford University who is known for his groundbreaking research on real-world organizational decision making, explains:

> Changes in technologies, practices, and products are character-istically described in terms of the triumph of the new over the old. Initially a new idea, institution or practice is introduced into a small part of the system. Ultimately it becomes pervasive. The stories use the power of retrospection to identify individual and organizational genius in this triumph of good over evil.[6]

We humans like stories which feature humans as heroes.

Innovation is a crap shoot. As such, it is subject to probabilities and chance. As such, innovation performance can be materially improved by the enlightened use of business analytics. Oil companies know this. Pharmaceutical companies know this. Consumer packaged goods behe-moths know this. Globe-spanning quick-service restaurants know this. Shouldn't you? To innovate without the assistance of business analytics is madness.

Chapter 8 puts a stake in the ground regarding what we will know and how we will come to know it in the future. The "future" is not out there waiting to be discovered. What China's gross domestic product will be in five years has not already been determined. Whether the North American auto industry will continue to decline is not pre-ordained. Right now a particular probability for each of a broad range of possible futures is calculable. The question becomes: Is what we can know (probabilistically) efficaciously actionable?

Setting up a process to examine the future rigorously and seriously is not easy.

> The future is uncertain. Attempts to predict it have a checkered history—from declarations that humans would never fly, to the doom-and-gloom economic and environmental forecasts of the 1970s, to claims that the "New Economy" would do away with economic ups and downs. Not surprisingly, those who make decisions tend to stay focused on the next fiscal quarter, the next year, the next election. Feeling unsure of their compass, they hug the familiar shore.[7]

Peter Drucker, the patron saint of management, claimed that "forecasting is not a respectable human activity, and not worthwhile beyond the shortest periods."[8] Furthermore, in the spirit of full disclosure, it is worth noting that forecasters' track records historically have been pretty poor. For example, in 1984, European journalists asked four finance ministers, four chairmen of multinational companies, four Oxford economics students, and four London garbage collectors to generate 10-year forecasts on a number of key economic variables.[9] In 1994, they assessed the results and found that company chairmen had managed to tie with the garbage collectors, with the finance ministers finishing last.

You will have to read further for me to prove that business analytics has materially improved. One thing remains constant: We want to know the probabilities of what is likely to happen so that we can do *something* about it.

We know that people get to the future at different times (i.e., there are people who are ahead of the curve, in the middle of the curve, behind the curve, and those who don't even know there is a curve).

We know that organizations and individuals who embrace business analytics will operate at a competitive advantage over those who do not. Bruce Sterling, the science fiction writer and social commentator, speaking at the 2006 PopTech Conference told a powerful story detailing the folly of trying to compete without the tools at hand:

> An engineering professor at Harvey Mudd split his students into two groups. The John Henry group had to hit the library, the encyclopedias and were forbidden to use the net. The Baby Hueys were forbidden to access ink on paper, and had to use Wikipedia and "bizarre blogger blither." He had to end the experiment because "the Baby Hueys were wiping the floor with the John Henrys."

We know that business analytics can expand our capacity for foresight. What cannot be known with any confidence, however, is how people actually will use this technology. A reporter once asked Theodore Roosevelt if he knew what the American people thought— that is, what their immediate desires were. "I don't know what the American people think," Roosevelt groused. "I only know what they *should* think." *The New Know* puts a stake in the ground and states unequivocally that executives should think much more analytically in the future. The true magic is to figure out how to make that happen.

## Can Futurists Be Trusted?

I am a futurist. As a futurist, I am required to expose myself to a whole lot of thinking from a whole lot of people in a whole lot of places. For that reason, I am very well traveled. I am on the road about 250 days a year. I am a promiscuous networker. I go through about 1,000 business cards every five to six weeks. The purpose of all this movement is not to serve as a lab experiment for the commercial airline industry. The purpose is to place myself inside a flow of human experience with an eye toward understanding what people are thinking about, worrying about, and spending money and time working on.

Futurists love and live for hinges of history. An analysis of the past quarter millennium reveals that historical hinges have tended to occur once every 50 years or so in the early Industrial Age, once every 20 years in the later Industrial Age, and once every five years in the Meso-Information Age.[10] We know that change happens and that it is accelerating.

We futurists are pretty good at the rough timing of change. Sadly, we are not terribly accurate about what shape the change will manifest. From the "Overture" of George Friedman's very provocative *The Next 100 Years: A Forecast for the 21st Century*[11] we learn just how wrong futurists have been:

> If you were a European living in London in 1900 contemplating the future you would be convinced that war was impossible and European dominance of the globe assured. In the Spring of 1914, economically, politically, culturally, educationally, everything was getting better in every way in most places. And then World War I happened. . . .

> If you were living in London in 1920, there would be many questions on your mind but one thing was certain—the peace treaty that had been imposed on Germany guaranteed that it would not soon emerge. And then World War II happened. . . .

> In 1940, Germany had not only reemerged but conquered France and dominated Europe. From the point of view of most reasonable people, the war was over. Futurists might question the thousand-year Reich, but conventional wisdom thought Europe's fate had been decided for a century. Germany would dominate Europe. . . .

> In 1960, the United States had the Soviet Union surrounded and, with an overwhelming arsenal of nuclear weapons, could annihilate it in hours. The United States had emerged as the global superpower. It dominated all the world's oceans, and with its nuclear force could dictate terms to anyone in the world. Stalemate was the best the Soviets could hope for— unless the Soviets invaded Germany and conquered Europe. That was the war everyone was preparing for.

> In 1980, the United States was seen, and saw itself, as being in retreat. Expelled from Vietnam, it was then expelled from Iran as well. To contain the Soviet Union, the United States had formed an alliance with Maoist China.

In 2000, the Soviet Union had completely collapsed. China was still communist in name but capitalist in practice. NATO had advanced into Eastern Europe and even into the former Soviet Union. The world was prosperous and peaceful. Everyone knew that geopolitical considerations had become secondary to economic considerations, and the only problems were regional ones in basket cases like Haiti or Kosovo. And then September 11th happened.

Every 20 years, a new bit of conventional wisdom. Every 20 years, a new surprise to render the conventional wisdom not only wrong but dysfunctional. This being the case, it is understandable that readers would look with justifiable skepticism at anyone claiming that a new age was upon us. Authors who pen business books with the adjective "new" in the title frequently overstate the novelty of the age, method, technology, and/or phenomenon they are examining. They mistake or misinterpret a contingent thing as a new eternal. Recognizing this danger on the front end, I undertook to make sure that *The New Know* was in fact something new, not just a fad or short-lived blip on the cognitive radar.

In addition to an extensive literature search, I conducted numerous in-the-field interviews with practitioners, C-suite executives, industry analysts, and journalists. I buttonholed a select group of people who, in my opinion, over the years had demonstrated a unique and uncanny ability to *know* when something big was going on. Most of my magi agreed wholeheartedly with my hinge of history hypothesis.[12] All this nosing about and amateur ethnography indicates unambiguously that we stand at a hinge of history that requires commentary, sensemaking, and, most important, executive action.

## What Exactly Is a Hinge of History?

A door hinge separates two distinct zones of physical space. For example, the hinge swings between outside and inside of a room and the hallway. In a similar fashion, a historical hinge is something that separates two distinct temporal spaces. Prior to 1492, the North American continent was viewed one way. After 1492 and the visit of Christopher Columbus, the New World was viewed quite differently.

Students of basic history, perhaps for mnemonic purposes, portray the historical landscape as featuring abrupt ruptures between one chunk of history, era, or epoch and the next. These historical Rubicons place significant importance and emphasis on hinge dates—the dividing line between one era and another. Such hinges of history are a natural part of how humans make sense of the world. "Chunking" information in this way is not a learned strategy but is instead a fundamental aspect of the human mind. Indeed, if you don't think in hinges, you are a little unhinged.

The more literary among you will recall that Shakespeare had his tragic period (the years 1601 through 1608, when he wrote *Macbeth, King Lear, Hamlet,* and *Othello*). Art lovers among us know that Picasso had his "blue period" (1901 to 1904). Less sympathetic observers of the IT scene would have you believe that we are only now emerging from the "We suck less" era of IT leadership.[13] Mark Twain, a close chronicler of how Americans thought, viewed the American Civil War as a hinge of history, observing that, in the South:

> The war is what A.D. is elsewhere: they date from it. All day long you hear things "placed" as having happened since the waw; or du'in the waw; or befo' the waw; or right aftah the waw; or 'bout two yeahs or five yeahs or ten yeahs befo' the waw or aftah the waw.[14]

I believe we are currently standing at a hinge of history. It may not be as significant as the hinge that swung between living in trees and walking erect, having fire and not having fire, and hunting/gathering and agriculture, but I am convinced and the rest of the book will attempt to convince you that in these last years of the first decade of the twenty-first century, the changes we are living through are as momentous and life changing as the dropping of the atomic bomb over Hiroshima on August 6, 1945, and the fall of the Berlin Wall on November 9, 1989.

Hinges divide the world into "before" and "after." Big hinges require major rethinking. Alan Webber, close personal friend, mentor, former editorial director at the *Harvard Business Review*, cofounder of *Fast Company Magazine*, author of *Rules of Thumb: 52 Trends for Winning at Business Without Losing Yourself*, and the craftsman of the magnificent afterword that concludes this humble tome, agrees with my hinge of history hypothesis, "The time has come to rethink, reimagine, and recalibrate what is possible, what is desirable, and what is sustainable," he says.

Bernard Brodie, a brilliant new addition to the Yale University political science faculty, was an important player on the national intellectual scene. The Naval War College had assigned his book *Guide to Naval Strategy* as a standard text for officers. Brodie had established a solid reputation as one of the nation's foremost naval strategists. On August 7, 1945, he went to buy the *New York Times* at a drugstore in the neighboring village of Woodbridge. The banner headline captured his attention: "First Atomic Bomb Dropped on Japan: Missile Is Equal to 20,000 Tons of TNT; Truman Warns Foe of a Rain of Ruin." Brodie read just two paragraphs of the story that followed, looked up for a few seconds, turned to his wife and said, "Everything that I have written is obsolete."[15] The atomic bomb had changed the world.

The New Know has changed our world too. The combination of massive computing power, massive expansion in data management tools and practices, and exponentialized increases in customer expectations have created a world so complex and a customer so demanding that unaugmented human cognition—by this I mean making decisions without the assistance of a robust business analytic tool set—is no longer good enough. What you need to know, whom you need to know, how you come to know and the very abbreviated time window available for making efficacious use of knowledge are transforming.

Lawrence Summers, director of the White House's National Economic Council and Charles W. Eliot Professor at Harvard University's Kennedy School of Government, senses that we stand at a hinge of history. "I suspect that when the history is written 200 years from now, it will emerge that something very important happened in human thinking during the time when we were alive, and that is that we are becoming rational, analytical and data-driven in a far wider range of activity than we ever have been before."[16] Business, government, and society are moving from a faith-based mode of operation to a fact-based way of working. Is your organization ready for this fundamental transformation?

Hinges of history are important moments. They are filled with opportunity and risk. One of the biggest risks is not being aware that one is living in such a moment. Margaret Lavinia Anderson, who teaches "History 5: The Making of Modern Europe, 1453 to the Present, at Berkeley" likes to share with her students a cartoon from the *New Yorker* that portrays a town crier progressing through a European city center declaring "The Middle Ages are over, the Renaissance has begun. The Middle Ages are over, the Renaissance has begun." The joke of course is that typically—at least historically—people in a given age or epoch are not savvy to the labels later generations will use to describe the world they live in. People in the Dark Ages probably didn't know they were living in the Dark Ages.

The term "Renaissance" was first prominently used by the French historian Jules Michelet in 1858, and it was set in bronze two years later by Jacob Burckhardt when he published his great book, *The Civilization of the Renaissance in Italy.*[17] The usage stuck because it turned out to be a convenient way of describing the period of transition between the medieval epoch, when Europe was "Christendom," and the beginning of the modern age.[18]

One of the reasons I wrote this book is to make sure that readers know we are standing at a hinge of history, on the cusp of entering a new age—the age of the New Know, an age when just showing up is not enough.

An age is made more memorable and easy to grasp if it can be labeled by a word that epitomizes its spirit. I thought I would throw "New Know" into the ring to give people a cognitive buoy to float on until a better phrase comes along.

When we were astride another major change point—the fall of the Berlin Wall—the *New York Times* held a contest for readers to name the new age.

[T]the majority of respondents were male and extremely pessimistic. Popular labels included the "Age of Anxiety," "Age of Uncertainty," "Age of Fragmentation," "Age of [Great and Failed] Expectations," and "Age of Disillusion [and Dissolution]." One reader from NY suggested the "Cold War Lite Era" . . . From Greenwich High School in Connecticut came the "Era of the New Meanies." And one wag from Santa Monica offered the "Age That Even Historians from Harvard Can't Name."[19]

The historian David Halberstam called the epoch "a time of trivial pursuits." When it came to foreign policy, there was one phrase that the Clinton administration could not seem to escape: "post–cold war era." The president hated the phrase. "What kind of message does *that* send? It defines where we are in terms of where we've been rather than where we're going. I'm tomorrow's boy, and I don't like being seen as doing yesterday's business."[20] During the Clinton administration, Strobe Talbott was ambassador at large and special advisor to the secretary of state on the New Independent States. When he visited Stanford University in September 1997, Condoleezza Rice, provost of the university, slipped in one dig: The namelessness of the 1990s, she said, spoke volumes about the aimlessness of the administration. Talbott reported back to Clinton, "She's wrong about us not having a sense of direction, but she's right about our doing a lousy job of explaining it."[21] *The New Know* is my attempt to make sure that very important patch of time we are currently traversing does not go nameless.

Foreign policy mavens will recall that the age prior to the fall of the Berlin Wall was called the cold war. The person responsible for that name and the strategy for it was George Kennan. Kennan continually counseled national leaders that they should stop trying to come up with a clever name for the era and concentrate rather on what should be done about the emerging challenges of the age. He advised members of President Clinton's foreign policy team to embrace the world's complexities and compose "a thoughtful paragraph or more, rather than trying to come up with a bumper sticker."[22]

Executives need to be very mindful of what is happening in the world—the whole world. Leaders need to recognize that we are living in a moment when decisions *really* matter; a time when the buttons they push, the systems they deploy, the employees they hire, and the relationships they create will materially impact their personal and institutional success trajectories. One of the most important things leaders can do is understand and master the realities of the New Know.

The primary purpose of *The New Know* is not just to make you aware of the information explosion that exceeds the human brain's capacity to process and the litigational implications of ignorance in the world just around the corner. This is an awareness *and* action book. This book celebrates human agency—the capacity of humans to make and impose choices; the ability of an actor to organize future situations and distribute resources.

Observers of the business book publishing scene contend that the typical best-selling business book confirms or caters to what people already know. Many publishers use the metaphor of business executives in bookstores as owners of TV sets where the "picture is not right." Buying the book is a bit like banging on a television set. You know something is off. You don't know how to fix it. So you just take a whack. Empirical evidence seems to indicate that reading the book will not fix the problem. Awareness alone does not solve problems. As such, awareness-only business titles can be very frustrating. The purpose of great business writing is to open up the set, learning how the parts work, and developing the tools to fix the pieces that might be broken.

Upon reading *The New Know*, I hope executives will come to understand what is broken, who might be available to fix it, and the various paths other organizations, in a variety of vertical markets, have taken in their analytic journey to the New Know.

## Notes

1. Longitudinal studies of executive behaviors conducted over 30 years at UCLA's Anderson Graduate School of Management's "Managing the Information Resource" Program; executive education classes taught at University of California Berkeley, Haas School of Business; E-MBA programs at the Fisher College of Business at Ohio State University and the W. P. Carey School of Business at Arizona State University; the CIO Lyceum Research Series sponsored by Cambridge Technology Partners; the CIO Leadership Network and CIO Executive Summit Series orchestrated by Evanta; and the IT Leadership Academy at Florida State College at Jacksonville.

2. My closest associates will tell you that I am not really a book-writing kind of guy. I love books. Some of my favorite people in the whole wide world are the hardworking librarians at MacArthur Library in Biddeford, Maine. I hugely admire writers. I write a book review column for the prestigious and exclusive *CIO Leadership Network* that seeks to induce some of the world's busiest people to take time to pause, reflect, and read. However, personally I prefer more intimate, less formal, more carbon-centric forms of information exchange.

Historically when called upon to put something in print, I have preferred the path of writing prefaces. Preface writing places one on the cover, allows one to set the tone for the work that follows and is a whole lot less time consuming. In my career I have written prefaces for four very successful books: Marc Farley, *Building Storage Networks;* George T. Geis, *Digital Deals: Strategies for Selecting and Structuring Partnerships;* Stuart Robbins, *Lessons in GRID Computing: The System Is a Mirror;* and Jim Davis, *Information Revolution: Using the Information Evolution Model to Grow Your Business.*

3. Gary Loveman, thought by some to be "the most successful Harvard Business professor in the history of the school—is the CEO at Harrah's, says there are two ways to get fired at Harrah's: stealing from the company or doing an experiment without a control group." Michael Schrage, a fellow with the MIT Sloan School's Center for Digital Business speaking at the CIO 100 Conference, Colorado Springs, August 2008.

4. Sarah E. Igo, *The Averaged American: Surveys, Citizens and the Making of a Mass Public* (Cambridge, MA: Harvard University Press, 2007).

5. Clay Felker, the founding editor *of New York Magazine,* popularized a form of journalism known as new journalism. New journalism uses literary techniques typically found in novels (storytelling, drama, characterization, and location) to render nonfiction in a more accessible and interesting manner. New journalism tells a story. In Felker's words, "Don't tell me about the Holocaust, tell me about Anne Frank." *The New Know* intends to tell the story about the people—the analysts, the people who collect, organize, manage, manipulate, and extract insight from the data that surrounds us.

6. James G. March writing in the foreword of Raghu Garud, Praveen Rattan Nayyar, and Zur Baruch Shapira, eds., *Technological Innovation: Oversights and Foresights* (New York: Cambridge University Press, 1997), x.

7. David Rejeski and Robert L. Olson, "Has Futurism Failed?" *Wilson Quarterly* (Winter 2006): 14.

8. Quoted from the audio book version of Jeffrey A. Krames, *Inside Drucker's Brain* (New York: Penguin, 2008).

9. Peter J. Williamson, "Strategy as Options on the Future," *Sloan Management Review,* April 15, 1999.

10. Carlotta Perez at the University of Sussex asserts that, starting with the onset of the Industrial Revolution in Britain in 1770, an industrial transformation has occurred roughly every half century. See *Technological Revolutions and Financial Capital: The Dynamics of Bubbles and Golden Ages.* [Northampton, MA: Edward Elgar Publishing, Inc., 2002]. The research of Clayton Christensen, Geoffrey Moore, and Ray Kurweil roughly substantiates the "every five years, a new era" hypothesis.

11. George Friedman, *The Next 100 Years: A Forecast for the 21st Century* (New York: Doubleday, 2009), 2-3.

12. Ramón Baez, CIO at Kimberly-Clark; Bruce Barnes, former CIO at Nationwide Financial Services; Colonel Curtis Carver, vice dean for resources at the United States Military Academy; John Chickering, chairman of the Association of Information and Image Management; Keith Collins, CTO at the SAS Institute; Barbra Cooper, CIO at Toyota Motor Sales; Alan Cullop, CIO at Net Jets; Bob Dethlef, CEO at Evanta; Dr. Richard Dietrich, chairman of the Accounting Department, Fisher College of Business, the Ohio State University; Malcolm Frank, SVP and chief strategy officer at Cognizant; Paul Gaffney, COO at Desktone, formerly director of supply chain at Staples; Seth Godin, top marketing consultant in the world; Louis Gutierrez, former CIO of the Commonwealth of Massachusetts; Joanne Kossuth, CIO at Olin College of Engineering; John Lever, deputy CIO at Naval Meteorology and Oceanography Command; Ben Levitan, managing director In-Q-Tel; Ashwin Rangan, former CIO at Walmart.com; Dr. Robert Rennie, CIO at Florida State College, Jacksonville; Moshe Rubinstein, professor emeritus of engineering at UCLA; and Alan Webber, former editorial director at the *Harvard Business Review*.

13. It has been argued in certain circles that IT, rather than focusing on truly delighting end customers with exactly what they want and need, tends to point to infamous cases of IT nonperformance claiming, "See, we aren't as bad as those guys." This mode of benchmarking has been labeled by snarkier elements of the analyst community as the "We Suck Less" strategy.

14. Mark Twain, *Life on the Mississippi* quoted in Eviatar Zerubavel, *Time Maps: Collective Memory and the Social Shape of the Past* (Chicago: University of Chicago Press, 2003), 90.

15. Quoted in Fred Kaplan, *The Wizards of Armageddon* (New York: Simon and Schuster, 1983), 9–10.

16. www.president.harvard.edu/speeches/summers_2003/hsph_deans_council .php

17. Jacob Burckhardt, *The Civilization of the Renaissance in Italy* (New York: Penguin, 1990).

18. Paul Johnson, *Renaissance: A Short History* (New York: Modern Library, 2000), 4.

19. James Atlas, "Name that Era: Pinpointing a Moment on the Map of History," *New York Times*, March 19, 1995.

20. Quoted in Strobe Talbott, *The Great Experiment: the Story of Ancient Empires, Modern States, and the Quest for a Global Nation* (New York: Simon & Schuster, 2008). 326.

21. Ibid., 329.

22. Derek Choller and James Goldgeier, *America Between the Wars From 11/9 to 9/11: The Misunderstood Years Between the Fall of the Berlin Wall and the Start of the War on Terror* (New York: Public Affairs, 2008), 13.

# Chapter 1

# The Art, Act, and Science of Knowing

F rom the Dark Ages (ca. 476 to 1000 A.D.), during the Renaissance (ca. fourteenth through seventeenth centuries), at the center of the Age of Reason/Age of Enlightenment (ending ca. 1800), and right on up through the Industrial and Information ages, the history of humans has been one of ever-increasing knowledge. Wanting to know and eliminating not knowing is a big part of the history of our species. We have spent 1,000-plus years seeking to eliminate ignorance.

## Why are Humans at the Top of the Food Chain?

Have you ever wondered why humans sit on the top of the global food chain? If we did the classic SWOT analysis (strengths, weaknesses, opportunities, and threats) for humans vis-à-vis other animals, our species would come up short on just about every dimension. Humans are at the top of the food chain because of our capacity to know. Our eyesight is not exceptional. We possess no ability to see the ultraviolet light that guides butterflies. We have none of the night vision that aids owls and ocelots. We cannot see as far as eagles. We have none of the echolocation by which bats and whales hunt and orient. We are olfactorily challenged, having a very primitive sense of smell. We cannot run as fast as the antelope or swim as well as the dolphin; nor do we possess the strength of the lion. So why aren't we lunch?

Mythology tells us that Epimetheus—whose very name evokes lack of foresight—forgot the human species when it came to doling out features and functions. By the time deeper-thinking deities arrived, it was too late: While other animals were well provided for, humans stood naked and defenseless. In desperation, Prometheus stole from the gods the tools of fire and crafts and gave them to humanity. Whatever the reason, humans are, by nature, deprived of natural qualities. Other animals are naturally equipped to survive. Humans owe their survival to empirical, technical, and moral knowledge, which they acquire progressively. The trait that separates us from the lower orders, the thing that generates our interspecies competitive advantage, and the behavior that places us at the top of the food chain is our ability to know.

## Recent History of Knowing

The Information Revolution did not start with the Internet. Alfred D. Chandler, the respected business historian at the Harvard Business School, argues that Americans have been on the information highway for at least 300 years.[1] My former boss, futurist Alvin Toffler, was one of the first to situate the Information Revolution in relation to the long waves of history.[2] William Wolman, editor at *BusinessWeek*, and Anna Colamosca believe that "by endowing libraries across the country, Andrew Carnegie created an earlier knowledge revolution in the United States whose scope at least matches that of the information revolution created by Bill Gates and his competitors."[3] Tom Standage, science and technology writer at *The Guardian*, business editor at *The Economist*, and author of *The Victorian Internet* weighs in:

> Today, we are repeatedly told that we are in the midst of a communications revolution. But the electric telegraph was, in

many ways, far more disconcerting for the inhabitants of the time than today's advances are for us. If any generation has the right to claim that it bore the full bewildering, world-shrinking brunt of such a revolution, it is not us—it is our 19th century forbears.[4]

The nineteenth century was a great age for facts but not necessarily a great age for understanding what the facts actually meant or for acting efficaciously. Charles Dickens's Mr. Gradgrind, the notorious headmaster in the novel *Hard Times*, has become a symbol for the excesses of out-of-context, fact-based reasoning: "What I want is facts. . . . Facts alone are wanted in life." What is wanted in life today is not just facts but the meaning of what the interrelationships of those facts mean.

Collecting or moving information around certainly is not new. Humans have been attempting to extract insight from rudimentary data sets for a very long time. Sara Igo at Princeton University tells us that gathering social statistics "useful for governing" goes way back: "Rulers have counted, administered, and made 'legible' populations for military service and taxation stretching back at least as far as William the Conqueror's *Domesday Book* of 1086."[5]

The knowledge industry is changing. In my periodic role as a professor, I am perpetually attempting to convince students that the reason we are going through the learning exercise is not for the grade, it is for the future period action that the knowledge imparted during class enables (which may or may not have something to do with the letter grade received). I. I. Rabi, a great man at the great Columbia physics department (he received his Nobel Prize in 1944 for finding a method of measuring the magnetic properties of nuclei), is remembered for his science, his many kindnesses, and a famous quote: "If you decide you don't have to get As, you can learn an enormous amount in college."

The path to knowledge is changing. Outside of America, access to knowledge has been quite a structured thing.

In South Africa . . . I had waited obediently year after year to get to the level at which "they" would begin to teach "me" the things I was able to handle. It has never occurred to me that I could learn what I wanted when I chose. In America,

> I was alarmed to see students who set about learning things on their own. I'm still embarrassed to admit to myself that I almost never studied anything I wasn't officially taught.[6]

The Internet makes self-teaching—and lifelong learning—the rule rather than the exception.

Historians ultimately will come to consensus on what to call the time period between the frenzy that was the dot-com bubble and the period before society finally enters the data cloud. For want of a better phrase, I call the 20-year interregnum we currently inhabit (1995–2015) the Age of Little Information. I come to this label not because the age exhibits a lack of information. Quite the contrary, it is during this epoch that information—previously locked away in analog form—is becoming widely digitized.

The New Know has changed our reality along 10 fundamental dimensions.

## New Know Reality #1: You Will Be Expected to Do Something with Information

All this newly digitized information has had, relatively speaking, little impact on behavior and little impact on organizational outcomes. Shareholders learned recently that digitized information does not necessarily mean managed and/or acted-on information. We are now exiting a historical moment of undermanaged and only occasionally acted-upon information to an environment requiring much more active, much more intense, much more aggressive information management. You as an executive will be held much more accountable for your data management behaviors. You will be expected to transform "data lead" into "knowledge gold" via the expeditious sensemaking leading to efficacious action. In the Age of Little Information, we were data vegetarians. In the New Know we will have to become information and knowledge carnivores.

Perhaps the thing that sets the New Know most apart from previous eras is that because there is more information and more ways of knowing, there is *more* competitive advantage to be generated from the informed and creative management of information and information technology. This flies directly in the face of some industry observers who contend that technology—being a purchasable commodity—has nothing to do with competitive advantage. With more things to know there are more places to exert knowledge leverage and more tools to create competitive advantage. Increasingly, your success in business, your standing in the community, and your physical/emotional well-being are related to the facility with which you and your enterprise can connect and then convert heretofore unimaginably large, complex, litigatable, and accessible sets of data into time- and context-appropriate action.

## New Know Reality #2: There Really Is More to Know

The New Know will be awash with data. Attendees at technology conferences around the world are barraged with charismatic sound bites telling us how much data, how much storage, how much bandwidth, and how much computer power we have at our fingertips:

> [M]more transistors were produced, and at a lower cost, than grains of rice.[7]

> [T]he number of transistors shipped in 2003 was 10 quintillion, or 10 to the 18th power—about 100 times the number of ants estimated to be stalking the planet.[8]

> The "pixel to pupil ratio" is so far skewed in favor of the pixels that only a small fraction of imagery can actually be processed.[9]

> Our ability to collect and store data exceeds our current capability to thoroughly process and exploit it. But, that's just the tip of the data iceberg.[10]

> Data storage—oh my gosh—the data was everywhere. Our CEO [chief executive officer] became a little cranky when he could not find how much we gave to the United Way one year.[11]

> [I]f all six billion people on earth used hand calculators and performed calculations 24 hours a day/seven days a week, it would take them 46 years to do what the top supercomputer can do today in one day.[12]

> A new blog is created every second of every day.[13]

> When I came to MIT 40 years ago there was one computer shared by thousands of students that cost $11 million. Your cell phone today is a million times cheaper; a million times smaller and

a thousand times more powerful. That is a billion-fold increase in capability in price/performance. We will make another billion-fold increase in price/performance of information technology over the next 25 years.[14]

Stephen Baker has written one of the seminal works in the field of analytics: *The Numerati*. In the book, we are frequently reminded about just how much information contemporary executives have to deal with:

> [T]he very air we breathe is teeming with motes of information. Sloshing oceans of data, from e-mails and porn downloads to sales receipts, create immense chaotic waves. In a single month, Yahoo alone gathers 110 billion pieces of data about its customers, according to a 2008 study by the research firm comScore. Each person visiting sites in Yahoo's network of advertisers leaves behind, on average, a trail of 2,520 clues.[15]

The network of remarkable people engaged in a variety of world-changing projects who annually assemble at the PopTech Conference in Camden, Maine (www.poptech.org) have historically used a subset of these factoids as base planning info-benchmarks:

| | |
|---|---|
| 1 billion PC chips on the Internet | 1 million e-mails per second |
| 1 million instant messages per second | 8 terabytes per second traffic |
| 65 billion phone calls per year | 20 exabytes magnetic storage |
| 1 million voice queries per hour | 2 billion location nodes activated |
| 600 billion radio-frequency identification (RFID) tags in use | |

Just about everywhere you look and everything you read touches on the topic of information inundation. Educators worry that information inundation imperils our children. Public safety officials—the designers of police cars—complain that there is not enough room in a car for all the communications equipment that needs to fit into it. Aviation experts worry about information overload in airplane cockpits. (The magnificent new Boeing Dreamliner has over 300 computer systems on board.) NASA scientists have a whole lot of data on their hands. For example, the VW Beetle–size Landsat 5 launched in 1984 has circled Earth at an altitude of about 700 kilometers more than 130,000 times. Sensors on the polar-orbiting craft collect data at seven different wavelengths from near ultraviolet to the far infrared. Except for central Antarctica and far northern Greenland, the satellite passes over each spot on land once every 16 days and can distinguish features as small as 30 meters across. Since Landsat 1 launched in 1972, 2.3 million images have been gathered.[16] The National Security Agency is rumored to overhear far more information than it can make sense of. Race car engineers are overwhelmed by the amount of information relayed back to them from sensors on the cars. Oil wells are now so heavily instrumented that they produce geysers of data points that are harder to process than the oil. Warfighters, formerly thought to be isolated in foxholes by the fog of war, now have so much information available that a special project, Force XXI, has been developed to help cope with foxhole overload.[17]

Processing power doubles every 18 months. Storage capacity doubles every 12 months. Bandwidth throughput doubles every 9 months. The cumulative impact of this is that within our lifetime, every molecule on this planet will be IP (Internet protocol) addressable. There will be an incomprehensible, mind-explodingly massive expansion in the amount of information floating around. There is more to know. Julianne Conry, an educational psychologist who studies ability testing at the University of British Columbia, pointed out that each time U.S. testing companies revise their tests, "You have to know more to be average."[18] It doesn't matter whom you talk to—storage vendors, strategy consultants, futurists, subscription research firms, or your teenage children—everyone knows that in the future, there will be *more* information. What exactly does this mean, given that "raw human intelligence is probably no greater today than in ancient Greece"?[19]

One of the immediate implications of the New Know is that professionals skilled in augmenting human cognition will fare well moving forward. A recent survey at *Network World* places modeling, data mining, and optimization in the top 10 skill sets for the new age.

Jobs are plentiful for workers who understand data mining and related fields, such as information on demand, content management, and unstructured information management, experts say.

"The world revolves around data. Anything you can do to develop data analysis, data mining and information on demand skills is incredibly critical," IBM's [Kevin] Faughnan says. . . . "There's a broad range of issues involved with managing very large amounts of data and being able to process it and extract knowledge from that data," Professor Peter Lee, head of the Computer Science Department at Carnegie Mellon University says. "One of the things we are starting to see from leading-edge places like Google is the need for graduates with the understanding and skill to cope in the new world of data intensive computing."[20]

Organizations are having trouble keeping up—and, sadly, the fact that there are more facts arriving at a faster rate of speed is not even the tip of the cognitive iceberg. Soldiers fighting battles with projectile weapons speak of the "fog of war" (e.g., confusion about what is going on). Info-warriors speak of the "fog of facts" (e.g., confusion about what information is to be believed, what information sources are credible, and what version of reality is to be acted on). In a world of multiple sources of information and 24-hour decision making, the very character of information is changing. A "fact" is no longer a "fact."

There are entirely new categories of knowledge available that were previously off most executive radar screens.

### New Know Reality #3: You Will Have to Know More about Knowing

The typical time-starved, information-overloaded, regulation-complying, mission-obsessed, multitasking contemporary executive probably does not give much thought to how the organization thinks, or even how he or she thinks within the organization. The New Know involves knowing more about knowing. A newborn infant has very little appreciation about the stages of sensemaking whereby a sensory input of an apple somehow emerges as an understanding of what an apple is or that it is good to eat. Receptors in the toddler's retina collect data, which is converted into information, knowledge, and understanding. All of this sensemaking is, for the most part, invisible to our conscious selves.

In a similar fashion, the way organizations come to understand their environment is, for the most part, currently invisible to most individuals in the organization. The New Know is defined by making visible organizational sensemaking. It certainly is not headline news that information has become the single most important asset in most organizations. Many organizations are not where they want to be or have to be regarding the skills, mindset, technology base, business processes, or reward system/culture needed to best protect, manage, and share this critical asset.

One of the major changes defining the new competitive environment is the requirement to know more about knowing. You are going to have to expand your ability to think critically about your own thinking. Experts sometimes refer to this as metacognition: knowing about knowing. The latest research on executive decision making posits that the best predictor of good judgment isn't intuition or experience or intelligence. Rather, it's the willingness to engage in introspection— specifically thinking about thinking.[21] We are on the cusp of a revolution in enterprise-scale thinking, decision making, and problem solving. A "ThinkQuake" looms on the horizon. Society is about to undergo a tectonic shift in how it thinks about thinking.

Driving this cognitive plate shifting are the RSS feeds, podcasts, blogs, old-media headlines, and evening news programs, which are increasingly filled with images and instances of current-generation leaders being asked by dissatisfied next-generation voters, customers, and shareholders the rhetorical question: "What were you thinking?"

Looking beneath the surface, those next-generation customers, sources of capital, and policy makers are *really* asking: "How were you thinking? Via what processes, using what data, and assisted by what tools did you arrive at your course of action?"

**ThinkQuake Task 1: Cognitive Cartography.** For a powerful exercise, try to draw a series of maps that depict how your organization thinks. Be aware not only of what your organization thinks; also be granularly aware of *how* your organization thinks. How are decisions actually being made? Where are they made? Who's making them? And what's prompting the decisions?

Also, and more subtly, be aware of how your organization thinks about how it thinks. Do employees think they're being led? Or do they think they're scrambling through their days without much thought? Do they think they're thinking, or do they think the organization's managers and executives are doing most of the thinking for them? Take some time and think about these things.

**ThinkQuake Task 2: Cognitive Reengineering.** Readers will remember the frenzy of process reengineering projects initiated in 1990, which aimed to modify or eliminate non–value-added activities from the workplace. I forecast a similar surge of cognitive reengineering in organizations around the world, which will result in the deconstructing and rearranging of assumptions, rules of thumb, data sets, information sources, and decision-making algorithms that support key processes.

### New Know Reality #4: Brain Science and Decision Science Are Converging

Scientists do not know how the brain works—yet. But they are sneaking up on it. Readers may be surprised to learn that neuroscience has been around for over 100 years. Neuroscience has progressed to the point that we at least know what we do not know.

The brain has been discovered to be a very complicated place. There are 10 to the eleventh power neurons, 10 to the fourteenth power synapses. Psychological research tells us that at "any given moment our five senses are taking in more than 11,000,000 pieces of information."[22] Human behavior is thought to be the product of physical processes in the brain.

The field of neuroscience began to nudge its way into general public awareness about 20 years ago with the advent of brain-imaging tools of all kinds—from computed tomography, to functional magnetic resonance imaging, magnetocephalography, event-related brain potentials, positron emission tomography (PET), near-infrared spectroscopy, and single photon emission computed tomography. With these tools, the human brain itself could be studied. Humans were now front and center and directly under the scientist's eye.

Every day, neuroscience is making advances in understanding the human mind. Brain-imaging techniques now show not just the structure of the brain but its inner workings. Advances in neuroscience are providing us with an expanding understanding of how the brain generates complex thought and behavior. We move toward a closer understanding of how the brain enables action (everything from a simple movement to a thought). To some extent, it is a simple truism that the brain is involved with all things that comprise our human existence. It follows, loosely, therefore, that understanding the brain will help us understand the human condition more fully.

As the workings of the brain become known, the legal system will reflect these changes. "The law is mainly about brains or, at least, the mind," said Stanford law professor Hank Greely, one of the directors of the year-old MacArthur Foundation–funded Law and Neuroscience Project. "If my fist hits your chin, what, if anything, I was thinking is crucial. If I was in an epileptic fit, if I was thrown from a car when I hit you, you don't convict me of a crime. . . . If I'm mad at you, we do."[23]

We are still in the early days. "This is baby science, first-step science, like genetics in the 1950s," says Dr. Michael S. Gazzaniga, a neuroscientist at the University of California at Santa Barbara and member of the President's Council on Bioethics.[24] Understanding thinking, argues Vanderbilt law professor Owen Jones, involves more than understanding how the parts operate. "There is more to thought than blood flow and oxygen demand."[25]

The big news is that the brain is not a blank slate. The brain possesses innate qualities that influence individual experience and opinions. There are things that can be known—that need to be known by executives seeking to maximize value from the knowledge assets available to the enterprise.

The example of the political polling industry may be an early indication of where all this brain research is taking us. Studies suggest that our basic political attitudes—liberal, conservative, or otherwise—may have genetic or physiological origins.[26] In the very respected journal *Science*, a group of scholars presented data that indicates that while no one has yet discovered a gene for, say, supporting the war in Iraq, there does seem to be an association between a person's biology and her politics. The researchers demonstrated that the brains of liberals and conservatives are physically and functionally distinctive, suggesting that people on either side of the ideological divide are actually wired differently.

Kevin Smith, a University of Nebraska political scientist who coauthored the *Science* study, says: "Our research shows that these reactions are so deep-seated, they're partly biological. Our biological makeup contributes to our political attitudes."[27] The work of Smith and his colleagues is driving an emerging field, sometimes called political physiology, that challenges traditional views of politics. What we know about what we know and how we think is changing.

Japanese researchers at ATR Computational Neuroscience Laboratories in Kyoto have evidently found a way to capture images from the mind's eye. Yukiyasu Kamitani and his team first scanned for patterns in their subjects' brain activity. Subsequently, those brain activity patterns were used to re-create what subjects were visualizing, and the output, while crude, was readable.

> "By analyzing the brain signals when someone is seeing an image, we can reconstruct that image," said Kamitani. "By applying this technology," said an institute statement, "it may become possible to record and replay subjective images that people perceive, like dreams." Added said Dr. Kang Cheng, a researcher from the RIKEN Brain Science Institute, "These results are a breakthrough in terms of understanding brain activity. In as little as 10 years, advances in this field of research may make it possible to read a person's thoughts with some degree of accuracy."
>
> The implications have not escaped the scientists. "If you have a technique that allows you to read out what people are thinking, we need clearer ethical guidelines about when and how you are able to do this," said John-Dylan Haynes of the Max Planck Institute for Human Cognitive and Brain Sciences in Leipzig, Germany. "A lot of people want their minds to be read—take for example a paralyzed person. They want us to read their thoughts. But it shouldn't be possible to do this for commercial purposes."[28]

## New Know Reality #5: The Environment Is Changing Our Brain

The information flood should be viewed as a permanent macroenvironmental change. Thinking in Darwinian terms, what adaptive pressures does this environmental change place on us? "Daily exposure to high technology—computers, smart phones, video games, search engines—stimulates brain cell alteration and neurotransmitter release, gradually strengthening new neural pathways in our brains while weakening old ones. Because of the current technological revolution, our brains are *evolving* right now—at a speed like never before."[29]

Gary Small is the director of the Memory & Aging Research Center at the Semel Institute for Neuroscience & Human Behavior and the Center on Aging at the University of California—Los Angeles. His research indicates that Internet searching and text messaging has made brains more adept at filtering information and making snap decisions. "The average young person now spends nine hours a day exposing their brain to technology. What we are seeing is technology affecting our evolution."[30]

### New Know Reality #6: Information Management Is the Essence of Leadership

In her stump speeches, Carly Fiorina, former CEO at Hewlett-Packard, talks about how, as an undergraduate at Stanford studying medieval history and philosophy, she was required to read one of the great works of western philosophy every week. These were big books written by deep thinkers, such as Aquinas and Maimonides. The students were told to distill these 1,000-page tomes into 2-page papers. Fiorina believes that distilling truth from overwhelming amounts of information is the essence of leadership. She believes that all of us are overwhelmed with information, and what sets great leaders apart is their ability to cut through the clutter and distinguish the truly important from the merely interesting.

While the public considers science as a field dealing with certainties, scientific observations actually reflect probabilities of occurrence. The proper representation of scientific finding is difficult. In a sense, the nature of science has been misinterpreted for years. How does scientific evidence get into court? Strict criteria regulate the introduction of scientific evidence.

In American courts, the judge has become the "gatekeeper" and allows "good" scientific evidence into the case while preventing "bad" scientific evidence (as well as irrelevant evidence) from entering the case. How should a judge, trained in the law, make such a determination?

Information management issues are just now exploding onto the sociopolitical radar screen. In the United States and around the world, the short-term legislative agenda will be heavily populated with information management–related bills. Many of these bills will become law. These budding changes and the associated societal awareness are emerging as a direct result of the fact that in a transparent and mondo-connected society, leaders are supposed to know things. And perhaps more important, they are supposed to do things about what they know. The persistence of known problems that remain unsolved is absolutely unacceptable to voters, consumers, and sources of capital.

But how do leaders—within the organization and within the political landscape—know things? And how can they change the ways they think about the things they know? Business analytics is at least part of the answer.

A major driver of the looming ThinkQuake is the existence and innovative use of information management tools for business intelligence and advanced analytics, which provide the ability to evaluate data and information in more detail than ever before. With these tools, organizations can not only rethink the ways they think, but they can also take control and rethink the ways they lead.

During the dot-com frenzy, strategy was said to be all about competing on the basis of business models. In the New Know, we will be competing on the basis of mental models: how we think, how we move from data to information, from information to knowledge, from knowledge to insight, and finally from insight to action.[31] Organizations will be required to make more transparent how the enterprise makes sense of its environment. We will be audited on what we know and how we came to know it.

John Seeley Brown, former director of research at the fabled Xerox Palo Alto Research Center (PARC) facility, repeatedly tells would-be innovators, "The job of a leader is not just to make decisions, it is to make meaning." I believe the role of the new leader in the New Know is to create an environment (tools, practices, incentives, culture) that enables employees/contributors to make sense of the world(s) they confront every day. The signal-to-noise ratio for many people in the workplace is out of whack. They don't know what is important. They don't know how the pieces fit together. They are not just looking to you to tell them what to do; they are looking to you to help them make sense out of this sea of data/information.

You might ponder what traits and capacities will generate competitive advantage in the totally searchable, panoptically surveilled, information-flooded future. Additionally, you need to ask yourself: "Is your organization ready for all this data?"

I was fortunate enough to meet and learn from Ram Charan, the CEO-whisperer, lecturer-extraordinaire (winning the Bell Ringer best teacher award at General Electric's famous Crotonville Institute), and academic (winning Best Teacher Award at Wharton *and* Northwestern). Professor Charan is quite adamant that:

> You need information that is detailed, up to date, and unfiltered, obtained quickly and at the source. This is what I call *ground-level intelligence.* The most important type of ground-level intelligence has to do with customers. Take, for instance, Wal-Mart's observation that for the first time ever its sales of baby formula were coinciding with twice-monthly pay periods, indicating that consumers were under severe stress and living from paycheck to paycheck. That's ground-level intelligence.[32]

Good data, the kind of data that generates powerful insights, is not just lying around waiting to be bumped into. Leaders have to be able to discern the "wish it were true" from the "is true" haystack. "Truthiness" was the American Dialect Society's 2005 word of the year, defined as "the quality of stating concepts or facts one wishes to be true, rather than concepts or facts known to be true."[33] Low-cost communications give rise to almost toxic levels of spin, hype, and empty rhetoric. Leaders are able to cut through all the noise. Does your organization filter its data?

## New Know Reality #7: A More Connected World

Kevin Werbach, assistant professor of legal studies at The Wharton School, University of Pennsylvania, points out: "We've gone from zero to close to three-and-a-half-billion people who have a mobile device and are connected to each other."[34] One of the transformational elements moving society to the New Know is something analysts at

Forrester Research call the "groundswell."[35] In today's infoverse, not only must we manage data, we must also sense and respond to how constituents sense and respond to data about our products, services, and situation. Josh Bernoff, vice president at Forrester, contends: "There's so much information flowing out of the groundswell, it's like watching a thousand television channels at once. To make sense of it, you need to apply some technology, boiling down the chatter to a manageable stream of insights."[36] There is so much information—six hours of video are uploaded to YouTube every minute—it would take you a whole year to view one day of uploaded content.[37] The new scarce resource in the next economy will be the human attention needed to make sense of information. The question is: How will we be able to keep up?

## New Know Reality #8: Math Matters

Whether in science or popular culture, math is in ascendancy.

Mathematics is now so widely accepted as the arbiter of truth in the modern world that it has become the backbone of disciplines ranging from physics (of course) to economics and sociology. Backing up a statement with mathematics gives it an aura of validity, even if the topic has to do something as mathematically messy as human behavior. The popular CBS television series *Numb3rs* provides a good illustration of the western world's belief in the power of mathematics. In each episode, two mathematical geniuses are brought in by the FBI to solve intractable cases. By using the magical power of complicated mathematics, they can predict anything from the location of a hostage to where a sniper will strike next. Like modern dragon slayers, the mathematicians always save the day . . . and the hostage.

Of course, *Numb3rs* is theater. In the real world, predicting human behavior is enormously complicated. Just ask the people who utilize math programs in an attempt to predict how people will vote or the next big thing in the stock market. Reading chicken entrails or going with a gut feeling often can be just as effective as attempting to crowbar human behavior into a mathematical model.[38]

However, many otherwise "normal" executives have a pathological aversion to math. This is not just unfortunate, it is dysfunctional. Some intuition about numbers, counting, and mathematical ability is basic to almost all animals. An approximate number sense is essential to brute survival: This is how birds find berry-rich (many) versus berry-poor patches of berries. This is how primates traveling as a couple know not to attack a gang of six. People use math to make decisions every day. We rely on our basic number sense to choose which subway car to ride in or which grocery line to wait in (based on a quick estimate of the number of people).

In the early stages of his career, Charles Darwin wasn't much of a mathematician. In his autobiography, he writes that he studied math as a young man but also remembers that "it was repugnant to me." Darwin ultimately came around concluding at the end of his autobiography that he wished he had learned the basic principles of math, "for men thus endowed seem to have an extra sense."[39]

A new study ranking the 200 best and worst jobs in the United States by CareerCast.com ranked mathematician the best job (lumberjack was the worst) according to five criteria inherent to every job: environment, income, employment outlook, physical demands, and stress.[40]

"In an age where you need to be numerate to do almost anything (from building bridges to conquering disease), governments anxiously compare their performance in mathematics with that of competitor nations."[41]

Math has some surprising uses. Math has helped add clarity to the existential question of how long we humans will exist. Princeton astrophysicist J. Richard Gott III, working only semi–tongue-in-cheek, piggybacks on the Copernican method (i.e., we humans are not privileged observers of the universe—we don't occupy a particularly unique place in space or time) to calculate that our species should last for at least another 5,100 years but less than 7.8 million years.[42] Gott begins with the assumption that you and I, not living in a special time, are probably living during the middle 95 percent of the ultimate duration of our species. In other words, we're probably living neither during the first 2.5 percent nor during the last 2.5 percent of all the time that human beings will have existed.

## New Know Reality #9: There Are Significant Downsides to Not Knowing

Michel Eyquem de Montaigne, a French Renaissance statesman (1533–1592) is famous for his question: "*Que sais-je?*" ("What do I know?"). That was the sixteenth century. Success in the twenty-first century requires materially expanding what you know and adding precision and efficiency to the processes (analytics) whereby you come to know. Or what? Here is a metaphor to keep in mind as you think about the New Know. If you are locked in a room with an elephant, it is useful to know where it will step. Every key process in your enterprise is locked in a room with an elephant—a critical process, serving a critical customer. Business analytics tells you where that elephant will step. In our elephant-in-locked-room metaphor, business analytics saves your toes. In real-life business, analytics will keep you from being sued.

Litigation occurs when an event causes one party to believe it has suffered damages as a result of the negligence (in this case, not knowing) of another party. The U.S. tort system cost $252 billion in 2007, which translates to $835 per person.[43] International observers contend, "America manages to be more unbalanced than other countries. This is partly because its legal system is out of control—an unstoppable clanking machine that has lost any ability to draw the line or respect common sense."[44] Lord Peter Levine, chairman of Lloyd's of London, was concerned that such costs were rising at a rate of 10 percent annually. One of the downsides to not knowing is exposure to possible litigation.

Another is the opportunity cost associated with misallocating resources. Perhaps the most fundamental challenge facing any enterprise is how to invest its resources: Which is the best reward or goal to pursue at a given moment? Classical economics would tell us that the solution seems straightforward: Consider all options, and pick the best. However, rarely will a decision maker have equal information about all options. Typically, the nature and likelihood of rewards associated with status quo behaviors are better known than those associated with more novel/less familiar initiatives. The challenge always seems to come down to whether to persist on the current course or to shift to another. This problem—often referred to as the exploration-exploitation trade-off—is ubiquitous, appearing at all levels and domains of decision making.

## New Know Reality #10: Knowing Can Change the World

If knowledge is power, then "knowledge about power should be especially empowering," says John Murrell, the very-much-in-the-know editor of *Good Morning Silicon Valley*.[45] He is talking about the new Google initiative designed to "display near-real-time information on your household's electricity consumption." The plan is to display overall household use, allowing comparison by hour and day and some extrapolation about patterns and appliances. About 30 Google employees have been testing the feedback mechanism. Studies indicate that access to home energy information results in savings between 5 to 15 percent on monthly electricity bills.[46] Murrell explains that while "it may not sound like much, but if half of America's households cut their energy demand by 10 percent, it would be the equivalent of taking eight million cars off the road."

Residents of Massachusetts are also involved in a New Know energy pilot. Using 15,000 meters, a subset of National Grid Customers will be able access their energy-use information via the Internet, by a thermostat readout, or through text messaging, and use the data to change their consumption patterns. "The whole point of doing this is to finally create a two-way conversation with our customers," said Marcy Reed, a senior vice president at National Grid. The company's pilot program is expected to cost consumers about $57 million, or less than a dollar a month for each of National Grid's 1.3 million electric customers. But program participants are expected to save 5 percent, or about $70 a year, on their energy bills.[47]

Change advocates from all fields of endeavor are excited about the possibility of putting new information in front of people in the hopes of changing behavior. Ken Peterson, communications director for the Monterey Bay Aquarium, was excited about his layer in Google Earth that shows the location of various types of fish, along with ratings for people about whether they should eat those varieties or substitute others.[48]

# Notes

1. "A close look at the record clearly demonstrates that North Americans got on the Information Highway in the 1600s and by the late 1700s they were experiencing traffic jams. To carry the analogy further, Americans by 1800 could see highway construction underway [the U.S. postal system and roads for the mail to travel on], traffic regulations [copyright laws], and a variety of information vehicles cluttering the roads [e.g., newspapers, books, pamphlets, and broadsides]. During the 19th century Americans applied electricity and creative tinkering to invent or highly develop key information technologies used around the world: telegraph, telephone, phonograph, and motion pictures, among others. In the 20th century, they continued to add more vehicles to the Information Highway, most notably the computer and its smaller version, the ubiquitous personal computer. In short, Americans have been preparing for the Information Age for more than 300 years. It did not start with the introduction of the World Wide Web in the early 1990s." A. D. Chandler and J. W. Cortada, eds. *A Nation Transformed by Information* (New York: Oxford University Press, 2000), v.

2. Alvin Toffler identified the "information age" as the third wave, arguing that there have been two universal technological revolutions, or waves, in the way humans have organized their socioeconomic affairs (the agricultural and industrial) with the information revolution being a third.

   "The deployment and use of increasingly powerful information technology is the key driver of this third wave in the same way that emergent farming and industrial technologies spurred the previous two waves or revolutions. As we emerge from the transitional period between the second and third waves, society will have been remade. This remaking is reflected in the way states interact, in the way society is organized and the sorts of economic activities which will be valued and provide employment." Christopher May, ed., *Key Thinkers for the Information Society*, vol. 1 (London: British International Studies Association/Routledge, 2003), 3.

3. William Wolman and Anne Colamosca, *The Judas Economy: The Triumph of Capitalism and the Betrayal of Work* (New York: Perseus, 1999).

4. Tom Standage, *Victorian Internet: The Remarkable Story of the Telegraph and the Nineteenth Century* (New York: St. Martin's Press, 2007), 213.

5. Sarah E. Igo, *The Averaged American: Surveys, Citizens and the Making of a Mass Public* (Cambridge, MA: Harvard University Press, 2007).

6. Emanuel Derman, *My Life as a Quant: Reflections on Physics and Finance* (Hoboken, NJ: John Wiley & Sons, Inc., 2004), 25.

7. Semiconductor Industry Association statistic, "A Law of Continuing Returns," *Los Angeles Times*, April 17, 2005.

8. Gordon Moore, Intel Developer Forum, www.intel.com/idf/us/fall2007/attractions/moore.htm

9. Todd Hughes, Information Exploitation Office, "The Mapping Revolution," DARPATech 2007 (accessed August 9, 2007).

10. Dr. Kendra Moore, Program Manager, Information Exploitation Office, "Patterns, Patterns, Everywhere . . . " DARPATech 2007 (accessed August 9, 2007).

11. Vice President, Enterprise Architecture, major pharmaceutical company.

12. www.lanl.gov/roadrunner.

13. http://technorati.com.

14. Ray Kurzweil, *The Singularity Is Near: When Humans Transcend Biology* (New York: Penguin Group, 2006).

15. Stephen Baker, *The Numerati* (Boston: Houghton Mifflin Company, 2008), 5.

16. Sid Perkins, "Watching Earth for 25 Years. Happy Birthday to the Workhorse Landsat 5 Satellite," *Science News*, March 5, 2009.

17. Richard A. Lanham, *The Economics of Attention: Style and Substance in the Age of Information* (Chicago: University of Chicago Press, 2006), 7.

18. Kevin O'Keefe, *The Average American: The Extraordinary Search for the Nation's Most Ordinary Citizen* (New York: Public Affairs, 2005), 27.

19. Alan Greenspan, *The Age of Turbulence: Adventures in a New World* (New York: Penguin Press, 2007), 505.

20. Carolyn Duffy Marsan, "Top 10 Technology Skills," *Network World*, March 20, 2009.

21. Jonah Lehrer, "The Next Decider: The Election Isn't Just a Referendum on Ideology. It's a Contest between Two Modes of Thinking," *Boston Globe*, October 5, 2008.

22. Timothy D. Wilson, *Strangers to Ourselves* (Boston: Harvard University Press, 2004) quoted in Stephen Baker, The Numerati (Boston: Houghton Mifflin Company, 2008), 23.

23. Reyhan Harmanci, "Complex Brain Imaging Is Making Waves in Court," *San Francisco Chronicle*, October 17, 2008.

24. Robert Lee Hotz. "The Brain, Your Honor, Will Take the Witness Stand: Researchers Probe How the Mind Determines Crime and Punishment, but the Science Isn't Beyond a Reasonable Doubt," *Wall Street Journal*, January 15, 2009.

25. Ibid.

26. Eve LaPlante, "Born to Party: What Does This Mean for Our Democracy?" *Boston Globe*, November 2, 2008.

27.  Douglas R. Oxley, Kevin B. Smith, John R. Alford, Matthew V. Hibbing, Jennifer L. Miller, Mario Scalora, Peter K. Hatemi, John R. Hibbing, "Political Attitudes Vary With Physiological Traits" *Science* [19 September, 2008], 1667–1670.

28.  "I Had the Weirdest Dream Last Night—Here, Let Me Play It for You," *Good Morning Silicon Valley*, December 12, 2008.

29.  Gary Small and Gigi Vorgan. "Your iBrain: How Technology Changes the Way We Think—How the Technologies that Have Become Part of our Daily Lives Are Changing the Way We Think," *Scientific American*, October 8, 2008, digital version: http://www.scientificamerican.com/article.cfm?id5your-ibrain.

30.  Belinda Goldsmith, "Is surfing the Internet altering your brain?" Reuters [27 Ocotober 2008].

31.  Tom Davenport, *Competing on Analytics: The New Science of Winning* (Boston: Harvard Business School Press, 2007).

32.  Ram Charan, *Leadership in the Era of Economic Uncertainty: The New Rules for Getting the Right Things Done in Difficult Times* (New York: McGraw-Hill, 2009), 16.

33.  J. Walter Thompson Ad Agency (JWT), "10 Trends for 2008," *Work in Progress* (November 2007). See also: www.americandialect.org/Words_of_the_Year_2005.pdf

34.  "A World Transformed: What Are the Top 30 Innovations of the Last 30 Years?" *Knowledge@Wharton*, February 18, 2009.

35.  Charlene Li and Josh Bernoff, *Groundswell: Winning in a World Transformed by Social Technologies* (Boston: Harvard Business Press, 2008), 81.

36.  Charlene Li and Josh Bernoff, *Groundswell: Winning in a World Transformed by Social Technologies* (Boston: Harvard Business Press, 2008).

37.  Bowen Craggs & Company, November 3, 2008.

38.  Sheilla Jones, *The Quantum Ten: A Story of Passion, Tragedy, Ambition and Science* (New York: Oxford University Press, 2008), 8-9.

39.  Julie Rehmeyer, "Darwin: The Reluctant Mathematician," *Science News*, February 11, 2009, web edition.

40.  Sarah E. Needleman, "Doing the Math to Find the Good Jobs: Mathematicians Land Top Spot in New Ranking of Best and Worst Occupations in the U.S," *Wall Street Journal*, January 26, 2009.

41.  "Let's Talk about Figures," *The Economist*, March 19, 2008.

42.  Timothy Ferris, Annals of Science, "How to Predict Everything," *The New Yorker*, July 12, 1999, 35; and J. Gott III, "A Grim Reckoning," *New Scientist*, November 15, 1997.

43. Towers Perrin, *2008 Update on U.S. Tort Cost Trends*. 4. See www.towersperrin .com/tp/getwebcachedoc?webc=USA/2008/200811/2008_tort_costs_trends .pdf

44. "The Hypocrites' Club," *The Economist*, March 13, 2008.

45. John Murrell, "Google Test Drives an Energy-Saving Plug-in," *Good Morning Silicon Valley*, February 10, 2009.

46. Sarah Darby, "The Effectiveness of Feedback on Energy Consumption: A Review for Defra of the Literature on Metering, Billing and Direct Displays," Environmental Change Institute, Oxford University (April 2006).

47. Erin Ailworth, "Utilities Plan to Let Consumers Watch Energy Use," *Boston Globe*, March 31, 2009.

48. Stephen Shankland, "Why the Ocean Matters . . . to Google," CNET, February 2, 2009.

# Chapter 2

# A Transformed World

During the summer of 1987, the president of Fujitsu invited Alvin Toffler (*ur*-futurist and author of *Future Shock*) and Dr. Richard Nolan (Harvard Business School professor and creator of the stages theory of growth) to address 40 of the top executives in Japan about the forces driving the changes then taking place.[1] Following their formal remarks, one of the Japanese executives approached the two speakers. He said, "You have concluded that everything needs to change, and that information technology is integral to all these changes. Is that what you mean by transformation?" Dr. Nolan thought for a moment and then responded affirmatively. The Japanese executive replied, "I accept your advice."

You don't have to teach at the Harvard Business School or be a world-famous, best-selling futurist to know that our world is fundamentally changing. What can be known, the processes whereby things come to be known, the people who do the knowing, and the actions taken because of knowing are transforming. You—as the insightful Japanese leader concluded more than three decades ago—have to accept the fact that the world is changing, and you have to do something about it. One of the most important and highest-value things you can do is embrace analytics.

## Analytics Makes Change Understandable

Few will reject the notion that change is all around us. If you dissect this change—technological change, economic change, political change, psychological change, competitive change, social change—you will find analytics as a key causal element. Things change because there is a New Know—someone knows something he or she didn't know before and has taken action. If you want to understand the transformations taking place as you read this sentence, you will have to understand analytics. If you want to act efficaciously on these changes, you will have to master analytics. This should not come as a big surprise. Since the beginning of the scientific revolution, math as been an important part of humanity's ability to make sense of the world.

Russian economist Nikolai Kondratieff argued that the global economy moved through "long waves" of economic development. My former boss and mentor, Alvin Toffler, wrote eloquently about three technological revolutions, or waves, in the way humans have organized their socioeconomic affairs: agricultural, industrial, and informational. We are now entering a fourth wave—the Analytical Age. Rapid change is being driven by perpetually expanding knowledge. Analytics gives us the insight to act on that knowledge. Those actions transform the world.

Thomas L. Friedman, best-selling author and brilliant pattern observer, is a perfect example of the New Know. Speaking at the Massachusetts Institute of Technology (MIT) on May 16, 2005, about his book *The World Is Flat*, this exceptional storyteller told the audience that the way he convinced his bosses at the *New York Times* to give him time off to write the book was to threaten the publication with his looming ignorance. From his perspective, his *Know* (i.e., the mental model and the mechanisms through which he made sense of the world) was no longer good enough.

Prior to writing *The World Is Flat*, Friedman's research oscillated between Lexus issues (i.e., world trade, technology, and finance) and olive tree issues (i.e., geopolitics and ethnic conflict). After September 11, Friedman went with the rest of the fourth estate (global press corps) to cover and obsess about the olive tree wars. He and his fellow journalists operated in this mode until January 2004. At that time, while on assignment in India doing 60 hours of interviews, he came to the conclusion that the lens, framework, and perspective he brought to bear on his foreign affairs beat were no longer good enough. As he recalls:

> I got progressively sicker and sicker—and it was not the food. A sense I got with each passing interview that while I was covering the Olive tree wars, while I was looking the other way the world—the globalization story—had fundamentally changed. Something really big had happened. I couldn't explain it. What happened—I had missed something.

> I came home . . . I called the publisher of the *New York Times*, called my boss Gail Collins the Editorial page editor and said "I have to go on leave. I have to go on leave immediately because my software needs updating. The framework through which I am analyzing foreign affairs needs updating. I am seeing things out there I cannot understand and explain. If I don't go off on leave immediately I am going to write something really stupid in the *New York Times*."[2]

Everywhere you look, in every industry, in every department of every organization, executives around the globe are seeing this pattern replicated. Something really big is happening. (Remember John Chickering's "advent of something big" question in his foreword in this book?) New data no longer fits widely held incumbent mental models. Who in your organization is charged with watching the patterns of data and raising their hands when reality is no longer explained by existing mental models and frameworks? Who says, like Friedman, "Whoa, if we don't rethink, we are going to say and do something stupid?" It is the analysts who typically see the early signs of change. And yet, in most enterprises, these important voices are mute.

Everyone is on a transformational journey. If the enterprise is not well down the path toward analytic mastery, what it is doing *is not* good enough. It is that simple.

In the Age of Analytics, as products and services become "lighter" (i.e., less physical and more digital), manufacturing and distribution costs—while still important—will be augmented with new metrics—the costs of know, the flow of know, and the costs of not-knowing. The information value chain—arguably a huge potential source of competitive advantage—is undocumented and unmanaged in most enterprises today.

Michael Porter, the über-strategy guru at the Harvard Business School, introduced the value chain to the business mainstream in his 1985 best seller, *Competitive Advantage: Creating and Sustaining Superior Performance*. The value chain identified this set of interrelated generic activities common to a wide range of firms:

- **Inbound logistics:** Includes the receiving, warehousing, and inventory control of input materials.
- **Operations:** Value-creating activities that transform the inputs into the final product.
- **Outbound logistics:** Activities required to get the finished product to the customer, including warehousing, order fulfillment, and so on.
- **Marketing and Sales:** Activities associated with getting buyers to purchase the product, including channel selection, advertising, pricing, and so on.
- **Service:** Activities that maintain and enhance the product's value including customer support, repair services, and so on.

The information value chain consists of several general information management activities:

- Data collection and storage
- Data processing
- Integration
- Knowledge application[3]

## Finance Industry: One of the First to Be Transformed by Analytics

Myron Scholes and Fischer Black are widely credited with starting a math revolution on Wall Street in the mid- to late 1970s. Their method of determining the value of derivatives (the Black-Scholes model)

provided the conceptual framework for valuing options and precipitated a plethora of new financial products, from options to hedging
strategies.

Prior to that, in 1956, Bill Fair and Earl Isaac (a mathematician and an engineer from Stanford) came up with the idea of
replacing loan officers with a computer. By quantifying such financial information as payment history, bank balance, and accumulated debt, the machine could ascertain the probability that a given
person would be able to pay back a loan. This was a credit score.
Everyone has one. Financial service firms that had consumer credit
card usage patterns and analytical models could identify people who
could be cross-sold other products, such as insurance and other fee-
generating financial instruments. Organizations using customer analytics could ascertain which customers to retain because of their
long-term profitability.

The head of customer analytics at a progressive retail bank recounts
the early days of analytics:

> [I]n 2001, we started out as "database marketing" in the home
> equity and mortgage area. . . .We built the first ever prospect
> and customer fused database which looked across the coun-
> try at every single adult and their mortgage lending behavior,
> their credit behavior, their real estate holdings, and their internal
> banking behavior. . . . It was a huge hit. Everybody wanted it. . . .
> So my department grew. . . . [We were] using primary and sec-
> ondary data mining—segmentation, targeting models—to cre-
> ate leads [lead generation] that were piped out to the branches.
> Everyone was taking all of that information and constantly
> using it for targeted programs.[4]

The Web page of GE Capital states:

> GE Capital Solutions provides financing and services to busi-
> ness customers of all sizes to help them grow. Our synergis-
> tic product offerings include: equipment leasing and lending,
> inventory finance, fleet services and franchise finance, globally.
> Leveraging our deep industry and collateral expertise, our top
> priorities are excellent customer service and being a great stra-
> tegic partner.[5]

What makes this powerful statement much more than just marketing copy is the aggressive and informed use of analytics. GE Capital and General Electric have embraced analytics in a big way. If you want to see analytics being done right, if you want to see how being smart about what helps your customer is being baked into organizational culture, you should visit GE Capital. Deborah Wall, customer insights leader for GE Capital Americas, has been a champion of analytics for her entire career.

> [H]ere's the paradigm shift that I'm seeing. I think that understanding consumer behavior—through analysis of spending patterns and being able to segment and target the market—is critical to the recovery of the financial services sector. And I think the use of data mining instruments on all the information that's being electronically collected now, to synthesize it and look at patterns of types of people, is where we have to continue to go. The paradigm shift that I'm seeing is that, because the consumer now has many choices, they're in the drivers' seat, so marketing becomes a science of understanding consumers' and businesses' patterns of behavior. Analytics allows you to align your strategy to fit the most profitable patterns. Analytics gives you a map for staying away from—for not serving—those pockets of the market where consumers don't align with your financial goals or your ability to serve the marketplace.[6]

The rapid and widespread embrace of high-end/advanced analytics by financial service sector employers gave rise to a variety of "financial math" programs in universities across the world.

## Healthcare Will Be Transformed by Analytics

The disciplines of genetics, physics and engineering, pharmaceuticals, psychology and psychiatry, and computer science are each experiencing an explosion of what can be known. This inside-the-discipline knowledge expansion is but the tip of the New Know iceberg. Each new development inside a discipline has implications on related spheres. To practice medicine today, you must keep up not only with what is going on inside your own discipline but also be cognizant of the evolution of related disciplines.

Dr. George Poste, director of the Biodesign Institute at Arizona State University, told a multidisciplinary audience that as medicine begins "focusing on the molecular enunciation of the causal mechanism of disease as opposed to symptonotology driving eventually to the domain of personalized medicine," there will be more to know.

Dr. Poste commented on the exponentialized increase in the domain of "-omics"—genomics, proteomics, and metabolomics. He cited a recent survey showing there were 72 different forms of "omics" currently in circulation.[7]

Researchers at Intel are building and testing a portfolio of devices that go far beyond the pulse-taking/pill-counting medical gizmos that define state of the art today. Eric Dishman, an anthropologist who works at a research lab at Intel outside Portland, Oregon, sees sensors eventually recording and building statistical models of almost every aspect of our behavior.[8]

One Intel prototype—the "magic Carpet"—features webs of weight sensors placed under kitchen tiles which allow medical professionals and/or loved ones to monitor and dispatch details on a patient's changing weight. The sensors also could inform caregivers/send an alert if the person being monitored (an elderly parent perhaps) failed to walk into the kitchen one day.

Reductions in the cost/size of sensors, expanded bandwidth, and improved modeling/analytics will enable continuous health surveillance. Stephen Baker explains that all these medical sensors providing all this data to already overloaded physicians make the case for analytics.

Only good math can sift through these floods of nearly meaningless data to provide doctors with specific alerts. This isn't easy. In one Oregon study, people's beds were wired to monitor their nightly movements and weight. One woman, researchers were startled to see, gained 8 pounds between bedtime and breakfast. A dangerous accumulation of fluids? Time to call an ambulance? No, her little dog had jumped on the bed and slept with her. Culling the pugs and corgis from the data will be up to the Numerati.[9]

Medical information used to be expensive and only available to healthcare professionals. The Internet has changed all that.

> [W]hile waiting in line at my local drugstore an elderly woman in front of me argued with the pharmacist. She was worried about the interaction of several medications she was taking.
>
> "No," the pharmacist kept saying, "that's wrong. There's nothing to worry about."
>
> Finally, steadying herself on her walker, the woman pulled a printout from her purse and shook it in his face. "I downloaded this information!" she told him triumphantly."[10]

Everyone following the exploding, expanding, evolving field of analytics talks about the impact the Internet has had. Today, not only is medical information available online; so too are healthcare analytics. Informed healthcare consumers using basic computational functionality (i.e., an Internet connection and a search engine) can now gain access to clinical trials. Armed with this information, they are changing the conversation they are having with their physician. There is a New Know going on here. Medical Web sites, originally designed for certified medical professionals, are increasingly making themselves patient-friendly.

Ian Ayres has written an important book about analytics—*Super Crunchers.* He succinctly captures how analytics is transforming the practice (at least the education) of future doctors.

> The *New England Journal of Medicine* published a description of rounds at a New York teaching hospital. A "fellow in allergy and immunology presented the case of an infant with diarrhea; an unusual rash ['alligator skin']; multiple immunologic abnormalities, including low T-cell function; tissue eosinophilia [of the gastric mucosa] as well as peripheral eosinophilia; and an apparent X-linked genetic pattern [several male relatives died in infancy]." The attending physicians and house staff, after a long discussion, couldn't reach any consensus as to the correct diagnosis. Finally, the professor asked the fellow if she had made a diagnosis, and she reported she had indeed and mentioned a rare syndrome known as IPEX which fit the symptoms perfectly. When the fellow was asked to explain how she arrived at

her diagnosis, she answered: "I entered the salient features into Google, and it popped right up." The attending physician was flabbergasted. "William Osler must be turning over in his grave. You Googled the diagnosis? . . . Are we physicians no longer needed?"

The reference to William Osler is particularly apt. Osler, who was one of the founders of John Hopkins, is the father of the medical residency program—the continuing cornerstone of all clinical training. Osler would be turning in his grave at the thought of Google diagnoses and Google treatments because the Internet disrupts the dependence of young doctors on the teaching staff as the dominant source of wisdom.[11]

Dave Hammond is arguably one of the smartest guys on the planet when it comes to health data. He used to be the chief technology officer at Dossia (www.dossia.org)—the frame-breaking consortium of large employers united in their goal of providing employees, their dependents, retirees, and others in their communities with an independent, lifelong health record. He is currently vice president of information technology and architecture at Cardinal Health—Clinical & Medical Products. Hammond is very concerned that information about what's happening inside of hospitals and how medical devices are used is very siloed. Analytics helps executives see the big picture. It changes:

> [H]ow we look at things. And you know, it's a classic case of possibilities arising from looking at the data. Before the fact people ask me, "Well, what are we going to get learn?" I say, "I don't know, but I guarantee we'll come out with pretty good ideas."[12]

## Retail Is on the Cusp of Being Transformed

Location, location, location has always been an important mantra in retailing. The physical, visual, and economic aspects of a new retail venture or modification of an existing franchise, concept, or brand require extensive analytical prework. Not doing sophisticated analytics borders on malfeasance in retailing.

David Friedman, economist, legal scholar and professor at Santa Clara University walks us through how some basic analytics can help retailers decide where to locate a new store.

> If you discover that old people on average do not buy very much of what you are selling, perhaps a retirement community is the wrong place. If couples with young children do all their shopping on the weekend when one parent can stay home with the kids, singles shop after work on weekdays [weekends are for parties], and retired people during the working day [shorter lines], then a location with a suitable mix of all three types will give you a more even flow of customers, higher utilization of the store, and greater profits. Combining information about your customers with information about the demography of alternative locations, provided free by the U.S. census or at a higher price by private firms, you can substantially improve the odds on your gamble.[13]

Immediately after World War II, retailers applied the logistics expertise developed during the war (delivering men and materiel to all points of the compass) to the targeted task of store operations. The things of retailing were "industrialized." The customers, subjected to long years of rationing, coupon books, and doing without, were, as Stephen Baker cleverly phrased it, "processed like card-carrying herd animals."[14]

Fast-forward 50 years, and you find the game has changed. It is no longer enough simply to keep the shelves stocked. You have to stock the shelves with things customers want to buy. Doing this requires mastering data mining.

To talk about marketing without talking about the Coca-Cola Company is probably malfeasant. My business professor colleagues concur that this global organization is a rich source of management lessons. I don't think it is possible to get a business degree from any school on any continent today without being exposed—typically on multiple occasions—to one of the world's most interesting companies. Established in 1886, the company owns four of the world's top five nonalcoholic sparkling beverage brands, employs over 90,000 associates worldwide (900,000 system employees), has operational reach in over 200 countries, generates approximately 1.5 billion consumer servings each day, and manages more than 2,800 products, 450 brands (13 of which exceed $1 billion dollars in sales).[15] Coke has a fascinating story, which has been recounted in numerous fabulous books over time. The first lesson we extract from Coke is that managing all this complexity requires some pretty sophisticated analytics. Just managing the information arriving from Coke's 10 million plus increasingly intelligent vending machines and coolers is a monumental data management task.

The second lesson is that marketing is hard work. Executives living outside of marketing typically have no idea what marketers really do. (Remember, this book is an ethnography of sorts. I went door to door asking analysts what they did and then asked the various tribes analysts interact with in the enterprise what *they* thought analysts did. In the course of my interviews, I learned that many marketing executives believed that analysts weren't the only misunderstood and underappreciated group in the enterprise.) Coke exemplifies this truth. The *Atlanta Journal-Constitution,* commenting on the arrival of Joe Tripodi at Coke in July 2007, pointed out the company "has been through at least seven chief marketing officers during the past decade": Sergio Zyman left in 1998; Charlie Frenette served from 1998 to 2000; Steve Jones, from 2000 to 2003; Dan Palumbo, from 2003 to 2004; Chuck Fruit, in 2005; Mary Minnick, from 2005 to 2007; and now Tripodi.

Thanks to the informed and balanced use of analytics, the chief marketing officer career killer—at least at Coke—has been turned off. At the 2008 annual conference of the Association of National Advertisers, Tripodi gave a keynote address under this session blurb:

> Coca-Cola is the world's most-beloved brand, with more equity than any other, but it was also a company in trouble and needed a big wake-up call. CEO [chief executive officer] Neville Isdell came in and re-invigorated the brand. All across the world, Coke came out with clever, new advertising and marketing and returned to a story of growth. CMO Joe Tripodi will detail how they staged their big comeback, and what Coca-Cola has planned to insure that this venerable growth brand continues to succeed.

In a world where the credit markets have dematerialized, financial markets have fallen, consumer confidence has plummeted, and unemployment in the United States is at a 16-year high, Coca-Cola has been able to demonstrate growth and bottom-line resiliency. Tripodi explained: "The secret formula for growth is that there is no secret formula. It's doing some of the basics really well." Chief among those basics is:

> [M]oving away from "spray-and-pray" advertising in favor of precision marketing—that is, targeting consumers with the right message at the right time . . . moving away from a "stack-high-and-sell-it-cheap" approach. . . . We're trying to figure out ways and working aggressively to inspire people in the stores and grab them. And we are advancing our understanding of the consumer, particularly through shopper insights.[16]

The company's new guiding strategy is to lead, innovate, engage, and collaborate. A big part of Coke's success is due to analytics.

Analytics is not a new thing at Coke. Many of those who preceded Tripodi to the top marketing spot were no strangers to the discipline. Indeed, the headlines trumpeting the arrival of Chuck Fruit as CMO in 2004 read:

> "Coke Names Chuck Fruit New CMO"
>
> "We've Got Enormous Talent"
>
> "Today's Consumer Is No Longer Captive"
>
> "Plans 'Examination' of 'Real' Campaign"[17]

CMOs are not stupid. Fruit understood that the world of marketing was transforming.

> Today's consumer is no longer captive. For brands to have meaningful relationships with consumers, first, we have to be more entertaining and engaging and not assume that they're waiting for us to come to them. Number two, traditional advertising— the 30-second commercial—will be a lot less effective. Having said that, it's still going to be, for the foreseeable future, the most potent form of brand communication for brands like ours, but we need to have a much more diverse and broader marketing communications mix, if we're going to be successful. . . .

One of my initial top-10 priorities is going to be a fact-based examination.[18]

There has been a proliferation of beverages in the non-alcoholic-ready-to-drink sector (NARTD). Ken Forster, group director of strategy, planning, and analytics for the Office of Chief Customer Officer at Coca-Cola, explains:

> There's a lot more choice out there. The days of just putting it on the shelf and having it sell are over. . . .we're having to compete, it's a tougher market for us. We are entering an age where thoroughly measuring our business, precisely segmenting our offerings and insightfully tailoring our services to specific customers are becoming areas of core competency.[19]

The new leadership at Coke balances a passion for the creative aspect of brand management and the precise analytics associated with fact-based marketing. The new chief executive officer, Muthar Kent, a 30-year Coke veteran, comes from the bottling side of the house—part of the business that always had an eye on the numbers.

Coca-Cola today is an environment that embraces measurability. In-store marketing (and the analytics therein) is now as important if not more important than broad marketing. The new mantra revolves around precision marketing. Forster explains how this has changed his world: "We need to be very precise in the way we spend our budgets and deploy our brands. Treating every customer's store the same? That's the world of the distant past."[20]

The world of direct marketing is not on the radar screen of many senior executives. It should be. Participants in this industry are very plugged in and frequently ahead of the curve in their use of analytics. I suppose the fact that some of the most sophisticated thinking on the planet in analytics helps companies like Bradford Exchange sell charm bracelets and cuckoo clocks (collectibles) appears incongruous to organizations in charge of national defense or automobile manufacturing. Many of the greatest minds in analytics currently work for or once worked in the direct mail world.

Remember New Know Reality #2 from Chapter 1: There *Really* Is More to Know. The data set in retailing that you must manage has become much more granular.

[I]n the West, where medical and cosmetic advancements are redefining our ideas about age and aging. The once-clear age-bound and taste-signaled markers of generations are dissolving steadily year by year, and marriage, parenthood and retirement are no longer predictable milestones on a path that marketers and demographers can reliably plot . . . [D]emography as we know it is dying.[21]

The über-analytic at a major insurance firm remembers his days at Bradford Exchange fondly:

> When someone comes in from a particular place, how quickly can we determine what they are going to buy next? How quickly can we determine their purchase sequence and their purchase types to really come up with the best optimum contact strategy for them? It became very customized. . . . It was all built on predictive models and we used SAS an awful lot. We would extract data out of the database, play with it in SAS and we built a little tool . . . you could go in, and remember, this was all visual art stuff, it's all collector's plates, pictures of Elvis and such and we built a tool that we loaded in the pictures of all the products and all the models and all of the customer segment stuff so you could click on a product [this was 1990ish so IT was still living in the basic ones and zeroes world] and you could bring up the model.

> You could look at the model and find out what else people who bought that product liked to buy and drill into response rates by customer segments and by offer type and fully understand who was doing what and what else can you should offer the person and whether a particular strategy was working and all this fun stuff. So it really automated a bunch of the marketing decision making that was going on in the company.[22]

During times of macroeconomic uncertainty that negatively impact the retail sector, executives in fields outside of retailing should think about cherry picking unloved analytic talent from the retail vertical.

## Grocery Stores Lead Transformation

I don't care what anybody says—groceries stores are economic miracles.

> [A] lack of wonder at what uncoordinated markets can achieve. Going to a grocery store for the hundredth or thousandth time is a pretty humdrum experience. As a rule it isn't going to elicit much of an intellectual response—though if it does, the response might be one of two kinds. The commentator Robert Kuttner once wrote of his dismay at the great number of breakfast cereals on offer in his local grocery. What a waste, was his point; who could possibly need all these different cereals? Can't we arrange things more intelligently? This is a leftist kind of response: "Put somebody sensible in charge and plan things better." The liberal response (in the *proper* sense of "liberal") is different: "How amazing that all these choices are available, so that every taste is catered to, and it's all so cheap."[23]

It turns out that all those cereals are there for a reason. The grocery industry is where some of the most interesting analytical work is going on. This is because consumers buy food constantly, which generates lots of patterns to observe and generate insight from.

If you were to create a list of the top 10 generators of customer insight, you would have to place at the top (or very close to it) the amazing people at Catalina Marketing (www.catalinamarketing.com/company/). Two things really surprised me when I first started talking the folks at Catalina Marketing:

1. Just how good they are at this analytic stuff.
2. How in the world is it that nobody really knows about them?

Everybody has heard of Coke, Walmart, Procter & Gamble, and FedEx. Who has heard of Catalina? From the company's Web site, we learn:

> Catalina Marketing is the global leader in behavior-based marketing solutions, providing brand manufacturers, retailers and healthcare providers with targeted marketing solutions to meet

growth objectives. Utilizing a sophisticated database, Catalina Marketing enables you to reach consumers and patients with precision targeting on a truly mass scale.

The scope and scale of what Catalina does is amazing.

[It] access[es] consumers' actual purchasing behavior to understand their preferences and more effectively communicate instore via incentives, advertisements, loyalty programs, sampling and more. High-impact promotions and advertisements are hand-delivered to consumers at the point of sale via a full-color printer. Catalina Health Resource communications are triggered based on patients' Rx purchase behavior (NDC scan) and delivered at the pharmacy via high-speed printers.

The company has access to more than 250 million transactions each week, reaching consumers in more than 23,000 U.S. and 7,000 international grocery, drug, and mass merchandiser stores. In healthcare, Catalina provides direct-to-patient communications in more than 17,500 retail pharmacies.

Catalina operates one of the largest online decision support databases in the world. I am very fortunate to get to talk to Eric Williams, the chief information officer [CIO] at Catalina, periodically. Not only is Williams smart, he is also a gifted communicator. He is able to make all the sophisticated analytical work going on at Catalina understandable. The road to analytical understanding—at least for me—goes straight through Catalina. Williams explained:

Catalina now is a 26-year-old company which holds a number of U.S. and international patents on the concept of issuing promotions, incentives and advertising based on consumer purchase. The original philosophy was very straightforward— [because] much of the advertising and promotion vehicles in the market were all mass executions, everybody got the same offer no matter how wealthy you were or how limited your financial position was, and irrespective of whether you had old children, young children, had pets or no pets, you got the same marketing activity. For years, everyone has said, "Wow, if I actually knew what you liked and what you did, I could find things that were more relevant and therefore more appropriate and therefore your response to those communications would be obviously more effective."[24]

Catalina was doing one-to-one marketing before the phrase "one-to-one marketing" existed. Here is the problem/opportunity. There is a product category: baby products. People in the business know that less than 6 percent of the consumers in the U.S. marketplace on an ongoing basis have children in diapers, young children under the age of two. But yet, in the age of mass marketing, the 94 percent of the market that did not have young kids at home received the same promotional flyer, the same coupons, the same marketing message. What a waste.

In 1983, Catalina Marketing conducted a pilot at Wegman's Supermarkets in Rochester, New York, that changed all that. Based on the products that were purchased, retailers and manufacturers could communicate an appropriate message to customers. The philosophy continued to expand over the years.

The basic idea of the five guys who started Catalina was that there had to be a better way to market to consumers to find things that were appropriate to their needs and their interests. This concept was born due to the development of scanning.

> That really was the transition that allowed Catalina and the whole concept of behavior-based marketing to come into play. Because once point-of-sale scanning became possible, it wasn't just $1.29 on the grocery key on an old mechanical register, it now was the UPC code of that unique product. Decisions makers said, "Oh, wow, we know that UPC code, it belongs to Procter & Gamble or Kimberly Clark's diaper products."

Catalina Information Resources would collect the data and turn it around in less than five hours.

> At midnight we would collect this information, the sales data of all the products in the store, and we would then build a database and provide that online to clients. Having this data allows people to ask questions like "How well are certain flavors

selling in a specific product line? Do I have sufficient shelf space to be able to accommodate that? Are my products always in stock?". . . [Y]ou could see the average sales each day of a product and very clearly see if I was selling six or eight units of a specific item every single day and all of a sudden Thursday and Friday I sold zero, you knew the only reason that occurred is, the product was out of stock.

Having this data and being able to analyze it transformed the grocery industry. Williams remembers:

The accuracy and the timing of the data was amazing to the industry. However, in my mind what was the most impressive . . . is that we were able to change the way direct store delivery was done. Historically, direct store delivery merchandise, cookie companies, chips, and bread companies and the like, all were spot sale companies. Those companies load their trucks with the merchandise that is needed or what they believe will be needed for that day on that traditional route. They load that truck with merchandise. The drivers head out at 5:00 A.M. and go to the first store. Goes in the store, brightens their merchandise set, and figures out how much they need of each of the products that their company supplies. They then go back to the truck they pull that product off and they actually change the ownership of that product at that moment in time. They actually pull the merchandise, go back to the back door of the store, the receiving clerk then checks that information in and then that data or that merchandise now becomes ownership of the store. The problem then with that model is that . . . if you ended up selling more rye breads that day than you did whole wheat in the trip, then by the time you get to your last few stops on your stops, you're out of rye. Because the warehouse didn't stock the truck with enough merchandise. What Catalina Information Resources was able to do was use that data to provide knowledge to these companies on what is selling so that they could more appropriately load the truck with sufficient merchandise to meet the sales of those stores.

The next thing that happened . . . which was quite impressive was that these companies realized, very quickly, that they should change their entire model from a spot sale company [to] . . . consignment sales. These companies . . . go to the store and they will stock the merchandise as needed to replenish the shelves and the store agrees to pay, based on the sales movement of the products on a weekly basis. So that the ownership of the merchandise is just like a regular consignment store— still retained by the original manufacturer.

Data and information changed the cash flow model of the industry. All this was going on during the 1980s. At business school, they tell the story about the early 1990s, when product ownership did not change until merchandise moved through the bar code scanner at the point of sale. This is the world of the zero-inventory retailer. As Williams says:

Many of these companies now work on a consignment basis, therefore there is no check-in, their inventory is much different, they have much less paperwork to deal with. It has been a major change in that model.

With analytics, retailer and manufacturer come to understand how their products are selling or not selling. On a granular basis, we can know what customers are buying, when they are buying, and with what frequency they buy. What loyalty is out there? Thanks to Catalina, it is now possible to have information the next morning regarding the U.S. marketplace and everything that is selling. Imagine the power of being able to tell any and every major consumer package manufacturer something about its product.

Analytics has the potential of telling brand managers and store managers something they don't know. Coming back to our recurring theme of big data:

At Catalina, our largest data repository right now has two years of history of approximately 150 million consumers in the United States and everything that has been purchased at the individual item level, UPC code, the price, the lane, date and time purchased for two years of all those customers. That represents . . . a little over 650 billion entries or rows in a data table. Tools from SAS—the SAS data mining technologies—go against that raw data set and are able to provide executives with insights that you would not normally think of.

Time after time, in market after market, we hear that organizations that are ahead of the curve in their use of analytics are materially out-performing competitors—even as the economy weakens. Because of the recession, most supermarket retailers have struggled to post same-store sales growth. Not the Kroger Co., which has consistently been notching comparable-store growth rates of about 5 percent in 2007 "According to Kroger senior management, much of the credit for that growth goes to a loyalty-card program."[25]

My brother Rusty and I were shopping the other day and he asked, "Why are these people always asking us if we want to get a credit card? They have to know we have a couple already, don't they?" While I can't pretend to know all the reasons why retailers train their customer-facing folks to push store credit cards, I do know that there are some informational advantages. Stores can use credit card data to determine spending pattern behavior. This in turn reveals the different charging patterns of different segments of customers, information that can be mapped to customer profitability. With the buying behavior captured, retailers can target their most profitable customers with a personalized campaign of couponing designed to stimulate behavior.

Paco Underhill, author of *Why We Buy: The Science of Shopping* and *Call of the Mall: The Geography of Shopping*, believes that, via analytics, retailers can manage every bit of the customer experience, going so far as optimizing the soundtrack that plays in the background. "One of the critical aspects if you are a Big Box retailer—Target, Wal-Mart, PetSmart—whatever is recognizing that there is an absolute predict-ability to who is in the store when. Therefore there is an appropriate moment to play Frank Sinatra or Death Camp for Cutie."[26]

## Advertising Is Being Transformed

If how we buy is being transformed by analytics, it stands to reason that how we are induced to buy must transform as well. The advertising industry is going through a massive transformation. As that transformation progresses, one of the bridges that has to be crossed is reconciling the art of advertising with the science of human behavior. Historically art and science have been thought to be polar opposites. Increasingly we find that they are very complementary.

> [Art] as a cultural force is generally regarded as intensely hostile to science, its ideal of subjectivity eternally opposed to that of scientific objectivity. But I do not believe this was always the case, or that the terms are so mutually exclusive. The notion of *wonder* seems to be something that once united them, and can still do so.[27]

As more and more advertising migrates to the Web (by 2010, 15 percent of global ad spending is expected to be online), advertisers have two objectives:

1. Figure out who is looking at a page.
2. Craft an ad in microseconds that appeals to that particular person.

This can be done only by blending art with analytics.

> Online advertisers are not lacking in choices: They can display their ads in any color, on any site, with any message, to any audience, with any image. Now, a new breed of companies is trying to tackle all of those options and determine what ad works for a specific audience. They are creating hundreds of versions of clients' online ads, changing elements like color, type font, message, and image to see what combination draws clicks on a particular site or from a specific audience.

> It is technology that could cause a shift in the advertising world. The creators and designers of ads have long believed that a clever idea or emotional resonance drives an ad's success. But that argument may be difficult to make when analysis suggests that it is not an ad's brilliant tagline but its pale-yellow background and sans serif font that attracts customers.

> The question is, "how do we combine creative energy, which is a manual and sort of qualitative exercise, with the raw processing power of computing, which is all about quantitative data?" said Tim

Hanlon, executive vice president of VivaKi Ventures, the investment unit of Publicis Groupe.[28]

Where we end up is a hybrid blend. Bant Breen, the president of worldwide digital communications at Initiative, the Interpublic Group media buying and planning firm, believes: "The traditional creative process right now is not structured to essentially deliver hundreds of permutations, or hundreds of ideas for messaging." He concludes: "There's no doubt that there will be a lot of data that can be collected that could be applied to the creative process."[29]

## What We Must Know about Customers Is Transforming

Sara Igo, associate professor of history, political science and sociology at Vanderbilt University contends that "modern market research arrived in 1911 with the establishment of the Harvard Bureau of Business Research." Many soon-to-be great enterprises are in the late stages of initial experiments (i.e., are at the end of a beginning) involving a pronounced transformation in the relationship they have with their customers. For quite some time, technology has allowed retailers to stockpile mountains of data regarding purchases. To date, few have really done anything exceptional with this information. Most retail systems and retailers still do not recognize individual customers. They are "clueless."[30] That is about to change. Analytics is driving this transformation. And analytics is changing.[31]

On February 5, 2003, the chief operating officer of the Coca-Cola Company, Steve Heyer, took the stage at the Beverly Hills Hotel to kick off the inaugural *AdAge* Madison & Vine Conference. His keynote address was a marketing manifesto announcing an end to traditional marketing thinking at Coke. Heyer made special mention of consumer resistance, noting that consumers now have an "unrivalled ability" to avoid advertising. With smart consumers in command of the technology to edit or opt out of marketing, Heyer said that the time had come for "transformational" change.[32]

In the 1970s, it is estimated that the average person was targeted by 500 to 2,000 ads each day. The latest estimate is 3,000 to 5,000 per day. Those following the infoverse mark 2003 as the year in which the amount of spam being transmitted each day finally exceeded the amount of legitimate e-mail. Despite all this outbound effort, this marketing carpet-bombing, customers remain strangers to most organizations today.

Segmentation has creatively dumped consumers into demographic buckets; some notable examples are Hispanics, yuppies, soccer moms, and the super rich. Success will require a much more granular understanding of who the customer really is.

Baker explains that we need to focus on customer behavior. He asks us to:

> Start by looking at the skinflints who, like me, forgo the pleasures of red and yellow bell peppers. In this green-pepper bucket I'll wager that I'm surrounded by people of all races. Both genders are represented. We drive all kinds of cars. Some of us hunt; other would just as soon outlaw guns. The district attorney might be in there, sharing bucket space with the FBI's most wanted killer. You could say we have nothing in common, and you'd be absolutely right—except for one thing: our behavior when it comes to buying bell peppers.[33]

The mass market is dead. The micromarket a brief blip on the radar.

> In its place, a nano-market is rapidly coming of age—an explosive proliferation of consumer segments, tastes, preferences, media and lifestyles that is splintering the marketplace into infinitesimally small pieces that are beyond the capacity of traditional marketing systems to recognize, much less adequately service and satisfy.[34]

One of the most transformed customer relationships comes from a surprising source—the utility market, erroneously thought by many to be behind the curve technologically. Becky Blalock, the award-winning chief information officer in charge of an award-winning information technology organization at an award-winning enterprise, recognized early that change was coming.

> [T]hose meters out there give us more information about how people are using power so that we know how to better project building power plants out into the future. [The digitized meter] is going to give us the ability, hopefully in the future, to inter-act with the customer in different ways. It could be that we are sending them pricing signals but we are also talking to smart appliances that are in the home.[35]

At the base of all this personalization and collaboration must be a solid foundation of facts—and world-class analytics to make sense of them. With facts in place, great creativity can be brought to bear on sculpting new products and services. Norwich Union, an insur-ance firm, conducted a data-gathering pilot on 5,000 automobiles and subsequently rolled out a "Pay as You Drive" insurance policy aimed at two different age ranges. The policy charges drivers based on when and where they drive. The data essentially bifurcated the generations, saying keep the elderly off the road during the morning rush hour and keep the young off the road at night.[36]

Just about everyone in the analytics business is very familiar with the fine work being done at CapitalOne.

> When you call CapOne, a recording immediately prompts you to enter your card number. Even before the service representa-tive's phone rings, a computer algorithm kicks in and analyzes dozens of characteristics about the account and about you, the account holder.

> [Analytics] transform[s] customer service calls into a sales opportunity. Data analysis of customer characteristics generates a list of products and services that this kind of consumer is most willing to buy, and the service rep sees the list as soon as she takes the call. It's just like Amazon's "customers who like this, also like this" feature, but transmitted through the rep. Capital One now makes more than a million sales a year through customer-service marketing—and their data-mining predictions are the reason why.[37]

## Business Models Are Transforming

Business models appear to be migrating from the "make-and-sell" mode of the industrialized past, through the "sense-and-respond" methods of the webified present toward the "anticipate-and-lead" ecosystems of the not-so-distant future. Michael Schrage, a fellow with the MIT Sloan School's Center for Digital Business, believes the future belongs to those organizations able to best construct and then analyze the results of innovative business experiments.

> I think the Web 2.0 companies are inventing the models we will use. Amazon, Google, eBay are conducting thousands of experiments. I personally talked to Jeff Bezos. One of the most important things he has done for the Amazon culture is instill a culture of experimentation that exploits Web 2.0 economics. These companies have built a culture around experimentation that gives them the best of both worlds—risk management and opportunity identification/exploitation.[38]

Robert Weisman is one of my all-time favorite journalists. He covers the "strategy" beat for the *Boston Globe*. He maintains that the essence of strategy is asking and answering "What is your company good at?" According to Weisman's research, capabilities-driven strategies are the ones that pay the biggest dividends.[39] Upon closer examination, the capabilities-driven strategies of strategic high performers are all enabled by analytics.

Whether we are talking about Wal-Mart Stores Inc. and its mastery of supply-chain management, Toyota Motor Corp. and its seamless orchestration of a global network of parts vendors and subcontractors, or Procter & Gamble's ability to consistently outinnovate the competition across product lines, deep examination proves that the companies exhibit a managed and deployed mastery of analytics.

## Logistics Has Been Transformed

The logistics industry is perhaps the first vertical market to truly embrace and broadly deploy analytics. It is not unusual for the person most knowledgeable about high-end analytics to end up being the CEO. A great case in point is Christopher Lofgren, PhD, the president and CEO of Schneider National Inc., a global logistics services firm. Another example is Pierre Haren, a PhD from the Massachusetts Institute of Technology, who is the founder and chief executive officer of ILOG. Working with the government of Singapore, ILOG was able to synchronize the flow of passengers into the new airport, making sure that visitors from mainland China wouldn't cross paths with travelers from Taiwan.

UPS provides a powerful case study to demonstrate what a difference well-managed analytics can make:

> Atlanta-based UPS moves over 15 million packages around the world in a day. . . . Dave Barnes, SVP [senior vice president] and CIO at UPS, states that his company had undertaken several time and motion studies to continuously optimize every step in the package delivery processes. These studies have revealed methods for loading the trucks in better ways through new heuristics and analytical methods such as training their drivers to fasten their seatbelt with their left hand while turning the ignition key with their other hand. Package routing information is constantly tracked and planned for each delivery truck, allowing for any changes in the routes if required by the customer or by other interferences such as traffic or weather.

> Years ago, customers would deliver their package to the nearest UPS collection center and wait a few days for an acknowledgement of delivery. Next, UPS and other logistics companies opened a number of physical centers where the packages could be dropped off and created online process visibility for customers to track the packages in transit. Following this, UPS and other leading companies offered home or office pickup of packages at predetermined times of the day. More recently, UPS is working on its business process capabilities to pick up packages from individual customers' premises at the times specified by its customers.

> A careful attention to business processes, integration of analytics, and capacity to dynamically reconfigure resources is

behind this transformation. UPS starts by focusing on the business processes at the individual truck and route level to load and route each truck in an efficient manner such that it improves the convenience for both its employees and its customers.

UPS' new routing analytics engine analyzes package delivery, weather, and traffic data to route each truck, minimizing left turns so that trucks are not held up at traffic junctions. This process improvement has reportedly saved the UPS fleet 1.9 million miles of travel per year.[40]

The logistics world requires close to real-time analytics. Building construction in Shanghai takes place at such a breakneck pace that the city's maps need to be rewritten every two weeks.[41]

## The Military Has Been Transformed

The first paragraph of U.S. Secretary of Defense Robert M. Gates's precedent-setting article in *Foreign Affairs* establishes in no uncertain terms that analytics will be a big part of how the Department of Defense does business going forward:

The defining principle of the Pentagon's new National Defense Strategy is balance. The United States cannot expect to eliminate national security risks through higher defense budgets, to do everything and buy everything. The Department of Defense must set priorities and consider inescapable tradeoffs and opportunity costs.[42]

Analytics is all about balance, about informed decision making. At the top of one of the most important enterprises in the world today—the Pentagon—analytics is critically important. Analytics plays a role strategically, tactically, and operationally.

One of the oldest military axioms in the book is "Know your enemy." Analytics plays a big and growing part of this. At the Defense Advanced Research Projects Agency (DARPA), social scientists are hard at work trying to predictively assess insurgent and terrorist patterns of behavior. Dr. Kendra Moore, program manager at the Information Exploitation Office, explains:

> Their actions are *not* random. Our challenge is to learn our adversaries' patterns and exploit them. Our ability to collect and store these data exceeds our current capability to thoroughly process and exploit it. But, that's just the tip of the data iceberg. Our challenge is to exploit all of this data . . . all of this rich, dynamic, multi-dimensional, ever-changing, and uncertain data . . . even as it is generated at increasing speeds, in multiple formats, in multiple languages, and at multiple locations . . . or at no location at all, in cyberspace.[43]

Coming back to a recurring theme regarding the New Know, we find from soldiers in the field that a whole new dimension of knowledge is necessary in contemporary combat. A commander from the Third Infantry Division commented on his march to Baghdad:

> I knew where every enemy tank was dug in on the outskirts of Tallil. . . . Only problem was, my soldiers had to fight fanatics charging on foot or in pickups and firing AK-47s. . . . I had perfect situational awareness. What I lacked was cultural awareness. Great technical intelligence . . . wrong enemy.[44]

Dr. Robert Popp, deputy director of the Information Exploitation Office, is doing very interesting work in the fields of computational social science. The office is working on predicting the "social weather."

> How are we to implement this new national strategy [winning over the hearts and minds of the local population by providing aid to improve their lives]? We believe the way forward is clear. It does not involve spending billions of dollars procuring more conventional ISR [intelligence, surveillance, and reconnaissance] or high-profile weapon systems to gain incremental improvements in precision, speed, or bandwidth. What is needed is a strategy that leads to a greater cultural awareness and thorough understanding of the threats comprising the new strategic triad [failed states, global terrorism, and proliferation of weapons of mass destruction].

What technologies must we develop to understand and influence nation states, societies, thugs and terrorists, WMD proliferators, and zealots of failed states?

I believe the path to understand people, their cultures, motivations, intentions, opinions and perceptions lies in applying interdisciplinary quantitative and computational social science methods from mathematics, statistics, economics, political science, cultural anthropology, sociology, neuroscience, and modeling and simulation.

Understanding and countering today's strategic threat that is inherently dynamic and socially complex is not easily reduced or amenable to classical analytical methods. It requires applying quantitative and computational social sciences that offer a wide range of nonlinear mathematical and nondeterministic computational theories and models for investigating human social phenomena.

These analytical techniques apply to cognition and decision-making. They make forecasts about conflict and cooperation and do so at all levels of data aggregation form individual to groups, tribes, societies, nation states, and the globe.

Because the analysis of conflict and nation state instability is inherently complex and deeply uncertain, no one social science theory or quantitative/computational model is sufficient. An ensemble of models—containing more information than any other model—must be integrated within a single decision support framework, to generate a range of plausible futures.[45]

Soon predicting social weather may become as popular and prevalent as regular weather forecasting is today.

Analytics has a massive role to play in day-to-day mission planning. Helicopter routes are optimized over insurgent hot spots in Iraq. Models of the best places to look are run prior to deploying ISR assets.

One of the largest radio-frequency identification device (RFID) projects in the world today involved Unisys creating full visibility for the global supply chain of the U.S. Department of Defense. Prior to this new system, the department was operating three different supply chains for the army, navy, and air force with minimal integration.[46]

Carl Gerber, a gifted data architect who has worked with McGraw-Hill, Procter & Gamble, and Tween Brands, remembers his early days in the U.S. Air Force putting together executive information systems designed to analyze and report on key performance indicators. "A general cares about how many fatalities there are per 100,000 hours of flying. This flight safety KPI is the most relevant example of using analytics I have seen in my career and it puts things in perspective for the business world."[47]

Analytics automates routine military decision making and amplifies/augments higher-level strategic decision making. Artificial intelligence technology will help automate military air traffic control. As airspace in target areas experiences increased air traffic due to the advent of unmanned aerial vehicles and other airborne weapons, air operation centers will be assisted by high-end analytics as they seek to manage airspace.[48]

## Science Is Transforming

It is not new nor is it news that the developed world is fragmented and has historically had trouble reaching consensus on most of the major issues facing the planet today. The one thing that just about every head of state, every elected official, every CEO, every university president, and a surprisingly large majority of the population agree on is that science matters. Not only does science matter—how one *does* science matters. Science is now widely understood as an engine of economic growth. Analytics is the fuel and lubricant that keeps the scientific engine running. Analytics is a big part of the future of science.

Francis Bacon, knighted in 1603, is thought of as the human catalyst of the scientific revolution. He suggested that appropriate analytical practice begins by observing the world as it really is, inventorying facts, and hypothesizing about why things happen the way they do. Scholars studying the history of science tell us that the scientific "attitude," the scientific "method," is made up of four major elements:

1. That the universe is an orderly and knowable system; that the very term *universe* etymologically is accurate—that there is one set of rules that applies throughout the system. No exceptions. No mysteries.

No supernatural inexplicables. In principle everything within the system is explicable within the terms of the system itself.

2. Systematic doubt or skepticism—originally set forth by the French philosopher Descartes. The Cartesian method is the application of systematic doubt to all of our assumptions, all of our perceptions. You have to test every hypothesis with empirical evidence.

3. Part of the equipment of the really great scientists is basic curiosity —a drive to know, to explore, to go further, to extend the boundaries of knowledge, to understand the way things really work.

4. Emphasis on precise measurement and the mathematical representation of hypotheses.[49]

Analytics is science. It is as simple as that. Science is the disciplined, replicable and systematic study of the structure and behaviour of the physical and natural world through observation and experiment with an eye towards explaining how things really work. Isn't this precisely what analysts do?

As we look at the practice of global science, assembling some foundational facts is a good place to start. The editors at *Seed Magazine* put together a powerful special report titled "The State of Science 2008." Some of the highlights include:

Considering that science is fundamental to the world's productivity, we collectively spend very little on it. On average, nations spend about 2.3 percent of their GDP [gross domestic product] on scientific research and development [R&D], or roughly one trillion dollars a year worldwide. [Total global R&D spend: about $994,424,038,000; Total U.S. R&D spend: about $343,747,500,000].

Today almost two-thirds of all American science and engineering degree-holders are working either in the for-profit sector or are self-employed; only 9 percent work for colleges or universities.

The commercial sector now does about 70 percent of all American R&D in dollar terms. And while the overwhelming majority of corporate R&D remains biased toward development and applied research, about a fifth of US *basic* research is still done in industry.[50]

In today's world, you cannot "do" science without information technology; more specifically, you cannot do science without world-class analytics. Scientists will need to be completely computationally and mathematically literate. By 2020, it will simply not be possible to do science without such literacy. In 2005, Microsoft assembled 30 of the world's greatest scientists from 12 nations to examine the challenges facing scientists in the future, paying particular attention to the impact of computing and computer science on the sciences. The highly respected scientists concluded:

> We are starting to give birth to "new kinds" of science and possibly a new economic era of "science-based innovation" that could create new kinds of high-tech sectors that we can barely imagine today, just as we could hardly have imagined today's rapidly growing "genomics" sector happening two decades ago.[51]

The future will feature "novel mathematical and statistical techniques in science, and scientific computing platforms and applications integrated into experimental and theoretical science. This combination is likely to accelerate key breakthroughs in science and benefits to society."

More and more science will involve running simulations. Will Wright, the famous video game pioneer (creator of *Spore* and *SimCity*), believes:

> "The quest to build a simulation is a scientific quest. Experimenting to test a hypothesis used to be the way to do science, but simulation is the new way. . . ."

There is, of course, nothing novel about humans making models and running simulations. In fact, some argue the ability is one of the defining characteristics of human intelligence. Say you run into a dog in the street. Based on what you know of the world and of dogs, you build a model in your head of the situation. You have a concept of what the dog is and what his relationship may be to you. Then the dog growls, and you begin, in Will Wright-speak, the "reverse engineering" process. Is the dog protecting his master, warning you to get off his property? Does it have rabies? Then you begin the simulation process in your mind, considering possible courses of action and their outcomes. What will happen if I run? Put out my hand? What is new, and what truly excites Wright, is the idea that now we can marry this abstract human ability with the powerful computational jaws of a PC.[52]

*Towards Science 2020* emphasized that we are transitioning from the

application of computing to support scientists to "do" science (i.e., "computational science") to the integration of *computer science concepts, tools and theorems* into the very fabric of science. This transition is thought to be ushering in a new revolution in science. A revolution is taking place in the scientific method.

"Hypothesize, design and run experiment, analyze results" is being replaced by "hypothesize, look up answer in data base." Databases are an essential part of the infrastructure of science. They may contain raw data, the results of computational analyses or simulations, or the product of annotation and organisation of data.[53]

Wright believes *very* strongly that the future of science, indeed the future of humanity, is closely linked to the future of computer simulation. He says:

It's an amplification of our intelligence, of our imagination really. Basically, scientists used to build these dynamic models in their imaginations, and they would sit there and they would imagine, or they might do a long math chain. But it was running to the limits of the abilities of the imagination. Now we have the ability to build elaborate models on the computer that no one person could ever fully understand using their own imagination.[54]

Down-to-earth challenges directly in front of us include "end-to-end scientific data management, from data acquisition and data integration, to data treatment, provenance and persistence."[55]

We know science is going to be a major agenda item going forward. We cannot be certain how big—probably it will not be as big as the quadrupling of funds for the National Science Foundation under President Dwight Eisenhower in 1957. We do know that moving forward, government science will be focused, intense, and engaged with the general public.

Most of the truly significant scientific figures of the seventeenth, eighteenth, and early nineteenth centuries were amateurs. In the twentieth century, most of the major figures in all branches of scholarship have been professional academics. Most started their careers with a university education, followed by research culminating with a PhD degree. Scholars of knowledge attribute this professionalization and standardization of science to the fact that since there was now more to know, only those who had access to the accumulated wisdom of humanity (i.e., large libraries and laboratories) located at universities could compete. The Internet and the microchip have changed all that.

> Email is as easy as walking down the hall. The Web, while not a complete substitute for a library, makes enormous amounts of information readily available to a very large number of people. In my field and many others it is becoming common for the authors of scholarly articles to make their datasets available on the Web so that other scholars can check that they really say what the articles claim they say.
>
> For a large and increasing fraction of the population, amateur scholarship, like amateur sports, amateur music, amateur dramatics, and much else, is a real option. These arguments suggest that, having shifted from a world of amateur scholars to a world of professionals, we may now be shifting back.[56]

One of the transformations of science is that Big Science may be giving way to "open science." Openness has always been an integral part of science, with scientists presenting findings in journals or at conferences. The open science movement encourages scientists to share techniques and works in process long before they are ready to present results. Thus, in those fecund moments, solo minds—rather than devising research questions, running experiments, and analyzing data alone—might link into the wisdom of the crowd. Open science has the potential of bringing disruptive but constructive change to the laboratory. Opening up science could speed discoveries, increase collaboration, and transform the field in unforeseen ways.

## Agriculture and Food Are Being Transformed

Imagine giving half a million cows a cell phone. Too weird? How about putting sensing devices on every cow in Kansas? Those devices would produce a lot of data. On a 7×24 basis you could count heart beats, moos, naps, water intake—whatever you want. Stephen Baker believes that:

> [T]he patterns in that data, analyzed mathematically, could point to all kinds of insights. The key was this: instead of veterinarians checking up on cows every few months, computers would be reporting on them every single minute. By tracking every animal and following its subsequent parts and byproducts as they were transported and sold, authorities could take a big step toward securing the nation's food supply. In a sense, wiring the cows would be akin to equipping each animal with a recording machine, like the black boxes airplanes carry.[57]

High-end analytics and supercomputers have been relegated—at least in the mind of the general population—to activities and problem sets somehow apart from day-to-day life. Nothing could be further from the truth.

> Figuring out the best way to transform a frozen pizza into a perfectly warmed pie, gooey on top and crispy on the bottom, is as much a computer problem as a work of culinary art. General Mills, maker of the Totino's and Jeno's brands of pizzas, would prefer not to whip up a thousand combinations of mozzarella cheese, tomato paste, crust and chemicals and blast them with microwave radiation. It's a lot cheaper and easier to model different pizzas using a sophisticated computer and only cook up the best candidates. To speed up the task, General Mills turned to computers containing high-powered graphics chips. . . . they need hardware that can analyze a vast quantity of data and do it much faster than standard computers.[58]

# Work Itself Is Transforming

In a litigious society, executives are being required to know—at an ever-deepening level of granularity—exactly what is going on inside their enterprise. This is very difficult, given the increasingly global and consolidated shape of the contemporary enterprise. Virtually every chief information officer I talked to had recently undergone or was currently undergoing some kind reorganization, merger, divestiture, and/or acquisition. Knowing what people do—heck, knowing if they are *your* people—is no small undertaking in today's rapidly changing workplace.

Julian Orr, one of the first and finest of a new breed of workplace ethnographers, explains:

[In the past,] it was easier for people to know what other people did because there was simply less to know. In the past, those who ran organizations were familiar with the production processes. They often designed the process and had even done the work themselves. Today, organizations are so complex that it is difficult for those in charge to have experienced much of the organization's work firsthand. Moreover, managers are often hired from the outside, and their experience frequently lies in completely different industries.[59]

Orr eloquently elaborates:

History tells us that work is the bedrock of any socioeconomic system. When a society's mode of production changes, so does the nature of work. It is primarily for this reason that the industrial revolution warrants being called a revolution. The industrial revolution marked a shift in what people did for a living and how they accomplished tasks. It signaled the decline of agriculture and handicraft and the rise of factory and office work as the primary means of making a living. Out of the crucible of the second industrial revolution [the late 1800s] came the time clock, the corporation, the union, the occupation of management, and even the very idea of "having a job" or of stringing those jobs together into a career.[60]

The complexity of contemporary work is so extreme; the organizational structure of modern enterprises so fluid; and the actual nature of the relationship existing between the enterprise and the individual actually doing the work (e.g., full-time employee, part-time employee, contractor, and/or offshore resource) so diverse that analytics are required to keep the whole thing operating smoothly.

You may not believe me. How about IBM? Stephen Baker has done us all a favor by introducing us to Samer Takriti at the Thomas J. Watson Research Laboratory. Takriti "leads a team building mathematical models of thousands of IBM's tech consultants. The idea, he said, was to piece together inventories of all of their skills and then to calculate, mathematically, how best to deploy them."[61]

People as math! People—*you* and *me*—as mathematical equations that can be modeled and simulated.

> One of Takriti's challenges is to help IBM develop a taxonomy of the skills of its 300,000 employees. On its balance sheet, IBM lays out the value of many other assets, from supercomputers to swiveling Aeron desk chairs. When strategists at the company are figuring out whether to sell a division or invest more money, they pore over these figures. They sketch out rosy and grim scenarios. They do the numbers.[62]

We are the numbers! Baker does a brilliant job envisioning what an "analyzed" workplace might look like:

> Picture an IBM manager who gets an assignment to send a team of five to set up a call center in Manila. She sits down at the computer and fills out a form. It's almost like booking a vacation online. She puts in the dates and clicks on menus to describe the job and the skills needed. Perhaps she stipulates the ideal budget range. The results come back, recommending a particular team. All the skills are represented. Maybe three of the five people have a history of working together smoothly. They all have passports and live near airports with direct flights to Manila. One of them even speaks Tagalog. Everything looks fine, except for one line that's highlighted in red. The budget. It's $40,000 over! The manager sees that the computer architect

on the team is a veritable luminary, a guy who gets written up in the trade press. Sure, he's a 98.7% fit for the job, but he costs $1,000 an hour. It's as if she shopped for a weekend getaway in Paris and wound up with a penthouse suite at the Ritz.

Hmmm. The manager asks the system for a cheaper architect. New options come back. One is a new 29-year-old consultant based in India who costs only $85 per hour. That would certainly patch the hole in the budget. Unfortunately, he's only a 69% fit for the job. Still, he can handle it, according to the computer, if he gets two weeks of training. Can the job be delayed?[63]

This is not science fiction. This is not distant future. This is happening *now*!

As IBM sees it, the company has little choice. The work force is too big, the world too vast and complicated for managers to get a grip on their workers the old-fashioned way—by talking to people who know people who know people. Word of mouth is too foggy and slow for the global economy.[64]

The analysts at IBM use math tools from multiple industries: Wall Street quantitative models regarding supply, demand, and commodity prices and economic and industrial engineering models for complex systems.

IBM is not the only company applying math to managing human capital.

John Challenger, chief executive of Challenger, Gray & Christmas, a company that tracks layoffs, said employers were being driven now not by compassion but by hard calculations based on data they have never had before. More than ever, he said, companies have used technology to track employee performance and productivity, and in many cases they know that the workers they would cut are productive ones. "People are measured and 'metricked' to a much greater degree," he said. "So companies know that when they're cutting an already taut organization, they're leaving big gaps in the work force."[65]

## Transportation Is Being Transformed

In aviation, sensing—at least the after-the-fact sort—has been with us since the advent of the "Jet Age." In 1958, authorities approved minimum operating requirements for the infamous flight data recorder. Historically, these "black boxes"

have served one function: recording the last information from a doomed flight. Recent technology, though, has allowed airlines to send flight data to a quick access recorder so that hundreds of details on routine flights can be collected and analyzed in flight quality programs. This allows airlines to detect errors in operations and maintenance that might otherwise go undetected. Japan Airlines is opening up this data to customers.

"Through this program we want to be as open as we can and show our customers how we are improving safety in our everyday business activities," said Akeo Misumi, director of the airline's flight data monitoring office. Japan Airlines has been steadily increasing the number of flights it reviews each year, collecting data from 320,000 flights in 2007

"You have voluminous data on modern aircraft, a large amount of flight data. I don't care what business you're in, if you have a device measuring the performance of your business, you should look at the data proactively to run a better business."

In the United States, more than 70 airlines participate in flight quality monitoring programs, known by their acronyms FOQA, for Flight Quality and Operations Assurance, and ASAP, for Aviation Safety Action Program.[66]

Taxi drivers in Japan have intelligent transportation systems that allow them to spot traffic delays and find open parking spaces rather than circling the block and contributing to vehicular congestion.

## Politics Is Transforming

One of the few desires that executives and politicians have in common—no matter the geography, the market, or the party affiliation—is the wish to see around corners. Everyone would love to know what the future will bring. Life would be so simple if we could do this. However, the dubious art of prediction has been thoroughly debunked. Indeed, a new subcategory of business best seller has emerged that questions the extent to which what comes next might be knowable.

Francis Fukuyama at John Hopkins, in addition to chronicling the challenges of forecasting I referred to previously, also wrote a very helpful article titled "The Great Disruption."[67] The essence of Fukuyama's thinking was brilliantly synthesized by *New York Times* political columnist David Brooks:

> The information economy began to disrupt the industrial economy. The feminist revolution disrupted gender and family relations. The civil rights revolution disrupted social arrangements. The Vietnam War discredited the establishment.
>
> These disruptions were generally necessary and good, but the transition was painful. People lost faith in old social norms, but new ones had not yet emerged. The result was disorder. Divorce rates skyrocketed. Crime rates exploded. Faith in institutions collapsed. Social trust cratered.
>
> As community bonds dissolved, individual autonomy asserted itself. . . . The combined result was a loss of community and social cohesion, and what Christopher Lasch called a culture of narcissism.
>
> . . . the Great Disruption produced ideological politics. The weakening of social norms led to fierce battles. . . . Personal became political. Groups fought . . . Politics wasn't just about allocating resources. It was a contest over values, lifestyles and the status of your tribe. This venomous style dominated politics straight through the two baby boomer presidencies—of Clinton and Bush.[68]

Brooks believes that we are now about to leave behind the ideological battles of the 1930s, 1960s, and 1990s. He believes we may be entering a more pragmatic, more analytical decade or two. Convinced that "the age of expressive individualism was coming to an end," Brooks concludes, "Obama aims to realize the end-of-ideology politics that Daniel Bell and others glimpsed in the early 1960s. He sees himself as a pragmatist, an empiricist."

Moving forward, we may anticipate a more fact-based, empirical approach to governing.

Governing is one thing. Getting elected to do the governing is quite another. Analytics has transformed this part of politics as well.

Useful formulations die hard, which is why commentators during the 2008 presidential election cycle will still be talking about red states and blue states, but the fact is red state-blue state is already a blunt tool.

By the 2020 election cycle—only four presidencies away— political strategists will be counting voters one micro-precinct at a time: sports fans, pet owners, international travelers, early risers, cancer survivors, heart-bypass veterans, Catholic school alumni, science majors compared to humanities majors, Mac users compared to PC users, American-car owners compared to foreign- car owners, Yahoo! browsers compared to Google browsers, single moms compared to married moms, and on and on.[69]

## Technology Companies Slow to Embrace Analytics

One of the biggest surprises for me in writing this book is to find that at the back of the pack, materially behind the analytical power curve one finds—believe it or not—technology companies. It is strangely ironic that many of the companies that create the technologies that allow us to know more—about our world, about our customers, about our competitors, about our operations—have not, for the most part, aggressively deployed analytical technologies themselves.

The top analyst at a financial services firm did a brief stint at one of the big hardware vendors. He was amazed at what he found.

Can you believe it? Here I was—at headquarters of one of the largest technology companies in the world, and they had never even heard of response analysis when they formed the database marketing group. To my utter horror, they would just send out mailers and nobody ever bothered to count up the responses. They just immediately moved on and mailed off the next thing and just kept it going. There was no concept of improvement, no concept of modeling, no analytics involved, and by launching some initiatives around "let's determine what's working for whom," we were able to significantly increase the response rates of all the direct marketing activity that was going on.

Say, for example, that I can determine without too much trouble that someone is in charge of IT, they are probably going to care about the system's features. However, if I find out that someone is actually in marketing, they are probably going to care about maybe user training costs. By partitioning off customer interests and responsibilities and asking—here's a novel idea—asking people what they wanted to get more information about, we were able to dramatically impact campaign effectiveness. Again, you scratch you head and go wow, boy, we asked our customers what they wanted and gave it to them.

Sales reps at this firm were deeply suspicious of the whole concept of direct mail. I had sales reps tell me flat out, You are taking food off my table. And we said no, what we want to do is, we want to use analytics to find customers who are going to buy high-volume, low-dollar transactions, take those off your plate and you sell them the big expensive systems and the big expensive service contracts and we'll handle the disk drives for you. Not too long later, we had a $5 billion division and the sales reps were richer than ever.[70]

# The Media Industry Has Been Slow to Transform

We live in a transformed and transforming world. And yet, in every era, in every field of human endeavor, leaders struggle to balance the realities of the world of today with the promises, opportunities, and uncertainties of the future. Confronted with new ways of thinking, preservationists frequently fight to maintain the status quo. The Catholic

Church, for example, couldn't accommodate a heliocentric view of the universe, prompting Galileo to renounce the fact that the earth revolved around the sun. The media and consumer electronics industries, despite their proud history of device innovation, provide rich examples of change blindness. In the paleo-moments of this industry, visionaries Thomas Edison and George Eastman (an 1893 approximation of Microsoft, Intel, and Sony) collaborated to create a successful business around Kinetoscopes (machines that allowed users to individually view 30-second film snippets). When it was suggested that they look into the idea of projecting to an audience in a theater setting, Edison replied, "There will be use for maybe about 10 in the whole United States. . . . Let's not kill the golden goose."[71]

Jack Valenti, one-time president of the Motion Picture Association of America, will be remembered for his famous 1982 testimony before Congress: "I say to you that the VCR is to the American film producer and the American public what the Boston strangler is to the woman home alone."[72]

As we all know, eight years later total revenue from home video surpassed revenue from theatrical releases.

# Notes

1. Richard L. Nolan, "Managing the Computer Resource: A Stage Hypothesis," *Communications of the ACM* 16 (July 1973): 399–403. This original stages theory of computer growth was based on the learning curve reflected through the data processing budget. Subsequent publications focusing on the stages theory as applied to organizational learning include Cyrus F. Gibson and Richard L. Nolan, "Managing the Four Stages of EDP Growth," *Harvard Business Review* 52 (January-February 1974): 77–88, and Richard L. Nolan, "Managing the Crises in Data Processing," *Harvard Business Review* 57 (March-April 1979): 115–126.

2. Thomas Friedman speaking at the Stanford Energy Crossroads: "Building a Coalition for a Clean, Prosperous and Secure Energy Future," 2 March 2007 (http://stanford.energycrossroads.org). Friedman elaborated on the "three great eras of globalization," explaining that Global 1.0 began in 1492 and ended in the early 1800s with the advent of global arbitrage. Friedman claims that that era shrank the world from a size large to a size medium. "Countries globalizing—Spain going to America; Britain colonizing India—you went

global through your country." Global 2.0 went from the early 1800s to 2000. "It shrunk the world from size medium to size small. Spearheaded by companies looking for markets and labor—you went global through your company. Global 3.0 moves out from 2000—shrinking world from size small to size tiny. Not spearheaded by countries, by companies but by individuals." Globalization 3.0 is "[r]eally new, really exciting and really terrifying. Individuals can now compete, connect and collaborate globally." During 3.0, the personal computer allows individuals to author their own content in digital form. The browser is a tool that brought the Internet to life—the implication being that "grandma and granddaughter—not just MIT computer scientists can compute/connect." During the dot-com bubble, the "ridiculous overinvestment of 1 trillion dollars into fiber optic cable in 5 years accidentally wired the world with the implication being that Beijing, Bangalore and Boston are now next door neighbors. Everyone can collaborate around their digital content. Global platform for multiple forms of collaboration."

3. A blogger provides several examples (http://liako.biz/2008/05/the-value-chain-for-information), accessed 14 Jun 2009.

   i. Mining Industry

   Data Collection—Drilling core samples.

   Data Processing—Combining information from the core samples to build a view of the underlying terrain.

   Information Generation—Taking the new terrain map and understanding it (i.e., that particular fold and type of mineral could indicate gold).

   Knowledge Application—Successfully mining the gold.

   ii. Academic Research

   Data Collection—Hypothesis and conducting some experiment collecting samples.

   Data Processing—Crunching the numbers to find facts and figures.

   Information Generation—Interpreting the facts and figures and producing a research paper.

   Knowledge Application—Publishing that paper in a journal for peer review.

4. Phone interview with author Spring 2009.

5. http://gecapsol.com/cms/servlet/cmsview/GE_Capital_Solutions/prod/en/about_us (accessed January 31, 2009).

6. Phone interview with author Spring 2009.

7. Dr. George Poste, director, Biodesign Institute at Arizona State University, speaking at the Transforming American Health Care Symposium on September 29, 2007, on the topic "Genetics and Computing: The Principal Drivers of Systems Biology, Molecular Medicine and e.Health."

8.  Stephen Baker, *The Numerati* (Boston: Houghton Mifflin Company, 2008), 155.

9.  Ibid., 158.

10. Ibid., 70.

11. Ian Ayres, *Super Crunchers: Why Thinking-by-Numbers Is the New Way to Be Smart* (New York: Bantam Books, 2007), 96.

12. Author phone interview with Dave Hammond Spring 2009.

13. David D. Friedman, *Future Imperfect: Technology and Freedom in an Uncertain World* (Cambridge, UK Cambridge University Press, 2008), 57.

14. Baker, *The Numerati*, 43.

15. www.thecoca-colacompany.com/ourcompany/index.html (accessed January 31, 2009).

16. Joe Tripodi,, "Balancing Inspirational and Operational Marketing: Marketing Imperatives for Growth,"Association of National Advertisers (Orlando, October 2008).

17. *Beverage Digest*, June 25, 2004. www.beverage-digest.com/editorial/040625.php

18. Ibid.

19. Author phone interview Spring 2009.

20. Author phone interview with Ken Forster Spring 2009.

21. J. Walter Thompson Ad Agency (JWT), "10 Trends for 2008," *Work in Progress* (November 2007).

22. Phone interview with author Spring 2008—the executive prefers to remain anonymous.

23. Clive Crook, "On Milton Friedman's Unfinished Work," *Atlantic Monthly*, December 12, 2006. See http://www.theatlantic.com/doc/200612u/nj_crook_2006-12-12.

24. Author phone interview Winter 2009.

25. Jack Neff, "Kroger: A Marketing 50 Case Study," *Advertising Age*, November 17, 2008.

26. Paco Underhill interviewed on NPR's *Science Friday*, "Understanding the Science of Shopping," December 12, 2008.

27. Richard Holmes, *The Age of Wonder: How the Romantic Generation Discovered the Beauty and Terror of Science* (London: Harper, 2008), xvi.

28. Stephanie Clifford, "Web Marketing That Hopes to Learn What Attracts a Click," *New York Times*, December 3, 2008. See: www.nytimes.com/2008/12/03/business/media/03adco.html?_r=2

29. Stephanie Clifford, "Web Marketing That Hopes to Learn What Attracts a Click," *New York Times*, December 3, 2008. See: www.nytimes.com/2008/12/03/business/media/03adco.html?_r=2

30. Baker, *The Numerati*, 43.

31. Advanced practices now do collaborative analytics extraorganizationally (i.e., my model talks to and informs your model, and vice versa). A broad trend is that higher-end analytics—once the purview of PhD-wielding "10-pound brains" are now available at the desktop and mobile device of normal workers.

32. I first became aware of Mr. Heyer's speech while reading J. Walker Smith, Ann Clurman, and Craig Wood, *Coming to Concurrence: Addressable Attitudes and the New Model for Marketing Productivity* (Evanston, IL: Racom Communications, 2005), 5. The speech may be viewed in its entirety at: http://www.pop2life. com/stevenjheyerspeech.pdf

33. Stephen Baker, *The Numerati*, 55.

34. J. Walker Smith, Ann Clurman, Craig Wood, *Coming to Concurrence: Addressable Attitudes and the New Model for Marketing Productivity* (Evanston, IL: Racom Communications, 2005), 35.

35. Author phone interview Fall 2008.

36. Caroline Muspratt, "'Pay as You Drive' with Norwich Union," *Telegraph*, October 4, 2006.

37. Ayres, *Super Crunchers*, 47.

38. Michael Schrage, a fellow with the MIT Sloan School's Center for Digital Business, speaking at the CIO 100 conference, Colorado Springs, Colorado, August 2008.

39. Robert Weisman, "Working to Strengths Is Survival Strategy: Narrow Focus May Help Firms Stay Agile," *Boston Globe*, December 7, 2008.

40. C. K. Prahalad and M. S. Krishnan, *The New Age of Innovation: Driving Cocreated Value through Global Networks* (New York: McGraw-Hill, 2008), 95.

41. Mark Leonard, *What Does China Think?* (New York: Perseus, 2008), 6.

42. Robert M. Gates, "A Balanced Strategy: Reprogramming the Pentagon for a New Age," *Foreign Affairs* (January/February 2009): 28.

43. Dr. Kendra Moore, Program Manager, Information Exploitation Office, "Patterns, Patterns, Everywhere. . ." DARPATech 2007, August 9, 2007.

44. Robert H. Scales Jr., "Culture-Centric Warfare," *Proceedings* (Annapolis, MD: U.S. Naval Institute, September 2004).

45. "Utilizing Social Science Technology to Understand and Counter the 21st Century Strategic Threat," DARPATech 2005.

46. Prahalad and Krishnan, *New Age of Innovation*, 88.

47. Phone interview with author Winter 2009.

48. "DARPA Advances Artificial Intelligence Program for Air Traffic Control," *Network World*, February 11, 2008.

49. Bruce Thompson, "Benjamin Franklin and the Enlightenment," *Stanford University History* 136, July 18, 2007, podcast.

50. "State of Science," *Seed Magazine* (December 2008). http://seedmagazine.com/stateofscience/

51. http://research.microsoft.com/en-us/um/cambridge/projects/towards2020science/; accessed 14 June 2009

52. "Putting God in a Box," *The Week*, January 13, 2006.

53. *Towards Science 2020*, is a report funded by Microsoft Research summarizing the work of the 2020 Science Group—over 30 scientists spanning biology, physics, chemistry, biochemistry, astronomy, genetics, medicine, mathematics and computer science, and 12 different nationalities. Coming from some of the world's leading research institutions and companies, the scientists were elected for their expertise in a particular field. The report synthesized collaborations emerging from a Venice workshop in July 2005. See: http://www.microsoft.com/presspass/press/2006/mar06/03-21MSR2020PR.mspx

54. Heather Chaplin and Aaron Ruby, *Smartbomb: The Quest for Art, Entertainment, and Big Bucks in the Videogame Revolution* (Chapel Hill, NC: Algonquin Books of Chapel Hill, 2006).

55. *Towards Science 2020*, 8.

56. Friedman, *Future Imperfect,* chap. 9, "Reactionary Progress—Amateur Scholars and Open Source," 123.

57. Baker, *The Numerati*, 1170.

58. Ashlee Vance, "Nvidia Chip Speeds Up Imaging for Industrial Use," *New York Times*, September 22, 2008.

59. Julian E. Orr, *Talking about Machines: An Ethnography of a Modern Job* (Ithaca, NY: Cornell University Press, 1996), ix.

60. Ibid., ix.

61. Baker, *The Numerati*, 20.

62. Ibid., 23.

63. Ibid., 33.

64. Ibid.

65. Matt Richtel, "More Companies Are Cutting Labor Costs without Layoffs," *New York Times*, December 22, 2008.

66. Christine Negroni, "Airline Black Boxes Get a New Role: Reassurance," *International Herald Tribune*, December 16, 2008.

67. Francis Fukuyama, "The Great Disruption," *Atlantic Monthly* (May 1999), 55–80.

68. David Brooks, "The Politics of Cohesion," *New York Times*, January 20, 2009.

69. John Zogby, *The Way We'll Be: The Zogby Report on the Transformation of the American Dream* (New York: Random House, 2008), 206.

70. Phone interview with author Winter 2009.

71. Scott Kirsner, *Inventing The Movies: Hollywood's Epic Battle Between Innovation And The Status Quo, From Thomas Edison To Steve Jobs* (New York: Cinema Tech Books, 2008).

72. Scott Kirsner, book signing (Portsmouth, NH, February 2009).

# Chapter 3

# The Analyst

*A New Animal in The Organizational Forest*

We have come to that point in the evolution of civilization, society, norms of behavior, and technology adoption and use, where most of what we do creates data, leaving a trail of informational crumbs. Via some process, these crumbs somehow come to reside in data repositories, databases, and/or clouds. High-performance organizations consistently, reliably, economically, and innovatively actually do something with that data. Someone in the enterprise takes that data and does something interesting with it. The people doing some of the highest-value and most interesting things with data are sometimes called analysts. These knowledge alchemists transform data into insight.

Analysts are probably the least understood and most under-the-radar animals in the modern enterprise today. One of the main reasons for writing this book is to help mainstream decision makers better understand who these people are. This book follows a line of business best sellers about analytics: Tom Davenport's *Competing on Analytics*, Ian Ayres's *Super Crunchers*, and Stephen Baker's *Numerati*. These are great books written by supremely gifted scholars. However, readers could come away thinking that analysts are not quite normal. For example, Baker in *Numerati* posits that "the only folks who can make sense of the data we create are crack mathematicians, computer scientists, and engineers."[1] I don't think this is the case. Analytics and analysts should be part of the mainstream and should not be ghettoized in special Mensa zones for the mathematically gifted but socially challenged. Analysts are real people—just like you and me.

Are they all the same? Are there separate and distinct analytical "tribes"? Do different types of analysts play well with each other? Do they play well with the rest of the animals in the organizational forest? Over the past two years, I did a walkabout in the Global 2000 (the top 2000 public companies in the world) conducting what many might consider a low-intensity ethnographic study of analysts. I essentially studied the analyst habitat. Where do they come from? Where do they live in the organization? How are they treated?

In this chapter I ask the question: Who are the analysts? Western societies have used anthropology as a mirror of sorts that allows and encourages a better understanding of ourselves through the study of others. By borrowing and bastardizing anthropological techniques, I hope to help nonanalysts come to a better understanding of the analysts' world and how it works. I collected a lot of data about a lot of "analysts" through extensive interviews. When quotes are presented in the chapter without attribution, they come from those interviews. This data revealed that the practice of analytics has evolved over time. Analytics and analysts of today are materially different from those of 10 years ago.

Ruth Benedict's landmark anthropological study of the Japanese, *The Chrysanthemum and the Sword*, has been accused of making getting to know Japan look too easy. I hope to be accused of the same transgression regarding analysts. For those who read Benedict's book, the Japanese, once inscrutable, were suddenly crystal clear.

My objective is to reveal, unmask, or unwrap the "real" analyst. I do this by accumulating comparative data from a series of field studies and interviews in different areas of the analytic community.

In anthropology, fieldwork is often used to expand the understanding of others, close or distant. Fieldwork usually means living with and living like those who are studied. I did not do this. In a vague way, of course, we are all field workers whenever we must make sense of strange surroundings and pass on our understandings to others. In its broadest, most conventional sense, fieldwork demands the full-time involvement of a researcher over a lengthy period of time and consists mostly of ongoing interaction with the human targets of study on their home ground. I did not go "native" with analysts, but I did spent a lot of time in the field with them, hoping to discover their cultural practices and attitudes. Who knows—after reading this book, anthropologists might come to recognize and appreciate analytics as an area worthy of more detailed anthropological inquiry. Like Margaret Mead, I went out into the field looking for general patterns. I sought to better understand:

- What do analysts do?
- Where/how do analysts spend their time?
- What does the rest of the organization think analysts do?
- Where did analysts go to school/what did they study?
- What was their first job?
- How are they evaluated?
- What does an "analytical" career path look like?
- What motivates analysts?
- How do analysts think (about themselves, about others, about problem solving in general)?

## What Do Analysts Do?

We asked all analysts we encountered to explain, in their own words, what exactly they did. Their answers, in alphabetical order, include:

- Answer questions from the business.[2]
- Build:
  - Databases.
  - Data marts.
  - Data warehouses.

- Models.
- Infrastructure/systems that enable businesses to ask and answer their own questions.[3]
- Parameter-driven inquiries.
- Tools.
- Transparent end-to-end information flows.[4]
- Cleanse data.
- Collect data.
- Conduct:
  - Data mining.
  - Primary research via focus groups.
  - Predictive analytics.
  - Promotion and campaign analytics.
- Enable:
  - Better understanding of who the customer is and where the customer is.
  - Total view of the customer.[5]
  - Better understanding of what the customer wants and how the customer wants it.
  - Customer segmentation.
  - Proactive asset management/maintenance.[6]
  - Risk management.
  - Revenue management (fire unprofitable customers).
- Generate:
  - Major routine reports (e.g., customer satisfaction via an info-portal).
  - Assertions.[7]
- Manage:
  - Databases.
  - Data marts.
  - Data warehouses.
  - Models.

According to the Institute for Advanced Analytics at North Carolina State University, the term "advanced analytics" covers a broad spectrum of activities, including data collection and integration, statistical methods, and complex processes for enterprise-wide decision making.[8]

A debilitating misconception by many outside the practice of analytics is to assume that all analysts do is "crunch numbers." Frank Wrenn, the gifted and eloquent manager of market research in the Customer Insight & Analytics department at Delta Air Lines, really put his finger on what analysts do when he said, analytics is "the ability to look at the data and then turn that into a story; to be able to draw from all kinds of information and turn it into a story."

Storytelling is a big part of analytics. After you crunch the numbers, after you generate insight, you have to do something with it. Analysts need to figure out what are we going to do with what we know. What recommendation can we put together to actually make a difference? Some of the information emerging from the analytic engines and processes is neat to know but has no operational impact. But certain insights do have ramifications to mandate change in a tactic or a strategy.

Zahir Balaporia, the soft-spoken but quietly passionate and impressively effective director of decision engineering at Schneider National Inc.,[9] is very active in analytical trade and professional organizations. He and his colleagues across industries agree that "most people don't really understand what we do." He is shocked that some analytical groups actually believe their work is done when the computer stops. "Analysts who say 'Here's the analysis, here's the numbers, and if you don't get it, then sorry, I can't help you' are missing the point. We have to give the data a voice so that it can tell its story and provide a direction for action."

Soyal Momin, director of research and population analytics at Blue Cross and Blue Shield of Tennessee, closes every year by having every team in his group craft "value stories" showcasing what the group has done and accomplished.

Another broadly held misconception seems to be that analytics is applicable only to certain parts of the business. While some areas offer an abundance of low-hanging analytical fruit, just about every department in every enterprise could benefit from a good analytical once-over.

Balaporia explains that unlike some analytical teams that focus on just one part of the business, "We are all over the board . . . we do stuff in customer retention/acquisition, dispatch optimization, pricing, call center operations, back-room process improvement, designing metrics, safety for our trucks and the motoring public."

Rosalee Hermens, CIO at Timberland, is a big believer in the power of analytics. She has courageously pointed out to various heads of business lines around the world that the processes in place were not designed and would not be able to generate the information they desired. To get the information they wanted would require changing the underlying business processes.

## Understanding Customers

Without a doubt, some of the most intensive use of analytics is in marketing, specifically analysis of customer data.

Chris McCann, president of 1-800-Flowers.Com, Inc. told me the story of how his firm used business analytics to identify and delight a key customer category—the person who lives to give. With the help of analytics, 1-800-Flowers.com, Inc. was able to create a persona that made this customer category come alive in the eyes of company employees. [10]

One interviewee told the story of when working at a large household products company, his team was trying to understand the difference between people who use toilet tablets that turn the water blue versus people who use chlorine-based tablets that don't turn the water blue. By determining what made these people tick, the analysts hoped that great sales and profitability might ensue.

Another analyst at a market research firm talked about creating profiles of health-conscious women who are also appearance oriented in order that marketing programs might be designed to reach out to them. An analyst at a direct mail retailer talked about how analytics could ascertain, if you had purchased Product A and Product B, there was a high probability that your next purchase would be Product Z.

The head of analytics at a hospitality company explained:

> With analytics you can measure ROI [return on investment] on a campaign or banner ad. Analytics also helps develop customer segmentation. Basically it is identifying the customers and then sending messaging that is relevant, appropriate and actually gets them to take action. We have this curriculum—how do we

move people from this bucket to the next bucket to the next bucket? We also started being more trigger based and more automated. This person has done this and this and this—they get this offer. We are really working hard to automate our generation of relevant and timely offers that drive value.

An airline might be able to identify a low-frequency, high-fare customer. Such customers are called splitters; they split their purchases between various airlines. Analytics might enable the airline to capture a greater percentage of those customers' premium fare business.

Eric Williams, the chief information officer (CIO) at Catalina Marketing, shared a fabulous example of using analytics to better understand and reach customers. As many readers know, soymilk has become quite the thing these days. Manufacturers of soymilk would like to intelligently target all consumers that they believe would be interested in the product.

The marketing team for any product is responsible for finding out who the target audience is. Is it females between 25 and 35? Is it kids or families with kids? Initial marketing for soymilk focused on consumers identified as being interested in their health. Evidently soymilk is one of these products that you like or you don't like. There is really no middle ground. But if you like it, you will constantly continue to use it.

One of the companies that manufacture soymilk went to Catalina Marketing and said:

> Okay, we are focusing on people who are looking for high-quality merchandise. We found people who are going after wholesome type of grains and other things, we've focused on all of those individuals, we've used your system very effectively but we think there is a new opportunity for us. We'd like to show people that *only* use milk or cream to lighten their coffee that soy is a much better product and doesn't change the taste of the coffee.

The soymilk manufacturer wanted to identify customers who are buying milk or cream to lighten their coffee, not to drink. The Catalina system could easily identify the people who bought milk, the people who bought coffee, and the people who bought milk *and* coffee. But how in the world could it determine how people used the milk after they got it home?

The Catalina analytics team went to work trying to figure this out. Catalina has a program called behavior-activated research. In many retail outlets, the bottom of the receipt tape asks you to go to a Web site to participate in a survey. Catalina printed offers to customers to participate in a survey based on their buying a certain product that it wanted to know about.

Williams explains:

> We printed an offer to give customers a $10 gift certificate good at the retailer where people bought fluid milk. We printed tens of thousands of offers. We had set up an interactive voice response Web site, asking them some basic questions. Somewhere buried in the question script was one that says, "Do you use milk to lighten your coffee?" Those that did were asked to respond to a number that was printed on the Catalina voucher, which gave us the ability to link the responses of this survey back to the transaction. Now we had a set of customers that answered the question affirmatively, that they did use milk to lighten their coffee. We could now take that subset and throw it at the data mining algorithm and say—tell me things about these customers that are common. We then executed the marketing campaign for the soy product and had some of the highest redemption rates we've ever had. So, we predicted who actually used milk to put in their coffee and not just to drink.

One of the reasons an organization wants to understand its customers is that once you have found them, you want to keep them and monitor any and all signals that might indicate that they are thinking of shopping somewhere else. Here again an example from Eric Williams at Catalina Marketing is illustrative.

All retailers have as one of their long-term goals the desire to keep people loyal to their store. Is there—via the wonders of analytics—a way for a retailer to know when a customer is on the cusp of defecting and to do something to circumvent that decision? Analytically here you are asking two questions: How do I know if a customer is going to leave my store? What can I do about it?

Williams explains:

> Most people would develop an ad hoc report that says, "Tell me all the people that provide $X amount and if that sales volume has dropped by $Y amount. So, if they used to buy $100 a week and now spend only $50 a week, maybe they're leaving my store." That was the traditional model. The challenge with that is that by the time that situation has occurred, that customer has likely already made the decision that they are leaving their store.
>
> What you want to do is to be able to predict that a customer is going to stop shopping at your store before it is noticeable in a loss of sales. So we did that. We threw a whole bunch of data at the computer for a set of consumers who did lapse the store and for a whole bunch of people who haven't.
>
> In this example, we did find that there was one key item that was a telltale product that if a customer used to buy this item, and then stopped buying this item, that there was a high percentage likelihood that this customer would stop shopping at that store. Do you have any idea what the product was? Believe it or not, it was fluid milk.

As the boundaries between supermarkets, drugstores, and discount stores blur to the point that most shoppers no longer think about retailers in terms of trade class, it becomes critically important for retailers and manufacturers to understand where the customer's head is at the time of contact/purchase. Understanding this would enable much more appropriate messaging and might enhance service recovery. Such situational awareness would allow airlines, when you check in at the kiosk, to say "Oh, sorry about your delay yesterday, here's a free drink coupon."

We are moving from a world where we "kind of/sort of" understand customers to one where we have granular, near-real-time understanding of their exact situation. Becky Blalock at the Southern Company[11] explains that her organization is moving to an automated metering infrastructure. It used to be the utility got one meter reading a month; someone physically walked by houses and got a reading about what electricity customers were using. With smart meters, Southern Company will have the ability to read the meter every 15 seconds. This empowers customers by sending pricing signals giving them the option to use less power when it is most expensive.

Consumer intelligence is a critical and foundational tool that needs to be demystified. Data mining in general and consumer behavior analysis need to be taken out of the "black box." We need clearer and simpler ways for everyone in the enterprise to understand what customers think/do/want. We need to render the link among profit/mission success, consumer behavior, and internal process transparent.

## Evolution of Analytics

Even though analytics has been around for a while, the language about analytics has yet to mature.

Wanda Shive is an analytic practitioner. She has served as chief financial officer, vice president of information, controller, and buyer. Her retail experience includes Food Lion, Babies R Us (formerly Baby Superstore), and Planet Music (a former division of Borders Group). After 25 years of cutting-edge work in analytics, Shive went back to school for a master's of science in analytics (MSA) from North Carolina State University, one of 23 students in the first graduating class. She is a principal at Waterstone Analytics. Shive agrees "that the word 'analytics' is misunderstood and misrepresented."

Analytics has run hot and cold over the past 20 years. Many tribal leaders recount a time—probably around 1997—when analytics was all the rage. Many believed that analytics was going to run the world. Then the dot-com boom came along, and everything exciting or valuable had to have the prefix "e" (e-logistics, e-commerce, e-gov, etc.).

Michael Rappa is the founder and director of the Institute for Advanced Analytics at NC State, which runs the MSA degree program. Prior to joining NC State, he was a professor at the Massachusetts Institute of Technology for nine years. Rappa believes that the environment has changed so much that a new graduate degree was needed; that is why he conceived of the MSA.

Rappa helped me understand that in the "old days," most data sets were handcrafted. Analytics was something you thought through in advance. You preconceived how you were going to analyze the data. On an *ex ante* basis, you knew what results you were seeking to gain and what you were trying to understand. Today's data is not so neatly structured. Just about everything you do and every process in the enterprise generates data, continuously and in massive quantities. Whether you want to analyze it or not, it generates data. The question for executives and students alike is: How are we going to analyze this data? Rappa elaborates on the importance of looking at data with new eyes:

> What are we trying to understand from it? So not only is there more data, but it really is different now too. It's messier. It doesn't have the neatness of something that's hand constructed. So we have this mass of data. How do we draw something useful from it? It's easy and seductive to say "Well, we have all this data, you know, let's analyze it" but it's really much, much more complicated than that.
>
> . . . [J]ust working with the vast amount of data that you have is always going to be a challenge, because the amount of data is always growing.
>
> . . . [T]hose of us who work with data know that it's really messy. And it's messy because it emerges as the outcome of lots of different things that we do and processes. The data is not necessarily the result of carefully designed, experimental studies to create particular kinds of data sets to analyze.

One of the questions analysts have wrestled with is for whom analytics should be performed—internal or external customers? One up-and-coming head of analytics at a services firm recalls that at first the analytical group at his company was set up as a for-fee service for customers. In that configuration, analytics placed more than $1 million on the top line. Time passed and senior management started thinking that that $1 million on the top line was great, but what if they took the entire investment in analytics and focused it on saving $1 million somewhere else in their business? They would reap the benefits of that $1 million *year after year* and probably could save a lot more than $1 million. So analytics became an internally focused, enterprise-wide shared service.

## Analyst Brand

Those who do analytics in the enterprise often are stereotyped inappropriately as "geeks." Anthropological research indicates that a given group's awareness of who they are and what they are doing is conditioned by their understanding of other people's awareness of who they are and what they are doing. Maine fishermen alter their work habits to suit what they imagine to be the tastes and preferences of Japanese tuna connoisseurs.[12]

I asked everyone I interviewed their thoughts regarding the general organizational attitude toward analytics.

A senior official in the intelligence community explained:

[There] is an insatiable desire for more. There are a group of people who you could refer to as power users or analysts, who are the keepers of the nuance of the data. There are relatively few executives who know how to access and manipulate that information. They know what they want to get out, but they can't actually lay their hands on or run the reports themselves.

A 20-year veteran in the highly competitive food business explains:

Analytics is viewed as extraordinarily important. Every decision has to be grounded in it, but it's underfunded and underresourced, dramatically. The expectations are extremely high, and the resources allocated to it are really low. Expectations continue to rise, and the resources continue to shrink. I am pretty sure this situation is somewhat universal.

One area where underfunding really gets in the way of being able to get full value out of analytical investments/activities is data quality. Several senior executives said they were uncomfortable trusting the outputs of various models, independent of how expertly created they might have been, because of inaccurate data.

We asked a prominent venture capitalist known for his 360-degree view of the technology industry what he thought of when he heard the phrase "business intelligence." His response: "big software, little analysis."

## Education of Analysts

Anthropologists examine the knowledge an individual has to have to function as a member of the culture. They ask "What does a person have to know to be considered a part of the group? Michael Rappa believes that the world has become so data intensive that new skills are needed—there truly is a New Know:

> We have all this data, now we really have to get it in the structure where we can analyze it. And now I think we're at the point where we need the people who have the skills to really understand the kind of analytical problem that this is and to be able to apply those tools intelligently and address the problems that our organization faces. The reason that we created this particular degree [the master's of science in analytics] was that realization that there was going to be a critical shortage of the kinds of people who understand enough about the data, and enough about the tools and methods to be able to apply them intelligently.

North Carolina State University created the Institute for Advanced Analytics with the specific goal to promote graduate education in the emerging field of analytics. Rappa and his team are intent on educating students to be prepared to work in the field after graduation. They did this by actually going out to the industry and examining what skills employers need most. They then proceeded to design a new degree— the master's of science in analytics (MSA)—from the ground up. Rappa recalls:

> We did something that I had never done before and I've been teaching for over 20 years. We started with a clean whiteboard and began by asking what do employers want? To answer this question we analyzed large numbers of job

descriptions for the kinds of people who I thought we would turn out. We went to career fairs, and talked with employers. What we found was, yes, employers need people with a technical skill level in math and statistics, or the quantitative orientation—but they want more. They want employees who have strong teamwork, communication and leadership skills. They want employees who can work well in multifunctional teams, who know how to use the complex analytical tools the organization uses, and who understand something about their business.

The analysts we talked to had undergraduate majors in computer science, consumer behavior, electrical engineering, finance, marketing, math, physics, and software engineering. There were a surprising number of English majors too. Analysts need to be good at math, *not great at math*.

The empirical evidence supports the fact that analytically astute, articulate, cross-disciplinary team players are in high demand. Rappa shares some data:

> We graduated the first class of two dozen students in May 2008. When employers came to interview students, you could tell how thrilled they were. They were seeing a different kind of student, one they don't normally see. Students who are technically strong *and* have the practical skill set to get the job done. These are students they could put in a position and know they can function at a high level from day one.

> I can't tell you how many times we had managers come here to recruit and learn about the program, who end up saying "I wish that they had this degree when I was in school."

Wanda Shive can't say enough great things about the MSA degree. She remembers:

> The MSA program weaves the science with the practical application of analytics. The wide variety of academic and

professional backgrounds of my fellow students enriched our experience. Understanding analytic methodologies is relevant to folks from all walks of life. I highly recommend the program and would do it all over again in a heartbeat.

NC State is certainly not the only source of world-class analysts, but it is a good place to start. We found exceptional analysts emerging from first-tier undergraduate schools, such as Dartmouth and Duke, big state schools (the University of Illinois), small state schools, small private colleges, and first-tier graduate schools (the Yale School of Management).

We asked Eric Williams where he managed to find his high-performing analysts.

It is very interesting. We actually find a lot of them directly from the major analytic houses in the U.S. So we find them from the IRIs [Information Resources, Inc.], from the Nielsens, those types of organizations. They are typically people who have a fair amount of history with them and are frustrated and tired of doing the same old things. So they are looking for some cutting edge services. They are looking for ways to be able to truly utilize the data and be actionable. That is something that is unique about Catalina. Information companies and reach companies being organizations like the IRIs and the Nielsens of the world, have information, but they can't do anything about it. They can report on it. And then you've got reach entities or media companies that can reach people but don't know anything about them. An example of that are all of the cable networks, ABC, NBC, the print services on down the line. We are the only entity in the world that is able to bridge that gap. You have the information and we can do something about it. So the analytic people out in the marketplace love coming here because they get to do the research and then they get to go and execute it. Then they get to do the analytics and see how accurate their assumption was.

We asked Zahir Balaporia at Schneider to describe the background of his analytics team.

> Most of our folks came out of what one would typically call industrial engineering or operations research programs from universities like Virginia Tech, Purdue, Georgia Tech, University of Wisconsin, and Northwestern. Most of them have advanced degrees in operations research, industrial/systems engineering, statistics, or computer science.
>
> My group has three roles: process engineers, logistics engineers, and research analysts. The process engineers are applying industrial engineering methods to the service industry. They're really looking at our business processes and using analytical techniques to help improve them. Our logistics engineers are more your classic operations research (OR) folks developing optimization and simulation models.
>
> Our research analysts have a strong quantitative analytics background but tend to have a heavier computer programming/computer science background. A lot of the stuff we do requires coding.
>
> For example, we developed and implemented a driver dispatch decision support system. On the team we have two great OR guys with good programming skills and a great computer science guy with good OR skills. When required we threw in a stats guy to help develop statistical profiles for driver waiting times that can be incorporated into the optimization model.

## Career Path

The more time I spend in the analytic habitat, the more convinced I am that independent of where a person might start his or her career, successful careers always end up in analytics. It is good to know stuff, and it is even better to know how to know. That is what analytics is all about.

Analysts who experience accelerated career success share three characteristics:

1. They work in an industry that understands the power of analytics.
2. They work in an enterprise that understands that analytics is a key source of competitive advantage and performance excellence.
3. They work for a boss who gets it.

This is the career trifecta.

Another key element of analytical career success is either having a good relationship with IT or being self sufficient in IT. Sometimes it helps to be both. George Jackman, director of applied insights and shopper marketing at Welch's, took an "IT sidetrack" to lead the process development and automation of the process for sales, planning, trade fund management, and analytics. Ken Foster was once director of retail sales and radio-frequency identification (RFID) programs on the IT side of the house and is now group director of strategy, planning and analytics for Coca-Cola's most important customers. Successful analysts are adept at spanning organizational boundaries.

Eric Webster, vice president of marketing at State Farm Insurance, is surprisingly articulate, urbane, and jovial given his very quantitative career beginnings:

> All I wanted to do was sit in a dark cube and have fun with my friends and write FORTRAN code, which was exactly what I did when I was hired by a company while I was going to grad school to write their marketing systems for them. So I came in and I had enough 2-liter bottles of Diet Coke that 15 months later out popped their marketing system.
>
> I was a programmer for one and a half years when the head of the company looked at the system that I wrote after a demo and said this is great, except that I have nobody that can use it. And I, of course, hung my head in shame and said okay, I guess I'll write the documentation and training, the bane of every programmer's existence. He replies, "No, you don't understand what I'm saying. I don't even have anybody that you can train. How would you like to come to marketing?" So, I came over and I became Mr. Analytics for this particular company.

Some companies actually are led by analytics. Dr. Christopher Lofgren is the chief executive officer (CEO) at Schneider National Inc. Dr. Gary Loveman is the CEO at Harrah's.

Analytics is a pretty safe place to be career wise. Analysts are rarely fired—they are attritted. *U.S. News & World Report*'s guide to the best careers published in December 2008 lists data miner as one of a dozen ahead-of-the-curve careers for 2009:

> Data mining is a great career for people who would enjoy using statistics to unearth patterns in data, using ever more powerful software. Opportunities are particularly good if you also have business sense and the ability to tease out the information that bosses really want to know.

From the IAA Web site (http://analytics.ncsu.edu/) we learn:

> The impact of the recent economic downturn on data mining jobs appears to be limited. CareerBuilder.com, the U.S.'s largest online job site, has over 800 data mining–related jobs— and nearly 1400 jobs in analytics—listed in the past 30 days. Although salaries for data mining analysts vary with education and experience, annual base pay for new recruits is frequently in the range of $80,000.

## Motivation

Analysts and analytics are all about making the enterprise better. Time after time we heard people mention reducing the time required for businesses to access the data needed to run the business. Rosalee Hermens, who as CIO frequently champions important analytic projects at Timberland, is passionate: "I set out to do whatever it takes to help us get information that actually gets us into the place where we can do things better."

A big motivator for most analysts is the quest to ask the right question. Isidor Rabi, the Columbia University Nobel Prize–winning physicist, told interviewers of an early influence on his sense of inquiry. When he returned home from grade school each day, his mother did not ask "Did you learn anything today?" but "Did you ask a good question today?" Gerald Edelman, a Nobel laureate in medicine, affirms that "the asking of the question is the important thing." Analytics and analysts allow the enterprise to ask great questions.

Deborah Wall, customer insights leader for GE Capital Americas, explains that she

> loves to understand what makes people buy what they buy and why they make the purchase decisions they make. Early on, I wanted to be able to understand and be able to analyze, quantify why consumers and businesses make the purchase decisions they make. I wanted to understand why the marketplace operates the way it does.

Carl Gerber, vice president of IT strategy and enterprise architecture for Essilor of America, says: "What matters to me is that I'm able to socialize the use of analytics and that we [IT] can uplift the organization's ability to compete using analytics. So I place more of an emphasis on using the tools than implementing the tools themselves."

Have you ever noticed how people in the food business are really passionate about what they do and where they work? It's very refreshing. An analyst in the industry told me what gets him up in the morning:

> It's talking to the customer . . . continually trying to figure out what makes them tick; what makes them anxious. It is continually trying to build credibility with them. Staying ruthlessly objective to the point where if we discover something significant that is not in our favor, calling them up and saying "Hey, guess what, we learned this and it's not good for us." Doing that stuff . . . builds tremendous respect and credibility.

Dave Hammond at Cardinal Health believes analytics is going to change every aspect of the healthcare industry. It is going to change how the medical device manufacturers behave. It is going to change how hospitals operate. And yes, it will change some of what the true heroes of healthcare—the nurses—do. Historically, every division, every department of every healthcare organization had its own technology architectures. These architectures were never designed to share data. At the end of the day, it is all about taking care of patients. What may be needed is a thorough analysis with a follow-on process reengineering in hospitals. Hammond is convinced that one of the very best ways for any company to make money in healthcare is to "keep people from making mistakes."

Analysts become very frustrated when the enterprise fails to take full advantage of what analytics can do. Several believe that, on average, most enterprises are capturing about only 30 percent of the value, leaving 70 percent on the table. As one interviewer said with a sigh, "You hear the term 'low-hanging fruit.' Well, in this company, the analytical fruit is so low I have to bend over to pick it up. It's on the ground."

## Managing Analysts

Analysts' roles span from entry level to executive management. Their functions involve planning, execution, and collaboration. A major subset of analysts' work (typically about 60 percent of analytics) is project based. There are short projects and long projects. At a clothing retailer, some of that project work might be with the catalog business: helping the company assess the effectiveness of the catalogs, creating insights so it can get more productive with mailings. Some is operational: people who actually are managing/overseeing the systems and processes whereby data is collected.

There is an administrative component: keeping track of what your people are working on. At the end of each week, Zahir Balaporia at Schneider National receives a brief written report of what happened last week. At the beginning of each week, he gets more face to face, engaging in half-hour conversations with project groups about what's on tap this week and what the next few weeks look like. Most conversations about analytics leave out the all-important aspect of people management. Analytic executives are responsible for people who have lives and careers and feel fulfilled and satisfied. Most of the analytic executives we talk to spend a good amount of time helping their people manage their careers. Does it make sense for an employee to move onto other things? And if so, what might be appropriate next steps?

The head analyst at a food company believes that managing analysts is a very different job from just doing analytics.

> How can I help my folks? Be it a specific initiative they're working on, a challenge they are facing. Can I grab more resources, or create more focus on those key issues here at the

headquarters office? Are there roadblocks I can knock down, funding I can secure? Stuff like that. One of my people might be working on an initiative when they encounter an issue with a customer. It might be brainstorming on what sources of information might we find that would support a given inquiry, and once we find them, how to best pick it apart and put it back together to build a compelling story.

Most of the senior analytic executives I spoke to were actually responsible for setting up the analytic department in the first place—that's how young the discipline is. Insurance is a fascinating business with a fascinating history. Many will be surprised to learn that marketing has not been a big part of that history for long. The head analyst at one insurance firm recalls that when he arrived at his company:

> There was no concept of a marketing department. Four or five of us were hired in from the outside. Previously the business had just sort of relied on agents to go out and find business opportunities. If agents wanted the home office to send some direct mail for them, we would, but by and large headquarters serviced the agents and our business plan every year was "Boy, I sure hope the agents write a lot of business. That would be great!"

> We sort of realized at some point that maybe being a little more proactive would be a good thing, so we went out and built a marketing department from scratch. We built a customer-centered database. Prior to this, all information was policy-centric. If I had to change an address, I had to go to the auto policy system and change the address and then go into the fire policy system and change that address and then go into the life insurance system and change that address. Marketing went and built a database that said: Here's a customer and you show me the products, as opposed to the other way around. By seeing the spectrum of products that people owned, we could then make intelligently cross-sell products. We had never been able to do this before.

These senior managers feel very responsible for creating an environment in which analysts can do great work. Managing the analysts and processes can be challenging due to the varied levels of both managerial and technical expertise existing in one area.

Analytics, like many technical disciplines, frequently faces the problem of an inverted age/expertise hierarchy. In a slowly changing society—which is to say in almost all of human history—older people, while they may not run as fast or even think as fast as younger people, know more. So it makes sense to have institutional structures in which, on average, older people have authority over younger people.

As the rate of change increases, so does the rate at which knowledge depreciates. The head of the research department knows much more about vacuum tubes than the young engineers whose work she supervises, but they are not researching vacuum tubes. But the faster the world is changing, the more ignorant the people in authority are likely to be, hence the more likely to make serious errors in their decisions.

One cannot solve the problem by simply inverting the age/authority hierarchy, appointing students fresh out of law school as judges, hiring the newest graduates of Cal Tech and Harvey Mudd to supervise research laboratories. . . . Managing a team of engineers requires knowledge of managing as well as knowledge of engineering. Some of the skills required for the job are in slowly changing fields, where the traditional pattern makes sense; some are in rapidly changing fields, where it does not.

One result of the situation is to reinforce the natural tendency of employees to ignore or evade the instructions of their superiors. The inverted hierarchy of expertise not only encourages employees to believe that they know how to do their job better than the managers they report to, but also encourages them to believe that they can get away with saying "Yes, sir" and then doing what they please. No old fogey of 45 is going to figure out what they are really doing. It is an attitude especially likely in employees with the sort of personality typical among bright young technophiles.[13]

Most senior leaders in analytics will readily admit that the people working for them are "a lot smarter" than they are technically.

Balaporia at Schneider clarifies:

They're much deeper than me. My job is to integrate. Where they go deep, I go broad. Because I'm going broad, I can help make connections between people, projects, and analytical techniques. So when we are discussing a project I might say "Bill, you should talk to Jeff because what you're doing is similar to something he did three years ago." The most important thing I can do is create an environment where they can maximize and multiply the impact of their analytical skills.

Sometimes optimization problems tend to stay in an optimization silo and data mining problems tend to stay in the data mining silo. We had a situation where we had an optimization model embedded within a simulation model. Why couldn't we take the results of multiple optimization runs and apply our data mining tools to the results and try to get to some insights? We got together for a quick meeting and talked about it and got the juices got flowing. Then I peeled off and left it up to them. So all I've done is plant the seed and created the environment for the idea to grow.

Successful analytic leaders spend significant time—25 percent or more—with other senior leaders across the organization, trying to build relationships such that that they and their people feel comfortable collaborating on analytic projects. Carbon-based relationship trust building is a big part of long-term analytical success.

Balaporia lays it out plainly:

At the end of the day, as with almost any business, it really comes down to trust. "Zahir says he can do this for me. I don't really have the time to figure out what he's talking about, or what analytical technique—blah, blah, blah—but I trust him. He's a good guy, he understands what I need. He's got all these smart analysts that are good at all this stuff and the project they did for my buddy over in another business unit went well."

There's a little less in depth of understanding of exactly what analytics is, so a lot of it comes down to trust.

Analysts are frequently misrepresented as cubicle-dwelling, heads-down wonks. Successful analysts maintain their credibility with the business and make constant deposits into their credibility bank by maintaining an informed perspective on the business and on the industry. One analyst explained, "I try to read everything I can get my hands on. What is the industry news? I process press clippings every morning. I see what the competition is up to, what we are up to."

An important though not publicly discussed aspect of the analytics game (at least 5 percent of total time) is making senior, senior management look really, really smart. This frequently involves working with the chief marketing officer (CMO) who in the course of trying to analyze the major shifts in a particular market typically has a couple of burning analytical questions. These questions arrive at the analytics department, which scrambles to pull together the data, perform an analysis, and generate insights. A scenario frequently played out in the apparel industry has the CMO taking the insight, interpreting it, and socializing it at the executive level.

## Analytics Everywhere

Analytics is not only a C-level undertaking. Ahead-of-the-curve practitioners embed analysts and analysis throughout the enterprise. In 1986, NetJets pioneered the concept of fractional jet ownership, giving individuals and businesses all the benefits of whole aircraft ownership and more at a fraction of the cost. Today NetJets is the worldwide leader with the most owners, the most experience, the largest fleet, and is laser-focused on safety. NetJets is arguably one of best run and best managed companies in the world today. From an analytics perspective, they have "data stewards"—they live in the business. Across the company there are 30 data stewards. Essentially they are analytic-type folks. They are looking at data and doing trending to generate a management dashboard. This is what CIO Alan Cullop calls a "reactive perspective."

They are also now looking to model data that is proactive and forward facing. They are modeling data in logistics and scheduling—all the information they have about demand. They put that through mathematical algorithms. That structured data produces flight plans for the next day. All of that planning and scheduling now is essentially done via computers. Cullop elaborates:

> We are at the beginning—we are at the doorstep of the HAL 9000 in the movie *2001: A Space Odyssey*. We are getting to the point now where we can build systems that can take data and do intelligent things with it thereby producing an improved outcome. We then take those improved outcomes, feed them back in so that you really create a chain of continual improvement. That's where the vision is.

> To me there is analytics, dashboards, decision analysis—there is a place for that stuff. Line managers need data with which to manage. You can't manage what you can't measure. There are those kinds of things. Then there are the parts I get really excited about: the proactive part of this. Where you are taking the data and you are actually taking those people who are thought to be the most complex thinkers in the organization and we are taking the tasks that they did repetitively and modeling that from a logic perspective using mathematics and algorithms—and we are producing results that are actually better than the people who were doing it—the quote unquote experts.

# Notes

1. Stephen Baker, *The Numerati* (Boston: Houghton Mifflin, 2008), 5.
2. "What is the total number of red shirts sold, in the Northwest region, over the last quarter as compared to sales of the same item last year in the same time frame?" Or short tactical queries, such as "What is the total number of red shirts in stock?"
3. At eBay, about 85 percent of the queries run on the company's data warehouse come from end users and are "exploratory in nature," according to Oliver Ratzesberger, eBay's senior director of architecture and operations.

Consultants in the apparel industry—thought by many to significantly lag in their adoption of analytics—estimate that 30 to 40 percent of executives' time is spent seeking out data to assemble spreadsheets.

4. Someone in the organization has to understand and then cause others to understand the end-to-end flow of crucial information elements (e.g., how data gets captured, used, manipulated, and managed across multiple parts of the enterprise). Many analysts are classic information junkies—they know where the data comes from, how it's been transformed, many of the nuances that aren't written down anywhere—and (most important) why certain data elements are extremely important to the business.

5. If you are in the hospitality/travel industry, you probably would like to know about customers' most recent experiences so you are not sending a promotion to a customer the day after his bags had been lost and/or he was delayed for 12 hours.

6. Sensors allow the Southern Company to measure things it did not measure in the past. Sensor reading in combination with predictive analytics helps to schedule equipment maintenance proactively.

7. "Some people think of pollsters as necromancers, trying to charm trends out of a jumble of dead numbers. Others act like we're con men, unintentionally or otherwise. How can we state with such assurance that Candidate A will win the election or that Product B is doomed to failure when we are talking to only a micro-faction of the public? I hear so frequently when this discussion comes up: No one ever calls me for my opinion . . . there's a little truth in all those characterizations. We pollsters are always looking for the secret incantation that will tease new truths out of the gigabytes of information stored securely in our computers. We also sometimes make astounding assertions." John Zogby, *The Way We'll Be: The Zogby Report on the Transformation of the American Dream* (New York: Random House, 2008), ix.

8. http://analytics.ncsu.edu/

9. Schneider National is a leading provider of transportation, logistics, and related services serving more than 80 percent of the Fortune 500 companies.

10. Panel discussion 17 June 2009.

11. Atlanta-based Southern Company has 4.4 million customers and more than 42,000 megawatts of generating capacity. It is the premier energy company serving the Southeast.

12. Robert J. Foster, *Coca-Globalization: Following Soft Drinks from New York to New Guinea* (New York: Palgrave/Macmillan, 2008), xvi.

13. David D. Friedman, *Future Imperfect: Technology and Freedom in an Uncertain World* (Cambridge, UK Cambridge University Press, 2008), 315.

# Chapter 4

# Where Analysts Live in the Organization

Teachers of young students are special people. They tirelessly and patiently undertake the incredibly important task of shaping the minds of future knowers. One technique for teaching U.S. geography is to show unlabeled cutouts of the states to students and ask them to identify them. Some states have very distinctive shapes (e.g., California, Texas, Ohio, and Florida). Other states (Wyoming and Colorado) are rectangular and look alike. Mark Stein in *How the States Got Their Shapes* tells us that while it is probably a good thing to know what a state looks like, it is much more valuable to know why the state is shaped the way it is (i.e., via what confluence of chance, history, culture, technology, and politics did the boundaries get drawn the way they were?).[1] In a similar manner, this chapter not only informs you where analysts live in the contemporary enterprise, it takes on the much more important and challenging task of making transparent the thought processes that have been and that should be used, going forward, when deploying analytical resources.

Organizational structure is one of the most important and visible levers employed by executives to improve performance and effect transformational change. As I examined the world of business analytics, it was natural to devote a sizable chunk of time discovering what people are thinking and what people know about deploying analytical resources. I started this examination by asking broad questions about how organizational structures in general were being transformed. With this as backdrop, I asked what I thought was a very simple question: Where do analysts show up on the organizational chart? I then drilled down seeking to determine if there were generally accepted rules of thumb about how analysts should be organized, and whom they should report to. I traveled around the world collecting empirical data regarding how analytic resources were structured.

## The History that Got Us Where We Are Today

The past two centuries of technology innovation—wireless telegraph, telephone, X ray, cinema, bicycle, automobile, airplane, Internet, the digital video recorder (TiVo), and cell phone— have collapsed time and distance. Technology change enables new modes of thinking about time, space, and organizational design. Rapidly expanding technology capabilities combined with a simultaneous cost contraction of per unit of computation/communication/collaboration has precipitated a general rethinking about how we physically, spatially, and psychologically organize our lives and our businesses. Information, knowledge, and insight play a large role in that rethinking. The result, for many enterprises, is a transformation of how people think about organizational structure.

The historically inclined reader will remember that advances in steam and water power enabled the creation of industrial factories, which gave rise to the second-order requirement for the general population to learn how to tell time (a New Know for that historical epoch), as workers needed to get to the factory at the same time. This is why so many classic early industrial factories had clock towers.

Railroads required nationalized and then globalized standardized time. The revered Harvard business historian Alfred Chandler, in his book *The Visible Hand,* details the managerial innovations required to solve the coordination problems associated with running a railroad: both eastbound and westbound on a single track.[2] These innovations developed after the public and Congress became increasingly alarmed by passenger train collisions.

David McCallum, a railroad superintendent for the New York & Erie Railroad, codified six principles for running a hierarchical organization in his Superintendent's Report of 1855. As author Clay Shirky describes:

> Most are what you'd expect [number one was ensuring a "proper division of responsibilities"], but number five is worth mentioning: his management system was designed to produce "such information, to be obtained through a system of daily reports and checks that will not embarrass principal officers nor lessen their influence with their subordinates." If you have ever wondered why so much of what workers in large organizations know is shielded from the CEO [chief executive officer] and vice versa, wonder no longer: the idea of limiting communications, so that they flow only from one layer of the hierarchy to the next, was part of the very design of the system at the dawn of managerial culture.[3]

## State of Organizational Structure Today

Organizational structures of large, complex multinational organizations are, by and large, out of sync with the worlds they inhabit. The market changes every day, every minute, and in the case of some vertical markets, every second. Organizational structures do not. Thus, organizational structure can understandably evolve to a point where it is out of alignment with the world/problem/customer it was originally designed to serve. This missynchronization frequently becomes a source of frustration—to employees, to customers, to executives and stockholders.

Historically, information architectures have been designed to deliver data to places, not to people and not to purposes. Just as our strategic thinking morphed to accommodate the reality that the mass market is dead, so too must our organizational thinking recalibrate to place person and purpose as the key informational design element.

Information architecture (i.e., decisions regarding what information goes to what people at what frequency to support what decisions) has vast consequences. Most existing information architectures in place today were designed to support the balkanized and hierarchical organizational structures of the railroad era. The historical behavior pattern has been to take the existing organizational structure as a given and deliver information and insight to it. This method can work, but it is suboptimal for the technologies and the opportunities in the marketplace today.

Ralph Szygenda, chief information officer (CIO) at General Motors, describes how the auto giant grew up as a collection of separate companies. Information was never meant to flow *across* the enterprise. Each major brand, including Cadillac, Oldsmobile, and Buick, had separate staff, procedures, information architectures, and agendas, and there was little coordination among them. They might have found shelter under the same umbrella, but, as one observer of organizational design quipped, "They were about as friendly as a group of strangers standing on a New York City sidewalk."

The information architecture at most companies reflects the characteristics of their products (category or price) or customers (age, gender, marital status, and income level). Some business-to-business companies slice their markets by industry; others, by size of business. Study after study finds that companies are having huge difficulties navigating with sufficient granularity among customer, product, and financial data. The data was collected for a specific purpose and is locked away.

Clayton Christensen, professor at the Harvard Business School believes that

> most companies segment their markets by customer demographics or product characteristics and differentiate their offerings by adding features and functions. But the consumer has a different view of the marketplace. He simply has a job to be done and is seeking to "hire" the best product or service to do it.[4]

A simple example will illustrate the issue. Consider the global overnight courier services marketplace. It consists of multiple competitors with multiple fleets of planes, trains, trucks, and personnel all designed to deliver with impressive six sigma reliability packages to places.

All too often, recipients aren't there to receive the package when it arrives, which is frustrating for them, the senders, and the couriers. The problem is that packages are directed to a physical location, which is static, but the intended recipient is mobile. Yet with information and technology available today, the delivery "address" could be a person who could be found in real time, anywhere.

How would that work? Imagine that a delivery company had access to your electronic appointments calendar and could locate you using the Global Positioning System via your vehicle or cell phone—with your permission, of course. The company could notify you of an imminent delivery and ask if a courier should bring your package directly to you right away, leave it at another location, or reschedule delivery for a more convenient time and place. Depending on your choice, you might "sign" for the package by verifying your identity through a smart card or a thumbprint. This kind of delivery would be a highly personalized service, made possible by combining several different types of information not commonly or economically available until recently.[5]

Corporations are long on data and short on the tools, methods, and talent for extracting value from it. Key information about customers, processes, employees, and competition is collected but not analyzed, distributed but not assimilated, guessed about rather than relied on. As a result, the status quo prevails and opportunities to improve performance, often dramatically, go unnoticed.

Historically, organizations and the concomitant information architecture that supports it have been designed to support nonchanging products and services to nonchanging customers. The problem with such organizational schemes is that they are static. Customers' buying behaviors change far more often than their demographics, psychographics, or attitudes. As Christensen observes:

> Demographic data cannot explain why a man takes a date to a movie on one night but orders in pizza to watch a DVD from Netflix Inc. the next.

Product and customer characteristics are poor indicators of customer behavior, because from the customer's perspective that is not how markets are structured. Customers' purchase decisions don't necessarily conform to those of the "average" customer in their demographic; nor do they confine the search for solutions within a product category. Rather, customers just find themselves needing to get things done. When customers find that they need to get a job done, they "hire" products or services to do the job. This means that marketers need to understand the jobs that arise in customers' lives for which their products might be hired. Most of the "home runs" of marketing history were hit by marketers who saw the world this way. The "strike outs" of marketing history, in contrast, generally have been the result of focusing on developing products with better features and functions or of attempting to decipher what the average customer in a demographic wants.[6]

Because organizational structure changes more slowly than the economic circumstances which surround them, in time most organizations become unfitted to the new competitive context. Most employees can sense when their organizations are not working well, but few know how to correct the situation. Truth be told, most organizations look the way they do not as a result of systematic, methodical planning. Rather, they have micro-evolved or nonevolved, as the case, may be over time. Organizational structure change happens in fits and starts, shaped more by at-the-moment/of-the-moment work-arounds and make-dos than some grand strategic design.

## A "Hot Mess"

Organizationally, the deployment of analytic resources in enterprises today could legitimately and accurately be described using a phrase popularized by Chelsea Handler, the irreverent late-night talk show host and stand-up comedienne, as a "hot mess." This is not a bad thing; it is just a thing, more reflective of the frequently primitive and undermanaged processes whereby important technologies enter the enterprise and are initially deployed than any reflection on the underlying technologies of analytics. "Banks have very disparate business intelligence [BI] technology systems," says Guillermo Kopp, vice president at research firm TowerGroup. "It's all over the place."[7] One manager of an analytics group describes the current organizational situation of analytics in this way: "In the past we were like the Aleutian Islands—our analytical activities covered a lot of territory, but they didn't attract much notice." As we will see in Chapter 7, despite being suboptimally deployed, analysts and business analytics provide enormous value to enterprises in every vertical market.

Across companies in the Fortune 500, the FTSE 100, the CAC 40, the NIKKEI, and the Hang Seng Index, analysts hold a bewildering array of titles:

- Chief analytical officer
- Chief customer officer
- Chief data officer
- Chief scoring officer
- Vice president of strategy
- Vice president of marketing
- Vice president of marketing science
- Vice president of research
- Vice president of information technology
- Vice president of direct and database marketing
- Vice president of database marketing and modeling
- Vice president of segmentation and target marketing
- Assistant vice president of customer insights
- Group director of strategy
- General manager of customer insight and analytics
- Director of applied insights and shopper marketing
- Director of customer marketing
- Director of business intelligence
- Director of decision engineering
- Director of strategic intelligence and analytics
- Director of research and planning
- Senior manager of enterprise data warehouse
- Manager of research and analytics

One of the things many executives might find surprising is that there are analysts all over the enterprise. Even human resource professionals frequently are unaware that in every global enterprise today there are at least three different analytic tribes actively engaged in data collection, manipulation, analysis, and distribution.

I asked the head customer strategist at one of the top brands in the world to inventory the analytic tribes at work in his company. He replied:

> At [our company], marketing is a highly analytic function ... probably much more so than our competitors ... there's a lot of analytics that go on there. The analytics they do is related to what I do, but instead of being focused on the customer and the shopper while they're in the store, they're focused on the consumer and their behavior at home and out and about.

This customer strategist explained that the analysts in marketing were trying to figure out customer wants, needs, and behavior in the general context of their life. "I'm trying to figure out, when they're in the store shopping, what are their triggers, hurdles, challenges, and how do we better create an environment that will compel them to buy, and specifically buy our product."

The strategist identified two distinct active analytical tribes in the Finance Department. "One is planning, so it's developing our long-range annual plans, and there's a ton of analytics that go with that, as well as continual reporting of analytics through the course of the year. And the other is like the controller's office, and the whole ... financial running of the back room."

I was surprised to learn that the information technology (IT) department at this high-brand company had its own analytics group, which the strategist described as being "very analytical, in terms of how things are working, what's not up to snuff, what's performing below expectations, vendor promises, or service level agreements." The supply chain group had its own analysts too. "The Demand Planning unit is a separate area with their own analysts. R&D [research and development]. It's a different slant on it, but they're constantly looking at the performance of our innovation pipeline." I asked if all these analysts who worked in different departments ever got together and shared notes. The answer was no.

Similarly, there are reporting relationships across the board. Some practicing the analytical arts report to the president of the enterprise.

Others report to the president of the business unit/division. Some report to the chief financial officer, the chief marketing officer, the chief operating officer (COO), the chief information officer or the corporate counsel. Some report to R&D. Clearly, analysts are everywhere working for everyone.

Some people take reporting relationships *really, really* seriously.

> "I resigned on the spot." So responded the marketing director of the independent British grocery store chain Safeway in July 1999 when he learned that he would report henceforth to the COO, not the CEO, of his company. It wasn't pride that motivated Roger Partington to leave but the deeper meaning of the change. In demoting his role, Safeway was in effect abandoning the direction he had been hired to pursue six years earlier as Safeway's chief marketing officer.[8]

## Thoughts on the New Normal

High-performance organizations are well down the path of rationally and aggressively restructuring their analytic resources.

Alan Webber declares in the opening of his book *Rules of Thumb: 52 Truths for Winning at Business without Losing Your Self*, "The time has come to re-think, re-imagine, and re-calibrate what is possible, what is desirable, what is sustainable. It's time to re-write the rules."[9] One set of rules that definitely needs to be revisited is how analytical resources are deployed. The deployment of analytical resources should be informed by several major developments:

- Concept of outside/inside goes away
- Decisions don't just happen at the top
- Matching analytical tools to market opportunities

### Outside/Inside Goes Away

A major change driving how organizations need to be structured has been the rendering irrelevant of the terms "inside" and "outside." Historically, what went on inside the enterprise was pretty much a secret to customers, investors, and regulators. Customer information exchange, when it happened at all, occurred at specially designed portals. Preapproved answers to anticipated questions were delivered to customers via a heavily trained, tightly scripted, and well-groomed staff manning Potemkin portals (e.g., showroom floor) via engineered processes. This is the world of the handcrafted data set Professor Rappa at the Institute of Advanced Analytics talks about. The world we live in today is not so preknowable.

Organizational "boundaries" have all but disappeared. In warfare, for example, there used to be the concept of a "front line"—the place where one engaged the enemy. Operational doctrine and recognition medals reflected the respect accorded to those most in harm's way. Evidence of the absence of a front line in the current evolution of war fighting is the new Combat Action Badge (CAB), awarded to soldiers "who personally engage the enemy."[10] The message is, in today's war, there is no front line. Everyone is engaged, everywhere. The implication is that everyone has to be smart. Everyone has to be connected to the organizational mission. Everyone has to be in the know.

The sandstorms that complicated logistics and support during the early days of the second Gulf War forced supply convoys to communicate via ordinary off-the-shelf walkie-talkies, which have a range of five miles. One supply convoy Humvee driver had to shout from a window to pass along an order to douse headlights, because he didn't know the frequencies for the radios used by the drivers behind him. He explained, "We're not the digitized division." We are all "digitized divisions" now.[11]

The same is true in the commercial and nonmilitary government sectors. There is no back room anymore. This fact has huge structural implications. It means that everyone and every process must be up to customer-facing standards. It means that every employee has to be cognizant of enterprise strategic direction and customer value proposition. Everyone has to *know* what is going on. Dave Duling, research and development director of data mining at SAS Institute, explains:

> It [business analytics] has really gone from a hard core, back-room technical research tool to a front-line tool. What that means is that the models, when they were in the back room,

were subject to a lot of human evaluation. Printed reports would be given to executives. Executives would then go and debate about what their strategy should be. Now the process and the models are being used directly. That puts a much bigger onus on the models to be robust, to be validated, and to be interpretable. It puts a much bigger burden on the statisticians. Statisticians who were building a few models a month are now building a dozen of models a month.

## Decisions Don't Just Happen at the Top

At the essence of organizational design is the question — rarely addressed explicitly—of: Who gets to make what decisions? The answer drives what information is delivered when and to whom. David McCallum, the creator of the first organizational chart, recognized that railroads were geographically too spread out to be controlled entirely from the top. "It would be like an emperor in Rome thinking he could micromanage the units fighting in India. The information just didn't flow quickly enough. So he divided the company into regional units, creating more managers and increasing their importance."[12] Enter the silo/fiefdom—an organizational phenomenon that has hampered the flow of cross-enterprise information ever since its inception.

Michael Hammer ranks "provincialism" as number two among the "Seven Deadly Sins of Performance Management."[13] Provincialism is the sin of letting organizational boundaries and concerns dictate performance metrics. Paul Gaffney, formerly executive vice president of supply chain for Staples and currently chief operating officer at Desktone, passionately agrees: "It is essential to avoid what I call 'the tyranny of the partial view.'"

High-performance enterprises recognize that the world is too complex to be known by executives at the top of the enterprise (a "partial view" from the top is not enough). The entire enterprise has to be actively engaged in sensemaking.

While hierarchies are not vanishing, profound changes in the nature of technology, demographics, and the global economy are giving rise to powerful new models of production based on community, collaboration, and self-organization rather than on hierarchy and control. "[S]upply chains work more effectively when the risk, reward, and capability to complete major projects—including massively complex products like cars, motorcycles, and airplanes—are distributed across planetary networks of partners who work as peers."[14]

The CEO at Procter & Gamble, A. G. Lafley contends that "someone outside your organization today knows how to answer your specific question, solve your specific problem, or take advantage of your current opportunity better than you do. You need to find them, and find a way to work collaboratively and productively with them."

The days when R&D workers go to their bosses and say, "What are we working on next?" are over. Organizations that thrive in the New Know recognize that sensemaking is all about the "collective us," not the "management we." Every employee needs to participate in looking around, in assessing where the economy is going, and in triangulating where the competitors are positioned. New Know enterprises collaboratively build the next vision of what the next product/service will be and where the company is going. At the base of this collaboration is information sharing. What information should be shared, via what media, and under what business/procedural arrangements is a key strategic decision.

Keith Collins, the chief technology officer at SAS Institute, is pleased that the responsibility for sensemaking is not outsourced to a special R&D or futures group. "The developer who has been on board for 3 months and the 20-year veteran—they each have the responsibility to understand their customers, understand their markets. They have the responsibility not only of fixing the quality of what they release but also of attacking the next opportunity."

## Matching Tools to Opportunities

To the typical executive, all analytics and analysts probably look alike. Actually, in the higher education and vendor community, analysts are frequently divided by discipline: statistics, forecasting, operations research, and data mining. The best-performing organizations are those now attempting to dissect key business processes into their constituent information flows. With the information flows broken out and the business problem identified, the best mix of analytical disciplines can be brought to bear.

In *Seeing What's Next: Using The Theories of Innovation to Predict Industry Change*,[15] Clayton M. Christensen, Scott D. Anthony, and Erik A. Roth give us a three-part framework for segmenting markets by information need: unstructured problem solving, pattern recognition, and rules based. They write:

> In the most demanding tiers of every market, problems have to be dealt with in an unstructured problem-solving mode. Take the health-care market. If you've got cancer, you go to the best oncologist money can buy, and she'll run a bunch of tests and analyze the data and develop hypotheses about what type it is and what type it isn't. She then embarks on a course of therapy, and the feedback from how you respond confirms or disproves her hypotheses. There are no pat answers to these kinds of unstructured problems.

> In the middle tiers of a market, many of the problems can be diagnosed and remedied in a pattern-recognition mode. Like type-one diabetes—if you're always thirsty, you urinate frequently, you're losing weight, and your eyesight is blurry, you have diabetes. The pattern is so clear it doesn't take nearly the skill to diagnose and treat conditions in the pattern-recognition area as it did up in the problem-solving mode.

> At the very simplest tiers of the market, things can be diagnosed and treated in a rules-based mode—like, if the test strip turns blue, you're pregnant. That takes even less skill.

> Over time scientific progress transforms issues that formerly needed to be dealt with in the problem-solving mode and pushes them down into pattern-recognition mode and from pattern-recognition mode down into a rules-based regime. That is the disruptive engine that enables people who didn't have the skill to play in the market before to do a better job than the unstructured-problem-solving experts historically could do. That's the role of technological progress, and that's the mechanism by which our lives get better.

During my research, I did not observe any analytic groups organizationally parsed to deal specifically with unstructured problem solving, pattern recognition questions, or rules-based inquiries. I assume that the more novel unstructured problems would go to analysts with a track record with such challenges.

Organizations are now engaged in delivering the deep knowledge that they possess direct to customer-facing employees. How exactly should you do that? What is the best way to organize the enterprise such that people on the front lines know what they need to know and have full organizational knowledge?

Say you are a hotel chain and you have conducted a major study of customer behavior—wants, needs, and so forth. You know certain things about people checking in at certain hotels, on certain days of the week, at certain times of the day. You do not have precise information, as every guest is different and every situation is unique, but you have statistically significant predictive models regarding general patterns of behavior. What is the best use of this knowledge? How should you deliver this knowledge to the front-line employee? Do you provide the late-night check-in associate with a single answer (e.g., a drink coupon), a simplified set of what-ifs? Do you provide an analytical engine at the associate's check-in terminal? Do you train each and every front-line employee in the fine points of forecasting and behavior modeling? You have extensive data on what visual clues and body language tell you about a guest's state of mind; how do you take advantage of that? Do you provide answers—"Do this"—or do you provide tools/analytical appliances to assist on-the-spot decision making?

## Power of Connected Analytics

Rosaline Franklin, the researcher who provided "the data . . . actually used" in Watson and Crick's hypotheses about DNA, was passionate in her belief that "science and everyday life cannot and should not be separated."[16] Thomas Barnett, geopolitical thinker and author, documents from a nation-state and terrorist standpoint that "Disconnectedness Defines Danger."[17] The number-one design point for the deployment of analytic resources going forward is to connect analysts with the great, grand, and glorious purposes of the enterprise. Most analysts today inhabit Mensa ghettos. All too frequently they labor in little departments, locked away in little cubicles working on less than enterprise-scale problems. Analysts and analytics can do so much more. The analytic tool box (statistics, forecasting, operations research, data mining, etc.) can create great value for the enterprise. In the research for his book *Competing on Analytics,* Tom Davenport discovered that at "Quaker Chemical, each business unit has a 'business adviser'—an analytical specialist—reporting to the head of the business unit."[18] The role acts as an intermediary between the suppliers (normally the IT organization) and users (executives) of data and analyses. The advisors not only stimulate demand by showing the business unit how analysis can be useful but, as intermediaries, explain business needs to the suppliers and ensure that business-relevant data and analysis will be provided. Wachovia has a similar arrangement in its Customer Analytics group, in which analytical teams are tied to particular business units and act as partners in creating and fulfilling analytical demand. Managers of these groups commented frequently that a relationship of trust between the analyst and the executive decision maker is critical to the success of an analytical strategy.

## Power of Conversation

Alan Webber, the former editorial director of the *Harvard Business Review* and cofounder of *Fast Company* magazine, always has his eye out for interesting organizational designs. One that caught his eye in the late 1990s was the physical layout employed at the old offices of Bloomberg News Service. The organization structured its physical office space to stimulate serendipitous conversation. In the 1990s, Bloomberg did three kinds of journalism: radio, TV, and print on seven floors in a New York City skyscraper. The elevator stopped only at the middle floor. You came to work in the morning and had to stop at the middle floor. The floors upstairs and downstairs were connected via a spiral staircase—no elevator. Webber observed, "People *have* to go up and down floors [on] a stairway in the middle of the building. People *have* to talk." People were constantly bumping into each other. "What are you up to?" "Oh, we just had somebody in on the radio program." "What did they say?" said somebody from the print side. All of a sudden they are in an accidental conversation that changes what they think about that day.

Additionally, "Every guest who comes in that building, . . . which is also where [the U.S. Public Broadcasting System's] *The Charlie Rose Show* is taped . . . is passed around to all the functions to maximize the value of the visit," Webber said.

The Bloomberg experience led Webber to ask a couple of questions about workplace design. "How is your company like a talk show?" The basic idea is that a leader's job is to create venues within the company where people can have a talk show–like experience. Whether it is the boss onstage talking to people inside the company, or outside the company, bringing people in for dialogue, conversation, or learning, the mission is to maximize the opportunity for productive conversation. The idea is we really learn through conversation and that is how we stimulate innovation. We have to design our work spaces such that our smart analysts are perpetually bumping into other smart people in the enterprise. Sadly, this is not the case in most enterprises today.

Webber and I believe that organizations which have great conversations can't help but have great performance. He is constantly reminding me that years ago, if you were working in a company and your boss saw you hanging around the water cooler, he or she would say, "Hey, what are you doing hanging around the water cooler? Go back to your desk and get back to work." In the world of the New Know, where ideas matter most, if your boss saw you at your desk, he or she would say, "Get away from your desk and go talk to somebody. You might actually learn something. Get into a conversation."

A success metric increasingly being used by more sophisticated analytic shops is "Did we change the business conversation?"

One of the first things you have to do as you seek to maximize the value of your investment in analytics and analysts is map the conversations your analysts are having and craft the conversations you want them to have: with whom, about what, and at what frequency. With that knowledge in hand, you are ready to rethink the physical layout.

One of the major trends in analytical organizations is letting the analysts out of the closet. CIOs have taken a big step out of the back room. At high-performance organizations, CIOs are now involved in active and frequent conversations with customer CIOs about exchange of information and the integration of systems. Doesn't it make sense for your analysts to be engaged in active and frequent conversations with analysts as your key customers?

A world-class analyst who has done high-end analytics for the U.S. Air Force, Procter & Gamble, McGraw-Hill, and a variety of retailers told me:

> One of the things that I'm promoting is the ability to push analytics out to the stores—store managers . . . get static reports today. We're trying to enhance their analytical experience in the stores, and we're finding technology infrastructure barriers to doing that. Namely, the stores are still on dial-up speed instead of dedicated broadband connections. And, believe it or not, we're having a tough time convincing senior management that they should invest in broadband to the stores to reduce customer time at the register and enable better access to analytics.

While the technologies, methodologies, and practices of analytics are quite mature—the executive conversations about business analytics sadly are not.

Historically, the most common approach to business intelligence was to assemble, case by case, business problem by business problem, department by department, a team of developers to build a data warehouse or data mart for a specific project, buy a reporting tool to use with it, and ultimately disassemble the team upon the project's completion. As you might expect, this approach to business analytics, where you perpetually started from scratch, with each team reinventing the wheel, was expensive and frequently resulted in incompatible business intelligence systems sprouting up throughout a company.

Establishing a business analytics beachhead in a key division working a critical business process has been a successful deployment strategy at many enterprises.

In 1907, there was a great need in America for private messenger and delivery services. To help meet this need, an enterprising 19-year-old, James E. ("Jim") Casey, borrowed $100 from a friend and established the American Messenger Company in Seattle, Washington. From these humble beginnings UPS has grown to become the world's largest package delivery company and a leading global provider of specialized transportation and logistics services. UPS understandably began its business analytics journey focusing on operations and logistics. With that capability up and running, the global firm began delivering analytical resources to customer management, assessing the likelihood of customer attrition, or preidentifying sources of problems for customers—before they occurred.

In the early portion of this decade, Procter & Gamble, known for crafting ahead-of-the-curve shared services capabilities, consolidated its analytical organizations for operations and supply chain and for marketing. Industry watchers and organizational theorists alike believe this will allow a critical mass of analytical expertise to be deployed to address P&G's most critical business issues. About 10 percent of the world's 2,000 largest companies have some form of business intelligence competency center, Gartner analyst Howard Dresner says.

In retrospect, many in the technology industry believe that one of the best and most prudent ways to move to the sought-for end point of business analytics—a standardized, rationalized, and optimized though not necessarily physically centralized approach to enterprise information management—is to create a business intelligence competency center (BICC). This is what industry leaders like Allstate, General Electric, McKesson, and BT have done.

Around 2006, the Global 2000 collectively came to the decision that business intelligence was the new black—the killer app for the rest of the decade. At the 2006 Gartner BI Summit, the world's largest advisory firm produced a strategic planning assumption forecasting that "by 2009, more than 60 percent of global 2000 companies and government agencies with cross enterprise, strategic BI initiatives will have formed BI Competency Centers."[19] The researchers at Gartner understood the need but misforecast the reality. They correctly forecast that analytics would remain a hot and mainstream investment area. They correctly understood as Bill Hostmann, Gartner research vice president articulated:

> The greatest burdens to BI success—by far—are shaped by organizational dynamics, including fragmented buying centers, multiple product vendors, multiple business drivers and a drive to standardize and consolidate at every level. There needs to be some sort of culture, leadership, skills and methodologies in place for establishing an overall BI architecture, a BI portfolio

and a set of BI standards—and a way to manage that program across the company. That's the role of the competency center.[20]

A BICC is a cross-functional team with a permanent, formal organizational structure. It has defined tasks, roles, responsibilities, and processes for supporting and promoting the effective use of business intelligence and performance management across the organization. Based on the recent "How Do You Plan for Business Intelligence?" survey performed by BetterManagement.com, organizations with a BICC see these benefits:

- Increased usage of business intelligence (71 percent)
- Increased business user satisfaction (48 percent)
- Better understanding of the value of business intelligence (45 percent)
- Increased decision-making speed (45 percent)
- Decreased staff costs (26 percent)
- Decreased software costs (24 percent)

A BICC provides a central location for driving and supporting an organization's overall business intelligence strategy. It enables an organization to coordinate and complement existing efforts while reducing redundancy and increasing effectiveness. The centralization of these efforts ensures that information and best practices are communicated and shared through the entire organization so that everyone can benefit from successes and lessons learned.

Decision making about organizational structure in regards to the deployment of analytical resources chronically suffers from an inability to see the big picture. Line of business executives, blinded by the glare of day-to-day, whack-a-mole responsibilities, fail to achieve the strategic mind-set that would let them contextualize the information management problem at hand. Rarely will one see a spectrum of innovative structural alternatives created to address information management problems. Time-pressured executives too often settle on the first solution that partially fits the problem at hand.

Future value-creating executives need to be able to set a much more robust table option-wise for deploying analytical resources. Many business schools fall embarrassingly short in their teaching of analytics and the appropriate use/structure of analytic resources. High-performing enterprises are breaking new ground and creating their own degree and certification programs in analytic decision making. José Ramirez, a statistician in the Electronic Products Division of W.L. Gore Associates, creates and delivers an impressive catalog of analytics courses for his colleagues. In a fashion similar to Microsoft offering training and certification in what is a core competency for it—programming and system engineering—so too will companies have to create curricula that helps their executives focus analytic resources on high-value targets.

At the base of that strategy, executives will need to be able to determine how solid is the linkage between the analytic resources deployed and business problem being addressed and/or the mission outcome being attempted. There are many ways to deploy analytic resources. Some are more cost effective than others. Has the organization evaluated how various structural alternatives alter the *cost of knowing*?

Forrester Research concurs that business analytics has reached a tipping point as companies move to expand access to decision support data beyond power users to a new and much larger realm of users, such as business executives and front-line managers.

### Medals Are Awarded at the End of the Race, Not the Starting Gate

On Mars, "There are no continents and there are no oceans, and thus there are no shores. Given patience, provisions, and a pressure suit you could walk from any point on the planet to any other. No edges guide the eye or frame the scene. Nowhere says, 'Start Here!'"[21] Regarding deploying analytic resources, where you start is not as important as where you end up.

In his book *On War*, Carl Von Clausewitz argues that no rational person should start a war without having a clear objective.[22] Ariel Sharon, Israel's warrior-politician, puts great stock in holding the high ground, controlling lines of sight, and measuring distances in terms of artillery range. Some might hypothesize that no rational person should deploy scarce analytical resources without having an enterprise strategy like Clausewitz's informed by Sharon's high-ground view/distance-to-target knowledge—and yet organizations appear to do so all the time.

Generations of business students have been drilled in the principle that "Structure must follow strategy." Organizations exist and are built for a purpose. The structure they take should reflect that purpose. Herein lies the true structural challenge for business analytics. Senior management ("suits") may not have resolved many of the ambiguities surrounding the real purpose of the enterprise. This lack of a mutually agreed-on purpose makes it difficult to select and execute a purpose-optimized structure.

## Strategically Deploying Analytic Resources

How should you deploy your analytic resources? It is probably best to start at the strategy level. Understand where the organization is trying to go, what it is trying to accomplish, and then determine what information, knowledge, and insight are required. This is not as easy as it might seem. Most organizations have multiple strategies in play at any one time.

Geoffrey Moore in *Crossing the Chasm*[23] tells readers that most global organizations probably have a subset of these strategies in play simultaneously.

- Get way ahead of the herd for competitive advantage.
- Go before the herd to address a broken business process.
- Go with the herd to ensure safety in numbers.
- Go after the herd to get increasingly better deals.

Each of those strategies might require a different type of analytics.

In his subsequent book, *Dealing with Darwin: How Great Companies Innovate at Every Phase of Their Evolution*,[24] Moore says that the million-dollar question is: Are analytical resources focused on creating information assets that facilitate establishing competitive separation? In 1980, William Synnott, then senior vice president of the First National Bank of Boston, introduced the world to the idea of the CIO:

> The manager of information systems in the 1980s has to be Superman—retaining his technology cape, but doffing the technical suit for a business suit and becoming one of the chief executives of the firm. The job of chief information officer

(CIO)—equal in rank to chief executive and chief financial officers—does not exist today, but the CIO will identify, collect, and manage information as a resource.[25]

In 1987, he moved beyond representing "information as a resource" and reclassified it as a strategic asset in his book *The Information Weapon: Competition through Technology*.[26]

Most business strategy books are, in point of fact, exercises in retrospective storytelling. They infer strategies from past performance. After the fact, business school professors provide eloquent post-mortem explanations of strategies, pinning down case study "butterflies" in classroom exhibition cases. Strategy seems easy enough once the passage of time has bagged and tagged it. Analytics can be hugely helpful in understanding competitive context and managing the difficulties inherent in having to make inferences quickly on limited samples. But the most important thing analytics can do is let you know something your competitor does not. Synnott presented the metaphor of the IT shop as an armory—a creator of capabilities ("information weapons") that deliver business advantage.

Usama Fayyad is the chief data officer (CDO) and executive vice president of research and strategic data solutions at Yahoo! He believes the CDO title

> described exactly what the executive team and the company were looking for: someone to lead all strategic data activities and to represent data as a strategic asset that *drives* business and that helps lead the company in new directions. I totally believe that most large companies will start appreciating this dynamic and we will see many more companies with this exciting and very much needed position.

## The Path Ahead

The CIO at a major apparel brand explained to me how analytics evolved in her company. "First of all, we had to prove that you could have data and that you could do something with that data. Once we established that, we were ready to create a governance structure around analytics."

The company put in place a business intelligence governance committee comprised of senior director-level people, people who are really good on the ground—get-things-done people. These people are smart enough to know what's going on and how things work today and how they might need to work tomorrow. The committee meets about every six weeks. When putting together the 2009 plan, the CIO—who heads up the enterprise business analytics initiative—told the committee:

> Based on your strategic objectives, this is what we think you want to do. But you tell us, because, quite frankly, we don't care what order we bring it in. And so they look at that stuff and make decisions about what's the priority order about putting the information together based on what we're trying to accomplish as a company.

Seasoned executives shared four rules of thumb for spinning up a new business analytics organizational structure:

1. Make sure to fix whatever problem/capitalize on whatever opportunity brought you to the place where you are actually changing organizational structure.[27]
2. Align the new structure with the stated strategy of the enterprise. (Often this new direction is what precipitated the reorganization in the first place.)[28]
3. Efficiently manage the processes you need today.
4. Be able to give "meaning" to why the organization was restructured and explain individuals' roles.

Most reorganization initiatives score top marks for the first two objectives, do reasonably well on the operational third objective, and do miserably on explaining why the reorganization was undertaken and what it will mean for the individuals involved.

The data indicates that two structural problem areas plague many business analytic organizations today: explanation and overspecialization.

## Explanation

The stories we tell ourselves (i.e., internal to the various business analytic organizations inside the enterprise: who we are, what we do, where we are going) and the stories we tell to the rest of the world are critically important, yet all too frequently they are left to chance. Words can and do have more than one meaning. Linguists tell us that the 500 most frequently used words in the English language have more than 14,000 meanings. In Dante's Hell, the worst sinners are "the fraudulent, those who misuse language to mislead and deceive; and those whose use of language fails to render a concrete and useful reality."

We live in a confusing world. A big part of leadership is using communication to part the fog of uncertainty enough to allow progress forward.

## Overspecialization

In the analytics world, particularly in large organizations, analytic professionals run the danger of becoming overspecialized and overidentified with very narrow skill niches. Mathematical techniques are very transferable from one field to another.

In the early 1970s, Irving Janis, the American psychologist, documented the tendency of undersocialized, overly isolated small groups to suffer from "group think." Among the symptoms:

- A cohesive core putting pressure on internal dissenters to fall into line
- A mutually reinforcing reluctance to consider alternative policies
- The dismissal and inattention to dissenting outsiders
- Frequent domination by a forceful individual

In some instances, workplace attitudes have gone so far as to be semibelligerent. High-skill technicians sometimes complain when placed on projects outside their specialty area. This severely constrains the flexibility the organization needs to meet the rapidly changing requirements of the business. Getting the right analytical skill to the right work assignment is almost impossible.

The Marine Corps, recognizing the danger of overspecialization, has as its base assumption and training mantra that every marine is first and foremost a rifleman. General Kevin P. Byrnes, the army's top training general, explains that the army has too many soldiers who have lost touch with their inner warrior. "Ask a junior enlisted who they are, and they'll tell you, 'I'm a mechanic,' not 'I'm a solder.' We need to change that culturally."[29] Analytic professionals need to rediscover their "inner businessperson."

One of the most important tasks facing analytic professionals today, and the one that is toughest to do, is to establish common methodologies, practices, and mind-sets across the enterprise.

## But When You Get It Right . . .

Business analytics is an amazing strategic lever. The senior management team needs to understand what business analytics is and what it can accomplish. Ramon Baez, the award-winning CIO at Kimberly-Clark, is very excited about the prospects moving forward. He explained to me in a phone interview:

> I am now working for a CFO that understands the power of standardization and analytics. This is important because you can't do analytics unless your data is common across the board. It takes a whole culture to understand the power of business analytics. It can't just be the marketing guys. It can't just be the sales guys. It really needs to be finance, sales, marketing, and supply chain. This place gets it. When I went to my interview for my current role, a big part of my discussion with the CEO and chairman of the company focused around decision support systems, business intelligence, and analytics.

At Kimberly-Clark, the enterprise business intelligence group reports to the CIO. People from across the enterprise come to the enterprise intelligence people and say, "Hey, this is what we are looking for from an analytic standpoint. This is the problem we are trying to solve. This is the issue that we are having out in the wonderful world of marketing or any other teams, and by the way, this is the kind of data and the kind of information that they want to be able to start making informed decisions quickly." Then that shared resource from the enterprise business intelligence team works with them to drive results and value.

## A Different Model to Build On

Readers seeking to build a world-class business analytics capability might want to examine the 12 organizational elements that guided the initial design of the Defense Advanced Research Projects Agency (DARPA):[30]

1. **Small and flexible.** DARPA consists of only 100 to 150 professionals; some observers have referred to DARPA as "100 geniuses connected by a travel agent."
2. **Flat organization.** DARPA avoids military hierarchy, essentially operating at only two levels to ensure participation.
3. **Autonomy and freedom from bureaucratic impediments**. DARPA operates outside the civil service hiring process and standard government contracting rules, a situation that gives it unusual access to talent, plus speed and flexibility in organizing R&D efforts.
4. **Eclectic, world-class technical staff.** DARPA seeks great talent, drawn from industry, universities, and government laboratories and R&D centers, mixing disciplines as well as theoretical and experimental strengths.
5. **Teams and networks.** At its very best, DARPA creates and sustains great teams of researchers who are networked to collaborate and share in the team's advances, so that DARPA operates at the personal, face-to-face level of innovation. DARPA is not simply about funding research; its program managers are dynamic playwrights and directors.
6. **Hiring continuity and change.** DARPA's technical staff members are hired or assigned for three to five years. Like any strong organization, DARPA mixes experience and change. It retains a base of experienced experts who know their way around the Defense Department but rotates most of its staff from the outside to ensure fresh thinking and perspectives.
7. **Project-based arguments, organized around a challenge model.** DARPA organizes a significant part of its portfolio around specific technology challenges. It works "right-to-left" in the R&D pipeline, foreseeing new innovation-based capabilities and then

working back to the fundamental breakthroughs that take it there. Although its projects typically last three to five years, major technological challenges may be addressed over much longer time periods, ensuring patient, long-term investment on a series of focused steps and keeping teams together for ongoing collaboration.

8. **Outsourced support personnel.** DARPA uses technical, contracting, and administrative services from other agencies on a temporary basis. This provides DARPA with the flexibility to get into and out of a technology field without the burden of sustaining staff, while building cooperative alliances with the line agencies with which it works.

9. **Outstanding program managers.** In DARPA's words, "the best DARPA program managers have always been freewheeling zealots in pursuit of their goals." The DARPA director's most important job historically has been to recruit highly talented program managers and then empower their creativity to put together great teams around great advances.

10. **Acceptance of failure.** At its best, DARPA pursues a high-risk model for breakthrough opportunities and is very tolerant of failure if the payoff from potential success is great enough.

11. **Orientation to revolutionary breakthroughs in a connected approach.** DARPA historically has focused not on incremental but on radical innovation. It emphasizes high-risk investments, moves from fundamental technological advances to prototyping, and then hands off the production stage to the armed services or the commercial sector. From an innovation perspective, DARPA is a connected model, crossing the barriers between innovation stages.

12. **Mix of connected collaborators.** DARPA typically builds strong teams and networks of collaborators, bringing in a range of technical expertise and applicable disciplines and involving university researchers and technology firms that are usually not significant defense contractors or Beltway consultants (neither of which focuses on radical innovation). The aim of DARPA's "hybrid" approach, unique among U.S. R&D agencies, is to ensure strong collaborative "mindshare" on the challenge and the capability to connect fundamentals with applications.

# Notes

1. Mark Stein, *How the States Got Their Shape* (New York: HarperCollins, 2008).

2. Alfred Dupont Chandler, *The Visible Hand: The Managerial Revolution in American Business* (Cambridge, MA: Harvard University Press, 1993).

3. Clay Shirky, *Here Comes Everybody: The Power of Organizing without Organizations* (New York: Penguin, 2008).

4. Clayton M. Christensen, Scott D. Anthony, Gerald Berstell, and Denise Nitterhouse, "Finding the Right Job for Your Product," *MIT Sloan Management Review* (Spring 2007): 38.

5. Glover Ferguson, Sanjay Mathur, and Baiju Shah, "Evolving from Information to Insight," *MIT Sloan Management Review* (Winter 2005): 51.

6. Christensen et al., "Finding the Right Job for Your Product," 38.

7. Nancy Feig, "The Next Level in Business Intelligence," *Bank Systems & Technology* [28 July 2006].

8. Jackie Fenn and Mark Raskino, *Mastering the Hype Cycle: How to Choose the Right Innovation at the Right Time* (Boston: Harvard Business Press, 2008).

9. Alan Webber, *Rules of Thumb: 52 Truths for Winning at Business without Losing Your Self* (New York: HarperCollins, 2009), 1.

10. Elizabeth B. Samet, *Soldier's Heart: Reading Literature through Peace and War at West Point* (New York: Farrar, Straus and Giroux, 2007).

11. Quoted in "The Doctrine of Digital War: How High Tech Is Shaping America's Military Strategy and Tactics: The Pros and Cons," *BusinessWeek,* April 7, 2003, 30–48.

12. David Weinberger, *Everything Is Miscellaneous: The Power of the New Digital Disorder* (New York: Henry Holt, 2007), 177.

13. Michael Hammer, "The 7 Deadly Sins of Performance Measurement," *MIT Sloan Management Review* (Spring 2007). The seven "sins" are: Vanity, Provincialism, Narcissism, Laziness, Pettiness, Inanity, and Frivolity.

14. Don Tapscott and Anthony D. Williams, *Wikinomics: How Mass Collaboration Changes Everything* (New York: Penguin, 2006).

15. Clayton M. Christensen, Scott D. Anthony, and Erik A. Roth, *Seeing What's Next: Using the Theories of Innovation to Predict Industry Change* (Cambridge, MA: Harvard Business School Press, 2004).

16. *Towards Science 2020,* Microsoft Research, 2.

17. Thomas Barnett, *The Pentagon's New Map: War and Peace in the 21st Century* (New York: Penguin, 2005).

18. Thomas Davenport and Jeane Harris, *Competing on Analytics: The New Science of Winning* (Cambridge, MA: Harvard Business School Press, 2007).

19. Gartner Business Intelligence Summit, "BI Competency Centers: From 'Should We?' to 'How Should We?'" Amsterdam, February 2006.

20. Ibid.

21. Oliver Morton, *Mapping Mars: Science, Imagination, and the Birth of a World* (New York: Picador, 2002).

22. Carl von Clausewitz, *On War* (New York: Barnes & Noble, 2004).

23. Geoffrey Moore, *Crossing the Chasm: Marketing & Selling Disruptive Products to Mainstream Customers* (New York: Harper Collins, 1991).

24. Geoffrey Moore, *Dealing with Darwin: How Great Companies Innovate at Every Phase of Their Evolution* (New York: Penguin Group, 2005)

25. William Synnott, speech, the Information Management Exposition and Conference, 1980.

26. William Synnott, *The Information Weapon: Competition through Technology* (New York: John Wiley & Sons, 1987).

27. Despite what the rank-and-file might think, organizations do not make structural changes lightly. There is always a reason why the "chairs" are being rearranged. The first step before drawing any new boxes on the organizational chart is to step back and ask, "What are we really trying to accomplish here?"

28. In the summer 2002, Microsoft unveiled a plan to realign the company into seven divisions. Each division has a de facto chief financial officer. This structural focus on tighter financial controls is consistent with the strategic situation the company finds itself in. Microsoft is changing "from fast-growth tech titan to [a] mature, slower-growing company akin to conglomerate GE." Byron Acohido and Kevin Maney, "Microsoft to Name Seven Finance Czars," *USA Today,* July 24, 2003. As one Harvard Business School academic characterizes the situation: "Microsoft wants to operate like a grown-up company, managing via the numbers and objective financial disciplines." There are many analogies one can draw between Microsoft's structural evolution (from adolescent to rule-sensitized adult) and the structure of business analytic groups inside large enterprises.

American Express has chosen a very centralized IT structure. It did so not just because of cost savings; it got tremendous cost improvement. At one point, American Express had 17 data centers. It now has two. The primary reason for the centralization was the need to be able to look at a customer as a single entity. This was and is the company strategy. If you are going to be American Express and you are going to treat a customer as a customer, your technology platform and your technology organization is going to have to enable that.

29. Eric Schmitt, "In New Army, All Soldiers Will Be Fighters," *New York Times,* September 7, 2003.

30. William B. Bonvillian, "The Once and Future DARPA," in Francis Fukuyama, *Blindside: How to Anticipate Forcing Events and Wild Cards in Global Politics* (Washington, D.C.: Brookings Institution Press, 2007), Chapter 6.

# Chapter 5

# Relationships Betwixt and Between

As a futurist, I frequently script "scenes" depicting the operational requirements of future worlds we might someday inhabit. As I look out over the contemporary landscape, I am perplexed by the low position on the organizational food chain occupied by the analyst community. After all, don't we live in an information society? From my vantage point as playwright of what comes next, I am pleased to forecast a starring role for future-period analysts, without whom our world would grind to a halt. This rosy projection is subject to one major caveat—that the analytic community develop mastery of relationship management.

I believe society is poised on the cusp of a renaissance driven by information management. The technologies are in place. Analysts must crawl out of their day-to-day transactional bunkers (store the data, move the data), move to the high ground of imagining how to use the data, and shape organizational cultures that appreciate and reward smart info-management behaviors.

The Achilles' heel of our discipline appears to be that analysts are (or perceive themselves to be) extremely bad at building connections outside the discipline. In this day and age, the inability to build personal networks is a terrible handicap. The story of our age is interrelatedness. As the great Argentinean author Jorge Luis Borges put it, "Everything touches everything." Analysts need to understand how human relationships work.

The most important career asset an analyst has is his or her portfolio of human relationships. One of the most powerful things at work in the contemporary enterprise is its internal and external network of human relationships. In the back of our minds, we sort of/kind of know that every enterprise operates through a series of human networks. And yet, surprisingly enough, for the most part, these networks are not managed and remain *invisible* to most decision makers. Very few enterprises have taken it upon themselves to systematically analyze the human networks via which decisions are made and actions executed. People in general and analysts in particular do not spend enough time managing their relationships. In the New Know, this will change.

The secret ingredient of your future career success is the depth and breadth of your network of personal relationships. In a complex world where knowledge is evolving much too fast for one mind to manage, your network of personal relationships becomes the steering wheel for navigating the just-over-the-horizon challenges you and the enterprise face. Most executives today are tragically unschooled in what personal networks are and how they work.

When most people hear the words "personal network," their minds typically jump to one or two places—social networking sites (e.g., Facebook, MySpace, YouTube) and/or the size of one's Rolodex. The success and growing popularity of technology-assisted social networking could be viewed at one level of abstraction as simply automating a quintessential human trait—our ability and natural propensity to work with others. In his book *The Company of Strangers: A Natural History of Economic Life*, Paul Seabright explains that *Homo sapiens* are the only animal that engages in elaborate task sharing—the division of labor, as it is sometimes known—between genetically unrelated members of the same species.[1] It is a phenomenon as remarkable and uniquely human as language itself.

# Why Are Relationships Important?

Have you ever wondered why some people are more successful than others are? Increasingly the trait thought to put particular *leaders* on the top of the organization is their ability to establish and manage dynamic networks of personal relationships. You probably did not know this, but your personal network—or lack thereof—says a lot about you. It says a lot about where you came from (e.g., socioeconomic class, educational background) and speaks volumes about where you are going (e.g., your ability to realize your full potential).

*Whom we know* influences *what we know* and *how we feel* about it. The personal networks you are embedded in exert powerful influences on the decisions you make and the actions that follow.

Hillary Clinton makes reference to an African proverb when she says, "It takes a village to raise a child." In that same vein, it takes a network of human relationships to capture full value from analytics. The days of the solitary, heroic genius-in-the-backroom working alone kind of analyst are behind us. Blanche DuBois, the heroine in Tennessee Williams's *A Streetcar Named Desire*, was not as wrong-headed as she may have seemed when she cooed, "I have always relied on the kindness of strangers." Humans unconsciously are natural psychologists, carefully monitoring one another's behavior and drawing subtle inferences about each other's mental states *without having the slightest idea we are doing this.* We are all, borrowing a term from biologists John Krebs and Richard Dawkins, unconscious "mind-readers."[2]

Analysts need to understand the strengths, weaknesses, biases, and behavior drivers of the various executives on the supply side of the house. Eleanor Roosevelt counseled Harry Truman that, "if you can get on a personal basis with Mr. Churchill, you will find it easier." If analysts can get on a "personal" basis with organizational leaders, having a positive and recognized impact on the enterprise will be much "easier."

Robert D. Putnam is a professor at Harvard. His book *Bowling Alone: The Collapse and Revival of American Community*, provided an accessible framework to better understand the relationship angst (i.e., why we feel so disconnected in a "wired" world) many in the analytic community may be experiencing.[3] *Bowling Alone* is a seminal piece of sociological scholarship that presents a sweeping statistical overview of several decades of decline in sociability and civic participation across the United States. During the first two-thirds of the twentieth century, Americans were becoming more and more connected with one another and with community affairs. The last third of a century witnessed a startling and dismaying reversal of that trend.

In the late 1960s, Americans in massive numbers began to join less, trust less, give less, vote less, and schmooze less. Putnam's key lens is "social capital." In his more recent work, *Better Together: Restoring the American Community*, Putnam sets forth a broad array of case examples documenting that social capital is not dead and is indeed being reborn in new forms.[4] Analysts need to build social capital. Communities like the Institute for Operations Research and the Management Sciences (INFORMS®) and SAS user groups are key areas where personal and institutional social capital can be created.[5]

## A More Nuanced Understanding of Relationships

Each generation manages relationships differently. Each generation most likely started managing relationships with a technology tool developed during their age. Baby busters (folks born from 1921 to 1945) might be most familiar with the Rolodex, a device where people kept their business cards. If you had a lot of business cards, you were thought to be "connected." Baby Boomers probably use an e-mail–based contact management tool (e.g., LinkedIn), while Millennials (folks born between 1982 and 2001) probably use Instant Messaging utilities.[6]

But just because you have a lot of *connections* does not mean that you are *connected*. Say you have tens of thousands digitized contacts in a device of choice. Say you left that device, unencrypted, in the back of a Chicago taxi. (In 2005, more than 85,000 phones and 21,000 personal digital assistants and pocket PCs were lost in Chicago taxis. Passengers left about 4,500 notebooks behind.) Would the finder of that unencrypted device now have access to your extensive personal network? Here is the big insight: It's not the size of the network that matters—it's the insight and impact of the network that is of chief importance.

## Paying Attention to What People Pay Attention To

Scholars tell us that economics is the study of how human beings allocate scarce resources. There can be little doubt that one of the scarcest and most precious resources in the world today is attention—the executive CPU cycles leading to choice, action, and outcome. Specifically limited is the attention we pay to "things" and the attention "things" pay to us. Lamentably and avoidably, many analysts are but passive participants in internal and external attention markets. This has to change. Failure to pay attention to paying attention is one of the top 10 career killers in our industry.

After speaking to dozens of midmarket and large enterprise decision makers, I recently launched a project seeking to chronicle frequently made and potentially avoidable crimes of attention. The preliminary data highlighted that the most frequently made and easiest to rectify crime of attention is ignorance that there *is* an active market in attention at work in your enterprise. It is dangerous and naive to believe that your organization will, as a matter of course, pay attention to the right things.

Organizations are not info plankton-sucking cetaceans gorging on each and every message that floats their way. Lisa Stone, a former researcher at Microsoft, coined the phrase "continuous partial attention" to describe the fact that individuals and organizations selectively attend to bits of information. How do you make sure that the right bits are processed by the right brains? Analysts might take a lesson from the chief information officer at a telecommunications firm who created a scorecard in which hundreds of performance metrics of various types are broadcast to PCs around the company, each occupying the screen for 15 seconds. The idea is to get everyone—not just senior executives—focused on information and what it means to that organization's performance.

Not recognizing the importance of managing and taking full advantage of positive "attention moments" is a crime of attention. The more politically oriented among you may remember that George H. W. Bush (forty-first President of the United States) had little flare for the dramatic. Presented with the major attention-focusing opportunity, the fall of the Berlin Wall, he opted out, saying "I am not going to dance on the wall." David Halberstam, the on-the-scene observer of presidents in action, goes deeper, explaining:

> Taking personal credit for any kind of larger success . . . conflicted with the way he had been brought up. He believed—in an age of ever more carefully orchestrated political spin, when the sizzle was more important than the steak—that if you did the right things, the right way, people would know about it. You should never call attention to yourself or, worse, advertise your accomplishments.[7]

Bush, who was thought unbeatable following the victory in the first Gulf War, was defeated in his bid for a second term.

Some observed strategies of leaders who excel at paying attention to what people are paying attention to include:

- Paying attention at the appropriate level of detail
- Being aware of where regulatory attention is being focused
- Paying attention (granularly) to what key current customers are paying attention to
- Paying attention (preemptively) to what future customers will be paying attention to
- Taming devices that steal attention
- Managing attention away from dysfunctional topics
- Paying attention to relationships

## Managing Relationships Requires Understanding Info-War

As commander in chief of the Continental Army, George Washington learned a lesson that many analysts come to appreciate too late in their careers: True victory is accomplished not on the battlefield but in the hearts and minds of those engaged. Public relations matters! George Washington lost more battles than he won. Despite this, he was eulogized by Light Horse Harry Lee as being "first in war, first in peace, first in the hearts of his countrymen." Is business analytics first in the hearts and minds of your chief executive and board of directors?

Analysts find themselves waging a high-stakes info-war. True victory lies in capturing the imaginations, respect, and energies of a broad and diverse set of stakeholders (e.g., suppliers, customers, and line-of-business executives). As mentioned in Chapter 1, soldiers fighting battles with projectile weapons speak of the "fog of war" (e.g., confusion about what is going on). Info-warriors speak of the "fog of facts" (e.g., confusion about what information is to be believed, what information sources are credible, and what version of reality is to be acted on). In a world of multiple sources of information and 24-hour decision making, the very character of information is changing. A "fact" is no longer a "fact."

Edward C. Prescott, winner of the 2004 Nobel Prize in Economic Sciences, is frequently heard to say "Economists create their own worlds." The über-implication of the Internet is that everyone has the capacity to create their own version of your world. Anyone—*anyone*—can be a sensemaker. Not a week goes by when a mind important to you (an info-target) is not presented with a version of "the facts" not consistent with or sympathetic to where you are going and what you are trying to do. You are at info-war. Research from the Information Technology (IT) Leadership Academy surfaced 10 best practices:

1. Recognize that you are at info-war.
2. Identify key info-targets (minds you want to make sure have a non-toxic version of the facts).
3. Create an info-map of information sources.
4. Create listening posts to monitor the buzz about analytics.
5. Creative "official" sources of truth—"voices" (work-for-you spokespeople like Brigadier General Vincent Brooks, who delivered daily briefings at Central Command headquarters in Qatar).
6. Create semiauthorized, carbon-based (i.e., human) "firewalls" (experts who know you, know what is happening in your analytics department, and generally know what you are doing/where you are going) who can be contacted when "it hits the fan."
7. Embed and empower storytellers in your organization (people who have good judgment and good powers of observation who can truthfully tell you and others what is really going on).

8. Create authorized information "moments":
   * Briefings
   * Blogs
   * Webinars
   * Lunches
9. Expand your organization's "smart width" (the understanding version of bandwidth). Broadband gives us more information. Smart width gives your organization more understanding regarding what all this information means.
10. Hire an ad agency (or first-year business students who will someday work in an ad agency) to review your "brand."

Perform these simple tasks and you are well on your way to being a successful info-warrior.

## Whom Do You Want to Have a Relationship With?

The personality traits of the people you want to have a relationship with are reasonably straightforward:

* They have to be smart.
* They have to be—and stay—current.
* They have to be honest; their job is to stimulate your thinking in new perspectives.
* They have to be funny. Nothing is less helpful than a bunch of blowhards who take themselves way too seriously.
* They have to be objective—they can't use this platform of trust to try to sell you something. There can be no conflicts of interest.

## Relationships with Peers

A key next-generation skill set is the ability to make a connection with high-attitude, high-skill colleagues. Sociability, oral communication, and the ability to nurture/induce the goodwill of others become critical.

In an effort to more quickly form associational networks, analysts will need to discard the generic titles presented in Chapter 4 and self-label in favor of neologistic badges of capability. Such badges are critical in the new work environment where whom you know (and who is willing to work with you) becomes a major determinant of earning power. Remember, media sources have become so personalized that we don't even have today's headlines in common. The ability to establish collaborative linkages with total strangers in a compressed time frame becomes a key skill.

## Analysts Need to Get in the Game

Most analysts are not suspended in a web of deep and respect-rich relationships with the senior decision makers pushing buttons and pulling levers in the corporate nose cone. Many spend their lives forever outside the corridors of power.

Augusto Vidaurereta and Tom Richardson are entrepreneurs and world-class systems integrators. They say that to win the game, you have develop relationships. When they say business is a contact sport, they mean that making contact and building relationships is the path to success.[8] Relationship Asset Management (RAM) represents a step-by-step plan for success in business or in any other field. The 12 principles that constitute the discipline of RAM are:

1. See relationships as valuable assets.
2. Develop a game plan.
3. Create ownership for relationships.
4. Transform contacts into connections.
5. Move into the win-win zone.
6. Get to know your stakeholders as people.
7. Build bonds of trust with all stakeholders.
8. Banish relationship killers.
9. When something breaks, fix it fast.
10. Get rolling and maintain momentum.
11. Maximize the long-term value of relationships.
12. Keep the wins coming, stakeholder by stakeholder.

Relationships are the single most valuable asset a company or person possesses. Many companies don't fully consider the role that relationships play in their business. Most companies don't fully understand the role that relationships play in reaching goals. It is important that you don't make the same mistake.

## Social Network Analysis: The Forgotten Piece of Business Analytics

The decreasing cost of computing, increasing connectivity, and rapid digitalization of critical business processes is bringing human networks into the growing category of things that can be measured, should be managed, and must be optimized. Social network analysis—the business analytics most people have never heard about—makes how the organization really works visible.

The science behind social network analysis is the same science behind how we understand customers, logistics, or weather. Social network analysis originated from the complex math used to explain subatomic physics. It is now being used to understand and manage human interaction in the workplace. Having an updated copy of the organizational chart is no longer enough (old know). The organizational chart merely reveals the formal hierarchy, the visible rules at work in an organization. The real story—the "ropes" of "learning the ropes" fame—can be revealed only by understanding how human networks operate within the organization. This requires math.

One of the most skilled practitioners of social network analysis in the world today is Karen Stephenson. We taught together at the Anderson Graduate School of Management. A pioneering social network theorist and classically trained anthropologist, she spent months studying ancient Mayan culture in the rain forests of Central America. She is now devoting her time to researching the behaviors of the modern tribes inhabiting corporate jungles. Stephenson is busy mapping the human relationships that form the human networks that drive the world of work. She has created what I refer to as a "Cliffs Notes for culture." Want to keep your job, be smart and fast, and drive your costs down? Focus on building and strengthening your human network, she says.

Stephenson began her journey to the pinnacle of social network analysis by being interested in the archaeological record of ancient trading patterns, the oldest available data about the roots of human exchange. This led her to anthropology and field archaeology research in the Middle East. A paper she wrote about algorithms for analyzing trade networks brought her to the attention of Harvard's anthropology department, which accepted her as a PhD candidate. Working part time in labs and then technology businesses to support her studies, Stephenson began to see parallels between today's organizations and the trade networks of ancient times. She hypothesized "a calculus of human exchange."

In her doctoral dissertation on the technology company Bolt, Beranek and Newman (BBN), the soon-to-be Professor Stephenson (with Harvard statistical scientist Marvin Zelen) devised a formula for ranking the significance of individuals as knowledge conduits. BBN cofounder Richard Bolt, who was still active in the firm at the time, had been close friends with Margaret Mead, the iconic and field-defining anthropologist. In Stephenson's interview with him, he said, "Well, if anyone can understand us, an anthropologist should." She began to use the formula from her dissertation to calculate how networks changed over time.

Relationships and the human networks by which they manifest themselves are a strategic issue. Any organization's ability to implement any new strategy depends heavily on the way knowledge courses through its networks. Stephenson and social network analysts around the world now use sophisticated mathematical algorithms to analyze the human flow of information around the corporation.

As you manage human relationships, you need to know that there are three kinds of network animals in the organizational forest:

1. *Hubs* are people who are the most socially connected in the enterprise. With the highest number of "direct ties," they hold a lot of face-to-face conversations.
2. *Gatekeepers* move information between parts of an organization or between hubs. If a gatekeeper likes you, you have a valuable information broker. If, however, the gatekeeper takes an aversion to you, he or she can really slow the process by withholding information.

Gatekeepers are information bottlenecks, controlling the flow of contact to a particular part of the organization, thus making themselves indispensable. In many manufacturing companies, managers of key assembly plants are well known as gatekeepers, protecting the plant's integrity (and their own position) by keeping a tight rein on the information flowing in either direction between the plant and the rest of the company.

3. *Pulse takers* have the most indirect ties. Stephenson says that they are "almost the opposite of hubs. They're unseen but all seeing." They carry a lot of influence, but it tends to be subtle. Stephenson's favorite famous pulse taker: Machiavelli. A pulse taker's patterns of connection show a distinct mathematical pattern, with links that are relatively sparse but frequently used and diverse. Every now and then someone gets colloquially recognized as the first to sense changes in the wind and to intervene in subtle but powerful ways. Stephenson likens pulse takers to "prairie dogs, poking their heads above the cubicle tops to see what's going on." Organizations are composed of tribes. Social network analysts claim that decision making can be examined the same way lab technicians analyze chemical reactions. Companies can analyze, engineer, and optimize their own human networks.

"Even I, after 30 years of research, can't see them by staring at the diagrams," she says. "You can only detect them through the mathematics"[9]—by which Stephenson means the algorithmic analysis of survey data. Companies can exert far greater control over their competitiveness and their future by putting the right people in the right places and fostering new opportunities for them to talk with each other. Trust networks release cognitive capability.

## Evolution of Relationships

Relationships with users and fellow executives evolve in stages. The most colorful example of this, recounted by an analyst at a Fortune 250 enterprise speaking on condition of anonymity explained that when the project first started, line-of-business users and IT employees working on the project would wave to the analytics team in the parking lot. As the project bogged down and a variety of things went awry, the business and IT staff still waved in the parking lot. As the project became increasingly delayed and overbudget, "the waves started to involve only one finger."

Successful relationships require a form of balancing act. Success requires a lot of face-to-face communications and fact-based case studies with real return on investment.

## Intense Focus on "Same Paging"

In the contemporary era, we have become more polarized—economically, socially, and politically—and less civilized (in the sense that we no longer feel compelled to speak civilly to one another). We no longer read the same front page, watch the same news, listen to the same music, or view the same TV shows.

This broad trend toward atomized, self-centered behavior manifests itself in organizations in the form of silos—clusters of people operating in their own space and concerned only with their own issues. It's also seen by many senior business executives as the number-one problem facing them as they seek to transform their organizations into leaner, more agile creators of customer-thrilling products and services. How do we get the entire enterprise on the same page, moving in the same direction?

In organizations with clear leadership and direction, focusing people on the same page becomes a channeling of energies. In organizations with weak leadership and ambiguous direction, focusing people onto the same page becomes a constant struggle against competing agendas and energies fragmented into unproductive pursuits.

Some practices that can be used to focus people on the same page include creating clear and precise tactical goals that are directly linked to the fiduciary interests of the business.

Many analysts do everything they can to minimize conflict. Jim Best, the executive once in charge of infrastructure at Larry Bossidy's Allied Signal, serves as a senior business advisor at Grand Circle Travel in Boston who does just the opposite. He believes you "polarize resistance or support so you know who is with the program and who wants to punch your lights out."

## Social Capital Is Teamwork Scaled Up

"Social capital" refers to social networks, norms of reciprocity, mutual assistance, and trustworthiness. High-performance organizations manage their social capital—both within the department and without. Teams and teamwork are an important form of social capital that analytic leaders must become adroit at managing. Dr. David Porter, assistant professor of management at Howard University, drove home three key points to a group of over 40 IT executives at UCLA's Managing the Information Resource Program:[10]

1. A team is different from a group.
2. A team is a group of people working together to accomplish a task. Teams have:
   • *Common goal*, mission, purpose or task, accepted by all members.
   • *Interdependence* within the team in accomplishing the task.
   • *Shared decision making* in how to do the task.
   • *Mutual accountability* for task performance.
   • A sense of *sink or swim* together as a group.
3. Building/forming teams is a good idea when:
   • Everyone's buy-in is needed.
   • There is no clear answer.
   • The task is complex.
   • There is too much or not enough information.
   • There is a strong bias.
   • Creative ideas are needed.
   • The problem crosses function.
   • The solution affects many people.

The effectiveness of teams should be measured on three dimensions:

1. **Output.** Tasks, decisions, products, and/or services to meet your goals and standards.
2. **Learning.** The experience of working together enhances the capability and willingness of all involved to learn—during the work experience—and opens their minds to future learning opportunities.

**3. Satisfaction.** The experience of working together contributes to the personal well-being and development of all involved. You enjoy the experience and would work together again.

Evidence from high-performing enterprises indicates that analytic groups that are connected to the constituents they serve, who in turn are governed by common goals and understandings of interdependencies associated with realizing those goals, materially outperform other organizations. One of the most positive effects of social capital is the ways that people in a relationship can reach goals that would have been far beyond the grasp of individuals in isolation.

## Analysts are Weak at Relationship Math

If you were to inventory all the sad tales told by analysts, the category that undoubtedly would top the list quantity-and quality-wise would be the lament that "I thought they liked me/I thought they valued what we were trying to do." Very few analysts in the business today do not have a story about being blindsided by users who failed to see the value of analytic resources. Knowing what people think about what you are doing and how you are doing it is a critical part of your personal career success. No one—not major news anchors, not the president of prestigious institutions such as Harvard, and certainly not analysts—is immune to outside opinion. Lord North, British prime minister during the American Revolutionary War, knew the importance of "counting votes in advance." He needed to know where other members of Parliament stood on the key issues of the day.[11] In order to move forward with relationship management, you will need to:

- Understand where you stand in the life cycle of career-critical relationships.
- Move aggressively to get everyone on the "same page."
- Understand what people *really* think about what you are doing and how you are doing it.

The relationship of CIA director Richard Helms with President Lyndon Johnson has been described as "golden." Helms explained to all who would listen that it was not his relationship with Johnson that mattered, it was the president's perception of the value of the data and the assessments that the CIA was providing him that carried the day. Being in a position to provide key information creates an opportunity to form important relationships.

Analysts are now in the process of migrating from the blocking and tackling activities of collecting and scrubbing the data to actually analyzing and interpreting the data. Glenn Wegryn, associate director of global analytics at Procter & Gamble, has been quoted as saying that 10 years ago, about 80 percent of the work in data analysis was obtaining, cleaning, and validating the raw numbers. It took so long that there was hardly any time to do actual analysis. Now, he says, the vast majority of the time is spent on actual analysis. "The power, capability, and cleanliness of the data is the biggest change."[12]

Irving Tyler, vice president and chief financial officer of Quaker Chemical, has a similar story about data quality. He says that in the past, people would bring loads of disparate data into meetings of senior executives to make the case for their projects. Now, he says, all the data is collected on a consistent basis and worked up into an understandable package before it's put before the senior executives.

# Notes

1. Paul Seabright, *The Company of Strangers: A Natural History of Economic Life* (Princeton, NJ: Princeton University Press, 2005).

2. David Livingstone Smith, *Why We Lie: The Evolutionary Roots of Deception and the Unconscious Mind* (New York: St. Martin's Press, 2004), 5.

3. Robert D. Putnam, Lewis M. Feldstein, and Don Cohen, *Bowling Alone: The Collapse and Revival of American Community* (New York: Simon & Schuster, 2001).

4. Robert D. Putnam, Lewis M. Feldstein, and Don Cohen, *Better Together: Restoring the American Community* (New York: Simon & Schuster, 2004).

5. http://support.sas.com/usergroups/ and www.informs.org/index.php?c=11&kat=COMMUNITIES

6. In *Connecting to the Net Generation: What Higher Education Professionals Need to Know about Today's Students* (Wahington, D.C.: National Association of Student Personnel Administrators, 2007), Reynol Junco and Jeanna Mastrodicasa

conducted surveys documenting that 97 percent of students owned a computer, 94 percent owned a cell phone, and 56 percent owned an MP3 player (iPod, Zune, Sansa, etc.). They also found: 76 percent of students used Instant Messaging (IM), a typical IM user was logged on to IM 35 hours each week, 15 percent of IM users were logged on 24 hours a day/7 days a week, IM users typically chat 80 minutes per day, 66 percent of IM users also use IM on their cell phone, 80 percent of IM users send messages to someone in their same physical location (dorm room or apartment).

7. David Halberstam, *War in a Time of Peace* (New York: Scribner's, 2001).

8. Tom Gorman, Tom Vidaurreta, and Augusto Richardson, *Business Is a Contact Sport: Using the 12 Principles of Relationship Asset Management to Build Buy-in, Blast Away Barriers, and Boost Your Business* (Indianapolis: Alpha Publishing, 2002).

9. Personal conversations with author at the IT Value Studio (Jacksonville, Florida 2007).

10. The "Managing the Information Resource" Program at the Anderson Graduate School of Management – UCLA is a week long, non-degree, residential program designed for CIOs and their direct reports.

11. David Mccullough, *1776* (New York: Simon & Schuster, 2006).

12. Glenn Wegryn, speaking at the INFORMS Conference in Phoenix February 2009. http://meetings.informs.org/Practice09/program.html

# Chapter 6

# The Evolution
of the Technologies
of Analytics

I am very fortunate to teach a group of switched-on future business leaders at the Fisher College of Business at the Ohio State University. One of the opening exercises I frequently give these hard-charging executive MBA candidates is to ask them to describe how information technology (IT) has changed over the past five years. The class typically scores top marks picking up on broad technology trends.[1] Most MBA students and the vast majority of business executives recognize that technology is a change management twofer:

1. Technology has the potential to change everything.
2. Technology itself (what it is, how much it costs, how we think about it, how we buy and deploy it) is changing.

The speed with which new technologies are coming to the market has increased dramatically. The amount of information external to the enterprise concerning new technologies is massive. How can executives render all that information "business relevant" (i.e., what does the business need to know)? How can executives keep up with the art of the possible?

In the business analytics world, keeping up with what the technology can do is complicated by the fact that the people who buy/approve technology purchases (typically IT) are not the people who actually use the application. As Alan Cullop, the very business-focused chief information officer (CIO) at NetJets, the world-wide leader in the fractional jet ownership industry, explains, "I never use the applications I deploy. This is all about the business and what they need."[2] While Cullop places value to the business at the top of his prioritization scale, my research indicates that, in many instances, the wishes of the business and the desires of IT are not aligned. In most parts of the technology adoption world, trusted gatekeepers validate, certify, and/or give their blessing to a given technology set. Walter S. Mossberg, who writes the "Personal Technology" column for the *Wall Street Journal*, is a particularly influential voice in the consumer technology space. Such an authoritative voice does not exist in the business analytics market.

If you were to ask those individuals responsible for bringing new technologies into the modern enterprise "What framework do you use?" chances are they would look at you as if you were crazy. The vast majority of decision makers, surrounded by all this technology change and changing technology, typically do not systematically employ frameworks to assist them in making sense of what is really going on. This is surprising given the fact that several very powerful and useful frameworks exist.

## Technology Evolves

A whole lot of very smart people have spent a whole lot of time thinking very hard about how technology adds value to complex enterprises. The one point on which all tech watchers can agree is that technology evolves. Three frameworks are particularly helpful in guiding decisions about investments in business analytics:

1. Dick Nolan's stages theory[3]
2. Geoffrey Moore's crossing the chasm model
3. Gartner Group's hype cycle

## Stages Theory

Dick Nolan's stages theory examines the technology change/technology adoption phenomenon from the point of view of how the organization learns to deploy and use a technology. It is one of the first, and in my opinion one of the best, frameworks executives can use to understand technology change. Nolan argues that any technology, as it enters any enterprise, progresses through a series of stages representing organizational learning (an S-curve). The simplest rendition of the stages model features:

**Stage One: Initiation.** Technologies are introduced into the enterprise via limited investment and contained experimentation designed to prove the value of the technology in the organization.
**Stage Two: Contagion.** During this stage, technology learning and adaptation take place; the technology proliferates in a relatively opportunistic and uncontrolled manner.
**Stage Three: Control.** The uncontrolled growth of Stage Two leads eventually to inefficiency, which creates a demand for management controls to cost-effectively guide growth to a more manageable rate.
**Stage Four: Maturity.** This stage is marked by a balance of managed controls and growth.

Nolan's model gives a CIO/IT-centric view of what is going on, focusing on how the IT organization learns to manage a new technology. In most organizations, IT is way behind where it needs to be to maximize value from investments in business analytics.

## Crossing the Chasm

Geoffrey Moore told audiences in 2006 that historically, you could understand a lot about the dynamics of what was going on technologically by keeping an eye on the famous law of the other Moore: Gordon Moore at Intel.[4] Every five to seven years, you would get a 10 to 100 times improvement in the underlying capability of computing, which would render obsolete whatever you happened to be doing at the time. The entire industry would rip and replace, literally swap out entire infrastructures, because the new gear was so much better, faster, and more powerful. Recently, while Moore's Law still applies, it has stopped explaining as much.

In his book *Crossing the Chasm: Marketing & Selling Disruptive Products to Mainstream Customers*, Moore focuses on how technology enters and moves through the market.[5] He attributes the flow (and nonflow) of technology to the preferences and behaviors of the people in the enterprise actually doing the technology adopting. If you have not read this book, you should. Moore started in the technology business doing research with Regis McKenna, one of the first and most respected Silicon Valley market research houses. The firm helped Apple, Compaq, Electronic Arts, American OnLine, Intel, Genetech, Microsoft, Lotus, Silicon Graphics, and 3Com through their formative years. Moore studies "discontinuous innovations." A lot of research has been done over the past 50 years, culminating in a model called the technology adoption life cycle. *Crossing the Chasm* embraces and extends this body of work by asserting there are six distinct time zones in the life of any technology.

1. Early market—when visionaries embrace new technology
2. Chasm—the gap between early tech adoption and mass market buy in
3. Bowling alley—niche-based adoption in advance of the general market
4. Inside the tornado—all-at-once mass market adoption
5. Mainstreet—aftermarket development
6. End of life

The rules for each of these technology time zones are different. The goal of good technology strategy is to align oneself with the forces in play in that time zone. Organizations tend to get good at one set of rules. When the market moves, behavior frequently does not change. As a result, organizations start doing dysfunctional things. Technology management jet lag sets in. *Crossing the Chasm* provides a model to avoid this. At each stage in the model (similar to Nolan's stages), Moore provides a set of rules about how to operate effectively.

A discontinuous innovation is a different kind of animal altogether. While a continuous innovation involves add-ons to existing products (e.g., whiter whites, brighter brights, better mileage), discontinuous innovations require new infrastructure. The end user community is going to have to adopt new behaviors. This is why so many discontinuous ideas fail—people perceive the risk/hassle associated with change as being significantly higher than the benefit. When pain is greater than gain, change *does not* happen.

A model developed by Everett Rogers at Harvard in the 1950s predicts how any community will respond when you introduce discontinuous innovation into the community. The model predicts that the community will self-segregate into five different types of responses—roughly equivalent to the standard deviations of a statistical curve.

1. Technology enthusiasts
2. Visionaries
3. Pragmatists/early majority
4. Conservatives/late majority
5. Laggards

A third of the people will make the "pragmatist" response. A third will make the "conservative" response. And the other third will be split between people making a very conservative response and those who are early adopters.

**Technology Enthusiasts.** These are the first adopters of new paradigms. They are technologically oriented. Fundamentally they just want to know how the technology works. According to Moore, they don't really care what it's for. They don't think that's their job. They think their job is to understand the technology—its properties and its principles. Technology enthusiasts typically don't have any money. Solution providers seek to seduce their minds rather than extract money from their wallets. They sometimes do this by providing early stage products at concessionary rates. These folks play a crucial role educating the rest of the population. In fact, if you do not win the approval of the technology enthusiasts, you are done. You are denied access to anybody else because the decision makers farther down the road will continually refer back to technology enthusiasts, asking "Did Earl say this stuff was okay?" If technology enthusiasts say a technology is okay, that does not mean the organization will accept it, but if the technology enthusiasts say it is not okay, it's out—the technology is over.

**Visionaries.** Visionaries are not necessarily technologically facile. What they have are wonderful strategic imaginations. Visionaries look at technology as an opportunity to create competitive advantage. Every time you hear the phrase "competitive advantage," think "visionary." These people are trying to create a gap between their organization and the other organizations they compete with. The way they create a gap is by going early. That means they go ahead of the herd. If they go ahead of the herd, they can't use references. They drive by the lights of their own imaginations. Pragmatists and conservatives wait for the herd. Visionaries make big, bold decisions. They drive the early adoption of the new paradigms. "I am going to go ahead of the herd. I've seen the new way. I will go first. I will set the trend."

**Pragmatists/Early Majority.** Pragmatists/early majority are the herd. This is a good word; it is not a pejorative term. It describes how pragmatists operate—they use herd behavior to make buying decisions. As opposed to analyzing the technology for competitive advantage, they want to know what everybody else thinks. As a pragmatist, I would ask a technical group to look at the technology but meanwhile I would start calling up other CIOs. I would start saying "So . . . are you going to WIN 95 this year? Me neither. Let's see, Web page, does everybody have a Web page? We have a Web page too. Next question: Does your Web page do anything? Ours doesn't either." So in 1996, you had to have a Web page, but it didn't have to do anything. We check around. "Do you have an @ sign on your business card? Okay, I have to have an @ sign on my business card." Pragmatists check with each other. They are staying with each other. We pragmatists figure that if we stick together, the standards stick with us. Everything moves with us. We are okay. "Moving with the herd" has historically been a popular way to make technology buying decisions. If you make the wrong technology decision, it doesn't really matter because we all made it together.

Pragmatists/early majority make up approximately 34 percent of those in a system to adopt an innovation. The early majority adopts new ideas just before average members of a system. The early majority interacts frequently with their peers but seldom hold positions of opinion leadership in a system. The early majority's unique position between technology enthusiasts and visionaries (the front part of the technology adoption life cycle) and the conservatives/late majority and laggards (those late to adopt the technology) makes them an important link in the diffusion process. They serve as an important conduit betwixt and between the system's interpersonal networks. The early majority thinks deeply before completely adopting a new idea. "Be not the first by which the new is tried, nor the last to lay the old aside" fits the thinking of the early majority. They follow with deliberate willingness in adopting innovations, but they seldom lead.

**Conservatives/Late Majority.** Conservatives/late majority do whatever pragmatists do, but they don't like it. These are the folks who want the benefits of technology without the experience. When you hear those in consumer marketing talk about "appliances," they are referring to conservatives. The difference between an appliance and a computer is that an appliance is not programmable. Therefore, you cannot be wrong. If the appliance doesn't work, it is the appliance's fault. It is broken. If a computer doesn't work, it's your fault. Being a techno-conservative is like computing without guilt. These people fundamentally don't trust electrons. Conservatives/late majority make up approximately a third of the members of a system. Adoption is semivoluntarily coerced via increasing network pressures from peers. The late majority do not adopt until most others in their system have done so. System norms must decidedly favor an innovation before the late majority are convinced. Just about all of the uncertainty about a new idea must be removed before the late majority feel that it is safe to adopt.

**Laggards.** Laggards are the last 16 percent of individuals in a system to adopt an innovation. They possess almost no opinion leadership. The point of reference for the laggard is the past. They often make decisions in terms of what has been done previously. Laggards tend to be suspicious of innovations and change agents. Laggards' resistance to innovations may be entirely rational from their viewpoint, as their resources are limited and they must be certain that a new idea will not fail before they can adopt.

## *Early Market*

The first thing that happens in the face of a new and emerging technology is the people who want to go in front of, ahead of the herd, break off and create a phenomenon called the early market. It is a real marketplace. You can make a lot of money here. The technology enthusiasts are out here because this is where the cool technology is. The visionaries are here because this is where there is opportunity to create competitive advantage.

These folks go early and create the early market. They create a lot of publicity and a lot of dollars—project-oriented dollars. If you are a vendor, at this point you tend not to have a lot of customers, but the projects you have are very visible. Then you hit the chasm—the gap between early adopters and mass acceptance—which emerges as a function of the visionary going ahead of the herd. Then, after a while, the paradigm matures and the chasm starts to shrink. From a visionary's point of view, that is bad. A new visionary comes in and thinks, "I could start with this new paradigm, but I would only get a little bit of a lead over people. That is probably not a good bet for me. I'm going to go try to find something weirder. This is too tame for me. This chasm is too short."

The pragmatist looks at this same space and says, "It's too wide." People have not moved yet. Fundamentally what happens is the market dynamics collapse. The market doesn't go anywhere. It just stops. A lot of companies that spent a lot of money getting to the early adopters (imagining that they were with the big herd) start pouring on the gas, ramping up production, ramping up marketing, and they crash into the chasm. In the 1980s, a lot of good companies collapsed into the chasm.

How can you cross the chasm? How can you shorten the time period to get across? You have to understand the dynamics of adoption on the other side of the chasm. The pragmatist segment has dominated high tech virtually since its inception, and still does. What characterizes the pragmatists' adoption pattern the most is something that ends up being called "the tornado": wide-spread adoption and hypergrowth.

Fundamentally, the tornado is simply the opposite of the chasm. The chasm occurs as a function of the pragmatists saying "It's too soon. It's too soon. Cloud computing? It's too soon. It's not ready for prime time." Pragmatists ultimately change their minds and decide, "Oh my gosh, it's too late." When that thought enters the mind of the herd, they stampede. The pragmatist herd does not adopt a little bit at a time. When everyone wants a technology at the same time, the demand swamps the market's supply mechanism. Right now we are on the cusp of a business analytics tornado.

The business analytics market currently is dominated by pragmatists who have gone before the herd. If you have been following Moore's argument, that last statement may give you pause. Wait a minute— pragmatists don't like to be alone. They like the herd. Why would they go before the herd? Who are the pragmatists who would go before the herd? That doesn't make any sense. A pragmatist is defined as somebody who goes with the herd. Well, yes. What would a pragmatist be doing this close to the chasm? Wouldn't they be happier back with the herd? The answer is that these are pragmatists who have *broken* business processes—key processes unique to their vertical market segment. Because the processes can't be fixed with existing infrastructure, these pragmatists are unhappy. Something has happened in the economic environment that requires these unhappy pragmatists to reengineer a business process—fraud in financial services, for example. All of a sudden the existing infrastructure, which worked fine, is broken. Unhappy pragmatists go to the people running infrastructure and say, "Can you help me fix it?" and they say, "No."

So these unhappy pragmatists look back across the chasm to see what is new coming down the pike that can help them fix their problem. The big requirement, unhappy pragmatists tell their vendors as they prepare to enter the bowling alley of initial technology adoption, is "You as a solutions provider have to bring 100 percent of the solution to my problem. I don't have any infrastructure that helps. If you don't bring 100 percent, this is not going to work." The notion of "the whole product" becomes incredibly important for solving this chasm-crossing problem. The SAS Institute is particularly strong in this regard.

Moore did significant research discovering that bowling alley strategies require technology vendors to identify a vertical market where a broken mission-critical business process is causing management enough pain that it would gamble on an unproven and/or unfamiliar technology.

This is step 1. Next the vendor must provide to that market not just a product but a whole solution. The objective is to become the hands-down/no-questions-asked leader in that niche, to saturate the community. Using the bowling analogy, after you have hit the first pin, you tip it such that it knocks over another pin. Each new market/pin should leverage the success and technology of the last.

## Gartner Group Hype Cycle

One of the most popular frameworks emerging from the buzz factory that is the Gartner Group is the hype cycle.[6] The "hype curve" refers to the very predictable cycle of emotions and expectations that accompany new technology as it enters the marketplace. The cycle has five phases:

1. **Innovation/Technology Trigger.** Something starts the ball rolling. Word emerges that "something is up." Excitement starts to build. People start thinking and writing about possibilities.
2. **Peak of Inflated Expectations.** Geoffrey Moore's early adopters and visionaries launch very visible pilot projects. Suppliers of the innovation talk up their high-brand customers. Analysts start hitting the trade show circuit. Journalists start writing "Is this the new thing?" articles. Airline in-flight magazines lead people to believe that if they are not involved, they might be behind. The stories in the press capture the excitement around the innovation and reinforce the need to become a part of it or be left behind.
3. **Trough of Disillusionment.** Early-stage pilot projects start bumping into reality. The visible, early-adopting big-name client stories are starting to get a little long in the tooth. Stories start surfacing about problems with performance. Questions about financial payback go unanswered. Stories about the technology not being what users expected start to surface. The media does an about-face from a tone standpoint. Whereas previously they were technology cheerleaders, they now play the role of skeptic, focusing on the challenges associated with generating value with the technology.
4. **Slope of Enlightenment.** Visionaries/early adopters stick to their guns and manage to make the technology work. Learning curve effects start to take hold. The press starts publishing "lessons

learned" and "best practices" pieces. Suppliers address issues with early beta releases. An ecosystem of knowledgeable professionals begins to emerge to assist risk-averse conservatives to embrace the "new" technology. Methodologies no longer have to be invented from scratch.

5. **Plateau of Productivity.** The technology is now deemed ready for prime time. The risk associated with the technology itself and the financial data demonstrating that acceptable returns are the norm rather than the exception lead to the possibility of a tornado developing. Adoption accelerates.

Most of the industry focuses on where a given technology might reside on the hype curve. The real power and value comes from the prescriptive suggestions the framework generates regarding managing the total technology adoption process inside your particular organization. A mindful approach using the stages, hype cycle, and chasm frameworks is a good way to look at the rapidly evolving world of business analytics.

## Where Business Analytics Sits Today

Technologically, the base portfolio of technologies comprising business analytics are, in Gartner Group hype cycle parlance, well along the slope of enlightenment and moving toward the plateau of productivity. With regard to the Moore chasm model, we have all the makings of a business analytics tornado forming. The most interesting model and the one that probably will have the most impact on the value your particular organization extracts from investments in business analytics in the near, mid, and long term is the Nolan stages model. Most organizations have not yet gone through the organization learning necessary to extract value from these powerful technologies. They are just entering Nolan's Contagion Stage.

Discussions with a wide variety of technology analysts (e.g., Aberdeen, AMR Research, ECM Scope, Forrester Research, Gartner Group, IDC, Nemertes Research, Nucleus Research, and Yankee Group), journalists, and practitioners lead me to conclude that business analytics really isn't a technology or an application. It is a capability built on a range of technologies (over 30 as of this writing),[7] practices, and strategic approaches. The ability to create value with the technologies of business analytics is a function of culture, organization, and analytical skills.

While the front end of what is possible with business analytics is always moving, the core technologies that enable exceptional insight are essentially mainstream technologies. The technology is very mature. There really is no technology risk associated with business analytics. The risk comes from whether your organization can migrate to a New Know mode of operation and actually observe, orient, decide, and act with the facts and insights that the tools now make available.

We all know that theoretically people don't *really* buy technology products. They buy the business benefits that technology products enable. Thus, the way to get full value from any investment in the technologies of business analytics would be to ask the question: Where can we create the most value for the business? This is exactly what John Deane, the personable and courageous former CIO at Wendy's, did not long after he joined that quick-service restaurant chain in May 2001. A business-savvy executive, Deane recognized that where you can impact the profit and loss statement the most are food cost and labor. Those are the two key operational elements that will or won't make a restaurant profitable.

The Wendy's team zoomed in on forecasting—one of the pillars of business analytics—as a possible high-payback/high-impact investment area. Previously, or so the story goes, forecasts were created by taking the last six weeks of data, throwing the high and the low out, and averaging the rest; that was the forecast. This might work in some enterprises, but an outfit like Wendy's is surprisingly complex. Think of every Wendy's restaurant as a small, build-to-order manufacturing plant. Don't forget that Wendy's at the time was the home of the custom hamburger with countless combinations. The shelf life for cooked food items was about 3 to 7 minutes; for salads, 3 to 4 hours. Further, menu items had to be delivered in about 90 seconds with the staff on hand, so the value of advance planning was critical. However, with no product mix information included in the old forecast, preprepped items such as salads produced a lot of food waste.

Using a data warehouse, Wendy's created a true statistical model, based on two years of data. It deployed predictive analytics such that analysts actually could predict for any of the 1,300 stores what each would sell with 95 percent accuracy by product mix by half hour. This is pre-2005. The capability to forecast key business processes has advanced materially since then.

## It is Time to Wake Up and Analyze the Data

*Blackwood's Magazine*'s "Battle of Dorking" (1871) is considered one of the most influential short stories ever written in the English language. It woke a sleeping England up to its shocking state of military unpre paredness.[8] It viscerally and very emotionally portrayed a once-proud England shamed and subjugated by external invaders. As a direct result of the article and subsequent book, Parliament passed laws, the military changed tactics, and politicians started getting busy. *The New Know*, while a work of nonfiction, similarly aspires to wake a sleeping cadre of senior management to the shocking state of analytic unpreparedness they find themselves in.

## What People Agree On

People have been thinking about technology and how to extract value from it for a long, long time. I examined the thoughts of major technology historians and synthesized them down to points of convergence— things everyone could agree on—and points of divergence—points where material differences of opinion prevailed.

### Technology Travels in Packs and the Interrelatedness of It All

One of the most frequently made mistakes in the technology forecasting realm is forecasting a single technology. Technology travels in packs. Spreadsheets didn't happen without personal computers, which did not happen without microchips. One futurist in 1900 might have anticipated rockets. Another futurist might have imagined nuclear explosives.

They never talked. The impact—the "what it means, aha!" part of the story—comes from combining the two. The fear of atomic Armageddon (e.g., missiles plus nuclear bombs), which was to become one of the central defining realities of the second half of the twentieth century, requires combining both vectors. Most forecasters analyze only one technology trajectory one at a time. The future will not happen that way. Keep interaction among technologies top of mind. History shows that the recombination of ideas is frequently the driving force behind technological creativity and subsequent commercial development.

A lot of very interesting technology in the near- to mid-term pipeline will arrive on the scene and add important context to what can happen in the business analytics space:

- Cloud computing
- Advanced robotics
- Three-dimensional printing
- Media distribution via game consoles
- Ultra-mobile/ultra-micro-devices
- On-body/in-body sensor technology

On the short end of longer term, we are going to see computing environments that allow same-time collaboration between people who do not speak the same language, do not live in the same time zone, and do not work in the same enterprise. Optical pickups/low-cost digital cameras and display technologies will deliver information to multitouch surfaces across the globe, allowing people to interact as if they were in the same room—before the end of the next decade.

User interfaces will become much more natural, making managing digital content (searching, authoring, editing, managing permissions and accesses) as easy and natural as having a conversation. The facts and data you need, whether they are in document, video, or aural format, will arrive at your workspace, wherever that might be, without the current hassle. Your ability to contribute meaningfully to the collaborations of the future is very much a function of your ability to master business analytics.

In fewer than 10 years, you will not have to "wonder" what your project team is up to. Social networking technologies such as Twitter now provide management with the opportunity to understand what workers are thinking/what matters to them via rendering the "tweet stream" machine-accessible, and thus making it available for analysis. Subject to your own preferences, you will be kept in the loop on all key project activities. One of the major technologies that will materially change the business analytics space is geospatial data. Information will now *know* where it is and, more important, where you are and when you need it. All enterprise data stores will be tagged to enable advanced mapping and navigation applications. In the future, you will be living in a world where you spend significantly less time searching for the right data.

## We Will Get Much Better at Modeling

Quantitatively aware executives *know* that—by definition—models are but representations of the real world. Efficacious models—models that help us make better decisions—are becoming more important to business success. Organizations need to become more adept at using sophisticated quantitative models. And yet many executives are not very comfortable with using such models. Executives have real trouble getting over the fact that models can be wrong.

There are several infamous cases of models mis-forecasting how the future would unfold. One of the most famous of these mis-tuned models is the one used—to great public relations effect and political impact—by the Club of Rome. This global think tank generated a series of high profile predictions based upon the first research to make serious use of computers in modeling the consequences of a rapidly growing global population. Things did not come to pass in the way or the time frame the model predicted.

At the base of Abraham Maslow's hierarchy of human needs is the physiological requirement of food. Running out of food is one of the most deeply rooted fears of all societies. Sadly, some of modeling's most visible missteps come from the repeated failure to forecast planetary food needs. Every college student remembers the personally quite upbeat but publicly quite pessimistic nineteenth-century demographer Thomas Robert Malthus.

Quite the numbers guy, Malthus introduced the world to the realization that things grow at different rates. He forecast that since human population increases at a geometric rate (1, 2, 4, 8, 16), whereas food production increases at that time were progressing at a more leisurely arithmetic rate (1, 2, 3, 4), without the population-decreasing effects of the Four Horsemen of the Apocalypse (pestilence, war, famine, and death), we humans would outbreed our food supplies.[9]

In 1850 (16 years after Malthus died in 1834), the world's population was 1.2 billion. We hadn't all starved. Society had not devolved according to Thomas Hobbes's forecast of a "war of all against all" (*bellum omnium contra omnes*). Lives, for the most part at that time, were not "solitary, poor, nasty, brutish, and short." Malthus's math was right (a key requirement for the New Know)—things do change at different rates—but his understanding of change (the essence of business analytics) was off.

Fast-forward 100-plus years; the food forecast again takes center stage in public consciousness. Global population had reached 3.6 billion in 1968 when Paul Ehrlich published the neo-Malthusian classic *The Population Bomb*.[10] "The battle to feed all of humanity is over," he notoriously declared. "In the 1970s the world will undergo famines—hundreds of millions of people are going to starve to death in spite of any crash programs embarked upon now."

Ehrlich's dire forecast was followed in 1972 when the Club of Rome came together to write *The Limits to Growth*.[11] Using five variables—world population, industrialization, pollution, food production, and resource depletion—the authors modeled the interaction of exponential growth on finite resources, returning to Malthus. And yet today, with a global population of approximately 6.8 billion, there are more overweight people than hungry people in the world.[12] What is with these modelers? Why can't they get things right?

Some attribute the fact that the *Limits to Growth* predictions were off the mark due to their failure to take into account basic economic principles (i.e., people change their preferences when the environment changes). David Friedman asserts that "in modeling the world, [they] had left out the role played by human rationality. It was as if they were trying to predict what would happen on a highway by extrapolating the path cars were following while ignoring the fact that each car had a driver with good reason to avoid colliding with other cars."[13] Modelers and modeling techniques have increased the sophistication with which they address the other driver scenarios.

One analyst told me, "Analysts are never wrong. Their models may be misused by management, however." A little hubris and a lot of truth reside in this provocative statement.

## *People Never Use Technology the Way We Think They Will*

What cannot be known with any confidence is how people actually will use business analytics. How will the pieces combine? The inventor of the telephone, Alexander Graham Bell, probably would not be surprised by the technical drawings of contemporary telephone systems. He would be quite amazed at such developments as telemarketing and phone sex. I am pretty sure the Wright brothers were not thinking about frequent-flyer miles when they launched from Kitty Hawk.

Linear extrapolation rarely paints an accurate picture. The personal computer was not a mainframe with a television screen. These devices make things possible that weren't possible before. This is the power of business analytics, not the technology pieces parts.

## *There Is Never Just One Opinion*

Information technology might seem to be the one area where foresight should be almost easy. And yet opinions frequently vary. Michael Goldblatt, former head of the Defense Sciences Office, liked to demonstrate to visitors that at any point in time, multiple points of view about a given technology set could exist. On the left wall of his office was a quote from the *New York Times* dated October 9, 1903: "The flying machine which will really fly might be evolved by the combined and continuous efforts of mathematicians in from one million to ten million years." On the right wall of his office, a quote from Orville Wright's diary, dated October 9, 1903: "We started assembly today."

## Trends

Business intelligence—now business analytics—has been at the top of the technology agenda for the past three years. I envision it staying there for the next decade. The sector has migrated from a data-centric orientation (i.e., "Why can't you get the numbers right?") to a decision-centric orientation (i.e., "What do we need to know to make the kind of decisions that will get us where we want to go?").

Business analytics is being baked into business processes. Everyone needs to become an analytical problem solver. Thus, everyone needs business analytics. This everyman-an-analyst phenomenon has precipitated a frenzy of mergers, acquisitions, partnerships, and alliances. Everyone is in the business analytics market these days. Every key business process—in every organization—in every vertical market is going to be:

1. Analyzed for efficiency and effectiveness.
2. Metered/instrumented for performance data collection and management.

There is going to be a New Know gold rush. Think reengineering with sensors and tightly calibrated performance feedback. The question is how, at what pace, via what technology, and at what cost will we make this happen? *Network World* recently ranked modeling (#1) and data mining (#7) as two of the most in-demand, recession-proof skills in the technology sector.[14]

Organizations have a lot of technology choices in front of them. Two tongue-in-cheek metaphors for technology adoption processes are associated with the technologies of business analytics: the large-mouth bass metaphor and the dog chasing a car metaphor. The large-mouth bass metaphor portrays technology buyers as only semisensate fish who will strike at any shiny object, forgetting that there is a hook attached to such behavior.

The dog chasing a car metaphor posits that technology buyers pursue the next "hot" thing—whatever device or practice is currently on top of the trade magazine hit parade. Rather than being a dog chasing the garbage truck or a large-mouth bass, be mindful about the capability you are trying to create. There are open source solutions. There are software-as-a-service options. The one option organizations do not have is not moving forward.

# Notes

1. They correctly observe: (1) Technology is becoming more global in nature (i.e., technology used to enable global business and innovative technology is now emerging from global sources); (2) technology enables collaboration; (3) technology product life cycles are shrinking; (4) there is increasing focus on mobility; (5) the vendor landscape/shape of tech supply chain is shifting; (6) complexity is increasing; (7) technology markets are still afflicted by "exuberances" and information asymmetries; (8) consumer is king; and (9) spending on business analytics is increasing.

2. Phone interview with author Winter, 2009

3. Dick is professor emeritus at Harvard and the Philip M. Condit Endowed Chair in Business Administration at the University of Washington.

4. Geoffrey Moore, "Digital 2.0: Powering a Creative Economy," Panel Discussion at World Economic Forum (Davos, Switzerland: 27 January 2006). See: http://geoffmoore.blogs.com/my_weblog/2006/01/dateline_davos__1.html

5. Geoffrey Moore, *Crossing the Chasm: Marketing & Selling Disruptive Products to Mainstream Customers* (New York: Harper Collins, 1991).

6. Jackie Fenn and Mark Raskino, *Mastering the Hype Cycle: How to Choose the Right Innovation at the Right Time* (Boston: Harvard Business Press, 2008).

7. The technologies include: appliances; business activity monitoring (BAM); enterprise content management (ECM); data visualization; data warehouse; data mart; digital asset management (DAM); enterprise information management (EIM); enterprise portal; enterprise search; extract/transform and load tools (ETL); master data management (MDM); metadata management; in-memory analytics; integrated search; online analytical processing; query; real-time performance management (RTPM); reporting tools; service-oriented architecture (SOA); social networking/Web 2.0 technologies (blogs, microblogging, wikis, user-contributed content, collaborative filtering, tagging, folksonomies); text mining; Web analytics; and Web content management.

8. "The story recounted, from the perspective of an old man living in the 1920s, an attack on England some fifty years earlier by a force referred to only as the 'the enemy' or 'the Power.'" Tom Reiss, "Imagining the Worst: How a Literary Genre Anticipated the Modern World," *The New Yorker*, November 28, 2005, 106. Lieutenant Colonel George Tomkyns Chesney had not intended the book

to be entertaining but to shock. By combining the two sensations "Chesney had accidentally invented the thriller." Literary critics view H. G. Wells's *War of the Worlds* to be an extrapolation of the "invasion novel" genre initiated by "The Battle of Dorking."

9.  Thomas Malthus, *An Essay on the Principle of Population* (1798).

10. Paul Ehrlich, *The Population Bomb* (Cutchogue, NY: Buccaneer Books, 1997).

11. Donella H. Meadows, Jorgen Randers, Dennis L. Meadows, and William W. Behrens, *The Limits to Growth: A Report for the Club of Rome's Project on the Predicament of Mankind* (New York: Universe Books, 1972).

12. It is not my attempt here to in any way minimize the very significant crisis associated with global poverty and hunger. My concern is that forecasts in this area have historically been off the mark. My colleagues at the World Bank are fighting an uphill battle—a battle that must be won. In the words of World Bank president Robert Zoellick, "While many are worrying about filling their gas tanks, many others around the world are struggling to fill their stomachs, and it is getting more and more difficult every day." J. Walter Thompson ad agency, "The End of Cheap," *Work in Progress* (September 2008).

13. David D. Friedman, *Future Imperfect: Technology and Freedom in an Uncertain World* (Cambridge, UK: Cambridge University Press, 2008), 317.

14. Carolyn Duffy Marsan, "Top 10 Technology Skills," *Network World*, March 20, 2009.

# Chapter 7

# Value of Analytics

*Knowledge, Strategy, and Innovation*

Futurists divide the world-to-be into three decision-spaces: knowns, known unknowns, and unknown unknowns. Knowns are things that, barring unforeseen black swan (totally unexpected) perturbations, will come to pass as a matter of course.[1] Demographic projections are a prime source of knowns. For example, within a relatively narrow range, we know, with a reasonably high degree of certainty, how many 25-year-old males there will be in China in 2034 because we know how many there are in 2009 and have a pretty good feel for the factors affecting the survival and geographic mobility of this cohort. During the cold war, we had a high degree of risk but also a high degree of stability. It was reasonable to predict an unchanging strategic future. We in the United States knew that the Soviet Union would be there, that the Warsaw Pact would be there, that there would be a North Atlantic Treaty Organization

(NATO) front in Germany. Knowing that all those factors would persist, engineering teams could spend 15 or even 20 years developing a battle tank for an unchanging theater strategy in Germany.

The uncertainty associated with the new world order has impacted the ability to project the strategic landscape for many years ahead with a decent probability of success. The absence of any such predictability has, in many ways, shaken our fundamental frames of reference.

Known unknowns are circumstances or outcomes that are known to be possible, but it is unknown whether they will be realized. Unknown unknowns are circumstances or outcomes that were not conceived by the planner/executive at the time when decisions were being made. Business analytics lets an executive know what decision space they are in. Oliver Wendell Holmes, American physician and writer (not to be confused with his son the Supreme Court Justice—Oliver Wendell Holmes, Jr.), ever aware of the interaction of knowledge and ignorance, used a spatial metaphor to illustrate it:

> Science is the topography of ignorance. From a few elevated points we triangulate vast spaces, including infinite unknown details. We cast the lead, and draw up a little sand from abysses we may never reach with our dredges. The best part of our knowledge is that which teaches us where knowledge leaves off and ignorance begins.[2]

Called by Winston Churchill the "organizer of victory" for his leadership of the Allied victory in World War II, General George C. Marshall served as the U.S. Army Chief of Staff during the war and as the chief military advisor to President Franklin D. Roosevelt. At headquarters, Marshall created a capability that twenty-first-century information managers would do well to emulate. Every morning authorized personnel could walk into Marshall's conference room and get a graphic yet accurate picture of exactly what was happening in every operational zone in which the United States was involved. The reason we manage information is to create meaning, which leads to action. This is the value of business analytics: It enables us to understand what is going on in the world.

In the geopolitical realm, we repeatedly see the enormous costs of not knowing (e.g., Pearl Harbor, Battle of the Bulge, and September 11).

The Central Intelligence Agency was created to ensure that another Pearl Harbor "never happened." In the weeks before December 7, 1941, the United States had collected enough information to establish a Japanese attack on Pearl Harbor as a known unknown. This part of the story is reasonably well known. What is perhaps not as well known is that on Sunday, February 7, 1932, at the outset of a U.S. Army-Navy war game called Grand Joint Exercise 4, Rear Admiral Harry Yarnell, commander of the newly commissioned U.S. aircraft carriers *Saratoga* and *Lexington*, launched *in simulation* a devastating attack on a sleeping Pearl Harbor.

> 150 planes, a mix of fighters, dive-bombers, and torpedo planes quickly moved into formation and headed through the night sky for Oahu. The strike formations used the battery of search-lights at Kahuku Point as a navigation aid to guide them toward their targets.

> Dive bombers and torpedo planes went to work on the ships lying at anchor along Battleship Row. Fighter aircraft peeled off and strafed the airfield hitting parked planes, fuel stor-age tanks and hangars. A *New York Times* reporter on the scene reported that the attacks were "unopposed by the defense, which was caught virtually napping."[3]

The "bombs" dropped were flour bags; they could be seen splat-tered on the navy's ships still sitting at anchor.

Taken totally by surprise, the Army Air Corps commanders sought to minimize the attack's results. They argued that the damage incur-red to the Hickam airfield was minimal and asserted that they had found and attacked Yarnell's carriers. Finally, they protested the attack on legal grounds: It was improper to begin a war on Sunday! The war game's umpires sided with the army. Their reports made no mention of Yarnell's attack but concluded that "it is doubtful if air attacks can be launched against Oahu in the face of strong defensive aviation without subjecting the attacking carriers to the danger of material damage and consequent great loss in the attacking force."[4]

Because there was no central office responsible for collecting and evaluating information, the numerous disparate bits and pieces of intel-ligence strewn among various sensing organizations—the Department

of State, War Department, Navy Department, and the White House—
remained unconnected. Coherent analysis and dissemination was
impossible. The "unintegratedness" of the info-pieces parts, this data-
but-no-knowledge frustration, led government leaders to create an
independent, unified intelligence agency, appropriately called the
Central Intelligence Agency. Making sense of all the data points was
difficult in 1941. It remains difficult today.

The Pearl Harbor story brings to the fore two business analytic value
truisms. The first is you need to collect, assemble, and interpret all the
information you are gathering. The second is you have to genuinely
want to question the status quo for change opportunities. You have
to want to know what is off the radar screen. You have to go out of
your way to think about known unknowns and unknown unknowns.

Unless a company is willing to change the way it does business on
the basis of what the data tells it, all the data it collects is worthless.

> Do stores want to run differently, do the retail directors, do the
> buyers? We all know that you can find "interesting stuff" in
> the data. The challenge is how you get the business to engage
> and be prepared to change processes or decisions based on a
> new more detailed source of customer understanding.[5]

The big insight—before you buy a piece of technology, before you
collect a byte of data, before you say the phrase "business analytics"—
you need to want to know. Independent of your technical budget, not
related to your personal math skills, and in no way related to your position in the organizational pecking order, your ability to create value
with business analytics comes down to one essential question: Are you
curious? We live in a world where just about everything is "knowable."
For us to know, however, we must hunger to understand.

## Business Analytics as Source of Strategic Understanding

You can't do strategy without business analytics. It's that simple. Why
bother creating a strategy if you aren't going to execute it? A recent
Booz & Company study revealed that employees at three out of every

five companies rated their organization weak at execution—that is, when asked if they agreed with the statement "Important strategic and operational decisions are quickly translated into action," the majority answered no.[6] "Execution is the result of thousands of decisions made every day by employees acting according to the information they have and their own self-interest. The Booz research showed that actions having to do with business analytics—how people made decisions and how they were held accountable—are about twice as effective as any other management program or initiative.

To move forward in uncertain times, managers have to have a clear sense of their roles and responsibilities. They must intuitively understand which decisions are theirs to make and have some degree of confidence that the facts with which they are making those decisions are legitimate.

George Geis, a professor at the Anderson Graduate School of Management, teaches the wildly popular mergers and acquisitions course. He creates the market modeling visualization tools (www.trivergence .com) used by many major players in the media and high-technology markets. Geis tells his students that while an executive used to be able to focus on a handful of competitors, the environment today is breeding new competitors coming from all directions. We are, in the words of Harold L. Sirkin, James W. Hemerling, and Arindam K. Bhattacharya of the Boston Consulting Group, "Competing with Everyone, from Everywhere, for Everything."[7]

Every sector is being impacted. Everyone has become a potential competitor . . . or a potential ally. Relationships are increasingly important. Intricate relationship webs define markets and competition. The end result of all this, in Geis's mind, is that you cannot do strategy—you cannot do market planning—without business analytics. Period.

Market modeling is a systematic method for analyzing and taking actions related to partnership and investment strategy in the globalized economy. Market modeling helps executives:

• Understand dynamic changes occurring within a market.
• Intelligently select partners.
• Decide on what types of deal structures to choose.
• Understand steps to take to implement deals successfully.

With regard to the mergers and acquisitions that emerge from a strategic exercise, there are eight end objectives:

1. Develop a *market overview* that depicts the *value activities* of the market—traditional, hybrid, or digital.
2. Build a *universe of players* relevant to the market being analyzed.
3. Design and build a *deal database* for the market.
4. Uncover *deal rationales* using direct deal analysis or by analyzing constellations of deals.
5. Within the context of your core competence, *determine your deal rationale* for complementary value activities that will contribute to a superior business model.
6. *Select* target partners for your company relating to each support value activity.
7. *Structure* the partnership or investment.
8. *Implement* the deal successfully.

The world has become too complex to try to figure out a strategy without using business analytics. According to Geis, "Linear value-chain analysis is no longer adequate to explain competitive positioning and partnering now that traditional, hybrid and digital activities are simultaneously occurring."[8]

Geis continues:

Accountants use financial information systems. Analysts build spreadsheet models. The HR department has a personnel system. Operations planners deploy enterprise resource planning (ERP) software. Sales managers have sales force automation (SFA) technology and customer relationship management (CRM) systems.

We need a systematic approach (e.g., business analytics) to develop information to support decisions relating to competitive positioning and strategic partnering.

Think of an industry as a picture puzzle with each piece representing a part of the chain of suppliers, manufacturers, and service providers that currently make up its structure. On the back of each piece is a number representing its value.

Now take the puzzle apart and change the shape of the pieces—cut them in half, attach them to others, discard a few, and create new ones. Then assign new values to each piece, but use a much broader and higher range of numbers. Winning . . . will be about shaping and owning the right pieces at the right time and putting them together in new ways.[9]

You can't do strategy without business analytics.

## Marketing to Customers

With business analytics, the art of marketing will be in the way marketers understand and satisfy customers better than the competition. In the marketing arena, business analytics has a proven track record of identifying the most profitable or desirable customers; in the credit markets, of identifying those with the lowest risk of nonpayment.

Many insurers have come to accept that success is not merely a matter of delivering superior products and services but of incorporating customer insight into enterprise strategy on an ongoing basis, creating a cycle of insight and action facilitated by transparency between front and back office.

Customers like to do business with smart companies and avoid doing business with dumb ones. When you show your customers that you see them the way they see themselves, or even better, when you surprise them with an insight about themselves they didn't realize until you revealed it, they put you in the category of really smart companies. That's the highest compliment a customer can pay you. It's how you make and keep a customer.

No two customers are alike. No two households are alike—even if they are right next to one another. Technology now allows media companies to route ads to specific households based on data about income, ethnicity, gender, or whether the homeowner has children or pets. Viewers may not realize they are seeing ads different from a neighbor's. But during the same show, a 50-something male may see an ad for high-end speakers and an age-related ailment while his neighbors next door with children may see ads for cereal, video games, and entertainment theme parks.[10]

## Customer Knowledge

One of the key values of business analytics is its capacity to help you know, to help you understand what is really going on. Clayton Christensen, a professor at the Harvard Business School, has spent his career as a successful entrepreneur and now as an academic trying to understand the driving principles behind success. He is a big believer in Toyota's *Genchi Genbutsu* (Go and See) approach. Go and See flies in the face of today's conventional wisdom. Businesspeople everywhere habitually complain about information overload: too many e-mails, too many memos, too many meetings. But the real problem isn't too much information; it's too much insulation. Christensen illustrates the process: To help your company's profitability, you first have to understand what drives the profitability of your customer. To do that, you have to look at and understand the customer's business.

Hill-Rom Co., a medical equipment company in Batesville, Indiana, was able to grow its share of the hospital bed market by figuring out how to understand what drove its customers' profitability even more astutely than the customers did.[11] Like most companies, Hill-Rom employees made contact with its customers' employees at many levels. Its senior executives visited with the senior hospital administrators. Company market researchers practiced *Genchi Genbutsu*—actually going to work as orderlies on hospital wards. Salespeople called on purchasing people. Service technicians interacted with hospital maintenance staffs, and employees in the financial departments of each company negotiated on how and when to pay for their purchases of beds. Unlike most companies, however, Hill-Rom convened regular meetings of all employees who had contact with the employees of specific customers in order to piece together an insightful view of the levers the company could effect that would improve its profitability. These meetings asked each Hill-Rom employee to look at the situation not from the point of view of his or her silo and job but from the point of view of the customer's profitability.

One of the many insights emerging from looking at the world through the customers' eyes was that nurses, who account for a significant share of hospitals' operating costs and whose interactions with patients strongly influence perceptions of the quality of care, were spending inordinate time on tasks unrelated to nursing—picking up things that patients had dropped and solving television problems, for example. By adding features and functions to their beds that obviated many nonnursing tasks, Hill-Rom differentiated its beds in ways that helped hospitals make more money.

The office superstore Staples is specifically interested in modeling how humans use information to make purchase decisions. It has created a Prototype Lab—a full-size store mock-up at the company's headquarters in Framingham, Massachusetts. It's all real and fully stocked, from the 24-pound paper marked on sale to the blister-packed pens hanging neatly side by side.[12]

The Prototype Lab is all about information—how it is used in decision making. The analysts in the lab watch their customers' eyeballs as they make purchase decisions.

With this data, Staples learned that its customers fall into two buckets of people: those who feel that asking for help is a personal failure and those who don't. It's the 60 percent who need help that determine the informational layout of the store. In the Prototype Lab, that's known as "way-finding," and it's where/how people think meets the way their bodies deal with space.

Imagine coming into Staples with a shopping list of 10 items. For you, the thousands of items Staples stocks not only are irrelevant, they hide what you are looking for. How much improved would your experience be if, as you entered the store, those 10 items were all that was in the store—and that was true each time you came? No matter what was on your list, you could go to a single shelf in front of the store, sweep the items into your basket, and be done with it. In the brick-and-mortar reality of "meatspace" retailers, this is impossible to do.

However, in a digital world, instead of having to be the same for all people, the delivered information set can instantly arrange itself for each person and each person's current task. Personalizing "information space" in the future will not only be possible, it will be required. Business analytics can assist in this endeavor.

In the previous section we talked about how, in order to do strategy, you have to have an effective business analytics program in place. The only way to win in the global marketplace is to *know*. One of the highest values associated with business analytics is the ability to know your customers—know what they want, when they want it, at what price, and via what delivery process.

The customer is changing. David Brooks observed in a recent *New York Times* column: "There used to be four common life phases: childhood, adolescence, adulthood; and old age. Now, there are at least six: childhood, adolescence, odyssey, adulthood, active retirement; and old age."[13]

## Real-Time Product Pricing

Undoubtedly it was a symmetry-loving Scotsman working in the early days of Adam Smith capitalism who came up with the idea of standardized prices. In the age of analytics, do we need to perpetuate the concept of the same price for every customer? In our hyperaccelerated present, it seems appropriate to consider the case of caffeine—specifically coffee. Consider the price of your morning cup of coffee. Retail pricing is viewed by many outside the curtain as one of the black arts of capitalism. As with most other businesses, a coffee retailer bases its pricing structure on a calculus designed to produce a profit after accounting for all of the various costs involved in production, logistics, marketing, and staffing. In many cases, this calculus is best described as an educated guess. The calculus is supposed to find a sweet spot that balances two concerns that must be brought together to conclude a sale: the minimum the retailer can afford to charge for each cup and still make a profit, and the maximum a person is willing to pay for that cup. Adam Greenfield, author of *Everyware: The Dawning Age of Ubiquitous Computing* believes that we will soon enter a new era of pricing. What your coffee costs and what you are willing to pay for it are constantly changing— perhaps as often as several times a day. According to Greenfield:

> The first fluctuates with the commodities market, transportation costs, and changes in wage laws; the second responds to moves made by competitors as well as factors that are far harder to quantify, like your mood or the degree of a customer's craving for caffeine. Nor does any present pricing model account for things like the variation in rent between different retail locations.[14]

In the future, the retail spot price of coffee might be a function of the actual cost of the jet fuel that flew this lot of beans in from Kenya, the salary of the driver who delivered it, the mass psychology of your particular market at this particular moment, and a thousand other possible elements. You are going to need business analytics to figure this all out.

Every firm can calculate simple descriptive statistics about aspects of its business (the average revenue per employee or average order size), but the most aggressive analytical competitors go well beyond basic statistics. They are using predictive modeling, for example, to identify not only the most profitable customers, but those with the most profit potential, or those most likely to stop being customers.

The business analytics landscape ranges from a spectrum of basic capabilities and value to extraordinary competitive differentiation. Base-level business analytics, which is necessary just to stay in the game, focuses on the knowns:

- What happened?
- How many, how often, where?
- Where exactly is the problem?
- What actions are needed?

Basic business analytics helps you react to the world as it happens.

More advanced business analytics moves executives into the all-important realm of understanding. Why is this happening? What if these trends continue? What will happen next? What is the best that can happen?

The greatest testimony to the value associated with business analytics is that investments in this area are going up. As the economic downturn touches every vertical market, enterprises are scrambling to look for ways to increase revenues and reduce costs. While overall information technology budgets become targets for cost cutting, business analytic programs are moving forward—in many cases, they are being accelerated. Organizations are using business analytics to evaluate lower-cost alternatives for moving forward. Business analytics can enable you to do more with less, leading to a win-win scenario that can contribute to both your top and your bottom lines.

According to Lora Cecere, vice president of consumer products at AMR Research, business analytics will continue to be "an area of investment through the downturn" as companies attempt to leverage insights across the enterprise. Dale Hagemeyer, research vice president of industry advisory services–manufacturing at Gartner, adds that "uncertainty underscores the need to sense and respond."

## Every Five Years: A "Do Over"

Historians are convinced that about every five years, humans living in the technocratic West slam into a step change that requires fundamental rethinking of how they live their lives and businesses. Dick Nolan, Harvard Business School professor, has guided organizations and individuals through these paradigm shifts many times in his career. He has spent his life explaining things. I was fortunate enough to work with him during the early days of his research on how computers impact and operate in organizations. "Suits" didn't know what to make of these machines. Nolan created the "Stages" framework (discussed in Chapter 6) that made computers and computing understandable.

When the Internet "changed everything," Nolan again applied his superlative analytical gifts first to understanding and then to explaining what can be done to prosper as the world changes. According to Nolan, executives need to be aware and treat seven symptoms if they want to thrive in the new environment:

1. Denying that the world has changed
2. Maintaining a complacent corporate culture
3. Responding with business as usual
4. Failing to cannibalize your product line before your competitors do
5. Letting egos get in the way
6. Always being in catch-up mode
7. Failing to adopt the new business model for the industry

In a world that essentially recompiles/reboots every five years, we are going to have to get much better at sensemaking. Appropriately calibrated business analytics can help.

## Applying Analytics to Innovation

Innovation has been a cover story, attention-grabbing, top-of-mind issue ever since Thomas Alva Edison started applying the principles of mass production to the processes of invention. And yet innovation remains an unsolved mystery for most organizations and many executives. Best-selling author and market researcher Geoffrey Moore repeatedly tells audiences that innovation has to be one of the most talked about, least understood, and poorly acted on words in the business vocabulary today. Innovation is fundamentally misunderstood by a lot of people.

Most organizations find themselves in a deep hole when it comes to innovation. The first rule of holes: Stop digging. The second rule of holes: Know where you should be digging. Very few organizations have brought the power of business analytics to bear on innovation strategy. Innovation is, for the most part, an unstudied and unmeasured activity. That is going to change. Let's get a couple of things straight. Innovation is not a synonym for invention. An invention converts cash into ideas. Innovation converts ideas into cash. The first thing we need to do is tighten up the language we use when talking about innovation. "Innovation" propels ideas to the first use or sale. An important follow-on metric is diffusion of technologies (the pace associated with widespread use in the market).

Another important concept: Innovation is not the artifact on the innovators workbench or drawing board—it is the bundle of benefits customers pay for and adopt. Innovation touches customers. A. G. Lafley opens his best-selling book *The Game-Changer: How You Can Drive Revenue and Profit Growth with Innovation* by stating: "My job at Procter & Gamble is to integrate innovation into everything we do."[15] He is passionate: "The customer is boss." You can't innovate without having a customer in mind. We have seen in previous sections that the best way to know the customer's mind is via business analytics.

We need to apply business analytics to understanding how the overall innovation process works in our enterprise *and* we need to use business analytics to obtain the customer insight that serves as a key input to the innovation process. Therefore, analytics *must* be a big part of the innovation process at your enterprise. Is it?

Tim Mason, chairman of Tesco.com explains, "There's 10,000 people over here, how are we going to do a better job for them?. . . With data, what we have to do becomes as plain as the nose on your face. It immediately changes the behavior of the business."[16]

Business analytics is assisting high-performance enterprises conceptualize, create and execute change initiatives. Examples of these companies include UPS, Continental Airlines, P&G, McDonald's and NetJets, to name just a few.

## Choice Architecture

Next-generation leadership is less Achilles and Hector (warriors doing battle and giving orders) and more Ulysses and Zeus (sculpting choices and working behind the scenes). The leaders of tomorrow will be exceptional choice architects. Choice architecture involves organizing the context in which people make decisions. A classic example of choice architecture is the placement of food in school cafeterias:

> The director of food services for a large city school system —without changing any menus, [ran] some experiments in her schools to determine whether the way the food is displayed and arranged might influence the choices kids make . . . directors of dozens of school cafeterias [were given] specific instructions on how to display the food choices. In some schools the desserts were placed first, in others last, in still others in a separate line. The location of various food items was varied from one school to another. In some schools the French fries, but in others the carrot sticks, were at eye level.

> Simply by rearranging the cafeteria, [the director was] able to increase or decrease the consumption of many food items by as much as 25%. [The] big lesson: school children, like adults, can be greatly influenced by small changes in the context. The influence can be exercised for better or for worse.[17]

Earlier I showed that business analytics is a powerful tool for understanding the choices people make. Does it not stand to reason that it would be a powerful tool for designing the choice architecture of an organization with an eye on making it easier for the enterprise to do the "right thing"?

If an organization used business analytics to understand the existing at-work choice architecture of the enterprise, improvable patterns would surface. Innovation initiatives could be positioned as being less threatening to high-status organizational players, less risky, and more fact based—experiments feeding into the decision-making apparatus of the firm. Can you imagine a day when executives would have to defend their not being innovative, not conducting experiments, not pushing the edge of the envelope in a risk-adjusted manner?

## Innovation Matters

Publishers of daily newspapers, editors in the trade press, deans at prestigious business schools, industry analysts, C-level executives, and people working in the information trenches have come to consensus agreeing that innovation is the key to:

- Personal career success
- Organizational success
- Success on the nation-state level

### Periods of Innovation

I asked independent analysts, IT Leadership Academy researchers, colleagues at the Ohio State University, and C-suite audiences around the world to chunk the immediate past into eras, paying particular attention to general attitudes toward innovation and information management. These information management periods were presented:

1985–1995: A period of efficiency and cost-cutting
1995–2000: A period of innovation and chaos
2000–2005: A period of efficiency and cost cutting
2006–Today and beyond: A period of simultaneous equations—innovation, growth, *and* efficiency

In 2005, Booz & Company conducted a study of the 1,000 biggest spenders in innovation, including the companies with the largest research and development (R&D) budgets around the world. According to the study, investment in R&D alone does not automatically generate profits, revenues, growth, or shareholder returns.[18] Instead, the study concluded: "The simple decision to invest in innovation is not enough." Not all new initiatives pass the "smell test" (i.e., are embraced by the market). In the mid-1980s, for example, new fragrance introductions averaged about 70 a year. The majority of these—more than three-quarters—failed.[19]

Experts are worried about the macro-state of innovation in America. Judy Estrin, former chief technology officer at Cisco and author of *Closing the Innovation Gap*, stated, "I have become more and more concerned about the state of our country and its innovation. We have a national innovation gap."[20]

I believe the secret sauce of highest-value innovation is business analytics: knowing where to look, knowing what questions to ask, and knowing what the answers mean. A key part of moving the ball forward—improving the trajectory of existing processes or jumping to an entirely new curve—is the ability to see things that don't quite make sense. Business analytics is all about pattern recognition. Things that don't fit (termed "anomalies" in the scientific community) frequently can serve as the source of new insight. Thomas Kuhn, philosopher of science, introduced the idea that revolutions in science arise from the recognition of anomalies. His work has created something of a cottage industry of change observers/commentors. He observed that the accumulation of anomalies—findings that cannot be assimilated into an accepted scientific framework, tradition, or paradigm—paves the way for scientific revolution.[21]

## Innovation Situation in Most Enterprises Today

Regarding the informed and insightful combination of business analytics with actively managed innovation processes, the market breaks into four groups:

| | |
|---|---|
| Ahead of the curve | 16 percent |
| On the curve | 23 percent |
| Behind the curve | 47 percent |
| Don't even know a curve exists | 14 percent |

## *Everyone Has to Innovate*

There is a misconception—dating perhaps from the early Industrial Age divide between brain work and brawn work—that only a special class of employee gets to innovate. This is *wrong*! I suppose that in Charles Dickens's day, the widespread practice was for managers to determine what work was to be done and for the workers to do it.

In today's workplace, everyone is a knowledge worker. Whether you are a truck driver at UPS, a line worker at Toyota, or a baggage handler at Continental Airlines, *you are a knowledge worker*. Success (i.e., unambiguously demonstrating progress toward mutually agreed-on business objectives) is less a function of telling people what to do than enabling them to make choices that move the enterprise in directions that are immediately nontoxic and advantageous in the future. Business analytics has to be embedded in the choice architecture of the enterprise.

Innovation "takes a village." It is a group effort. By definition, innovation involves at least two audiences—the benefit creator and the beneficiary. Frequently it involves many more. In the critically acclaimed and fondly remembered PBS Series *Connections* (1979), James Burke, the British science historian, demonstrated how developments in science, society, and history were interrelated (i.e., "connected").[22] Innovation also tends to combine multiple perspectives. Facts, numbers, and analytics are what will facilitate this border crossing.

Most who study innovation (e.g., dissect past innovations to see how they actually happened) believe that many innovations come to be as the result of synthesizing, or "bridging," ideas from different domains. Peter Drucker, management guru, stated that 60 percent of innovation comes from outside your industry boundaries. The most surprising creative insights result from connections among different bodies of knowledge. This is why getting analysts out and about is so critically important. Paul Saffo, the technology forecaster, believes, "An advance in a single field never triggers substantial change. Change is triggered by the cross impact of things operating together."[23]

Jane Jacobs, the urbanist and author of *The Death and Life of Great American Cities*, believes that it is this cross-pollination, this collision of diverse ideas that make cities vibrant hubs of creativity.[24]

Innovation must become the business of every employee. In the coming years, innovation will have the same status that quality assurance had in the 1990s—a distributed process and a collective responsibility.

Innovation does not happen only in Silicon Valley. Venture capitalists (clever and connected though they may be) are not the sole source of innovation. Innovation happens everywhere. North America is not the only place where ideas are being converted to cash. Innovation is rapidly accelerating outside the United States.[25]

## Innovation Does Not Have to Be Device-Centric

Innovation scholars repeatedly fall into the trap (it is a fetish, really) of celebrating devices rather than focusing on the benefits that the devices enable. For example, to celebrate the thirtieth birthday of the *Nightly Business Report*, the Emmy Award–winning PBS business program, a panel of experts assembled at Wharton and selected the top 30 innovations of the past 30 years.[26] They focused on things. This august panel composed of innovation "experts" admitted having trouble defining what innovation really is.

One of my favorite innovation tales is the classic story of how the product Listerine came to be. It is recounted fabulously by Rob Walker, anthropologist/consumer columnist at the *New York Times Magazine*.[27] Most consumers do not realize that Listerine, the market-leading mouthwash, started life as a disinfectant in the 1870s. The Lambert Pharmacal Company, the makers of Listerine, wanted to increase sales during the 1920s. Management, convinced that exogenous factors would not lead to a sudden spike in demand for disinfectant, took matters into their own hands. They invented a problem the product could solve: "halitosis." In the book *Soft Soap, Hard Sell*, historian Vincent Vinikas relates that someone at Lambert "discovered" the phrase "halitosis" in a British periodical.[28] Subsequent advertising campaigns placed in the popular mind the idea that halitosis (bad breath) was a widespread problem that many people had and didn't recognize because not even their friends would tell them. Listerine was positioned as the answer.

Analytics—the based-in-reality understanding that the disinfectant market was not growing and would not grow—led this organization to experiment. Repositioning Listerine as a halitosis buster involved little or no innovation in the product itself. The exact same product became relevant in whole new ways. Walker believes there was no change in what was inside a bottle of Listerine. There was a change in the people who bought it.

## Innovation Transcends Macroeconomic Circumstance

Colonel Curtis Carver, a career active duty army colonel and the vice dean for resources at the United States Military Academy, told a group of senior decision makers that "Bad times are the Best times to prepare for the Good Times."[29] High performance organizations aggressively innovate during good times and bad.

The belief that innovation rarely happens in periods of low growth could not be further from the truth. Adversity is one of the great drivers of innovation. Currently there is an absolute frenzy of process improvement business analytics going on in support of innovation initiatives aimed at saving companies money. There seems to be a misconception that innovation applied to legacy processes is somehow not as important, dynamic, or high-payback as innovation associated in doing totally new things. Key organizational processes are being analyzed, digitized, and optimized. Big improvements are being made. One utility was able to reduce costs by 20 percent while simultaneously and materially expanding service—all via business analytics. If you listen carefully, you can hear the analytic saws and hammers banging away in every "with vision" enterprise in the world.

## Innovation Is Transforming

As an anthropologist charged with studying the individual and aggregate behaviors of the multiple tribes that make up the modern enterprise, I am obligated to track changes, trends, and anomalies in language. Two words you will rarely see in close association are "analysis" and "innovation." We need to change that. We need to analyze innovation. In fact, the foundation stone of most of the major innovations changing our world today is world-class analytics.

We need to use our superior understanding of process to optimize innovation within the enterprise. We live in a world that is barreling toward multiple-decimal-point measurement of just about every-thing. In this world, when things do not go right, people want to know why. The lack of precision with which most enterprises discuss innovation—a concept/practice critical to success—is both surprising and unsustainable.

Digital technologies have completely transformed the opportunities and the opportunity costs to explore and test ideas. Innovation—actually the market response to innovation—can be simulated computationally. Experimentation—the systematic analysis associated with turning what seems like a good idea into a testable hypothesis—is arguably one of the highest-payback exercises in the contemporary organization.

Michael Schrage, a fellow with MIT's Sloan School's Center for Digital Business and one of the world's true experts on the econom-ics and ergonomics of innovation, believes that "digitally enabled web-enabled experimentation is going to have a bigger impact on business value creation and economic value creation than the quality movement."[30]

Schrage is quite passionate when he tells leaders that "good ideas are bad, that good ideas are useless. Nobody buys good ideas. The real chal-lenge, the real test, the real opportunity is how do you turn good ideas into good hypotheses that lend themselves to quick, easy, rapid, cheap test-ing?" Schrage only half jokingly suggests that the high-multiple companies of the early decades of the twenty-first century will be those possessing a CEO—a chief experiments officer.

Ian Ayres and the people at CapOne would seem to agree:

What really sets CapOne apart is its willingness to literally experiment. Instead of being satisfied with a historical analy-sis of consumer behavior, CapOne proactively intervenes in the market by running randomized experiments. . . . In 2006, it ran more than 28,000 experiments—28,000 tests of new products, new advertising approaches, and new contract terms. . . . Is it more effective to print on the outside envelope "LIMITED TIME OFFER" OR "2.9% Introductory Rate!"? CapOne answers this question by randomly dividing prospects into two groups and seeing which approach has the highest success rate.[31]

C. K. Prahalad and M. S. Krishnan—two truly exceptional academics—
title a chapter in their book "Analytics: Insights for Innovation." They
explain:

> Competitiveness favors those who spot new trends and act on
> them expeditiously. Therefore, managers must develop insights
> about new opportunities by amplifying weak signals. These
> weak signals emerge from insights derived through a deep
> understanding of a wide variety of information. . . . The new
> competitive landscape requires *continuous analysis* of data for
> insight. Analysis that is only episodic and ad hoc [as when a
> senior manager commissions a specific study, say, to assess the
> impact of oil prices on shopping patterns] or periodic [such as
> actual sales compared to forecasts] will not suffice. Traditional
> analytical approaches are often asynchronous with business
> changes. Hence delays in recognizing, interpreting, and act-
> ing on the trends are emerging as critical impediments to
> competitiveness.
>
> Foresight is a result of understanding, through structured and
> unstructured data, the unfolding of competitive dynamics. There
> is value in identifying new patterns of relationships, predicting
> the behavior and evolution of systems, and mitigating risk. In an
> N=1 world [i.e., where every value proposition must be custom-
> ized for the individual], the behavior of individual consumers
> as well as broad patterns of change must be understood.[32]

One of my favorite examples of analytics at work comes from
several national internal revenue services. It is known that not everyone pays his or her taxes adequately. Tax collectors build a database of
declared income and consumption patterns. They look for big-ticket
items, such as travel, cars, plasma TVs, deposits and withdrawals from
banks, stock market activity, and the like, to spot patterns of tax evasion. As with many analytic projects, successful identification of tax
evasion requires integrating massive amounts of data from multiple data
sources.

Remember Karen Stephenson, the expert on social network
analysis? She is convinced that "if I wanted to increase learning in a

company, I would take a gatekeeper in an innovation network and put him or her with a pulsetaker in an expert network. That's an algorithm for facilitating the distribution of knowledge."[33]

Organizations known for being innovative tend to embrace the idea of "radical transparency." For our purposes, "transparency" means "able to look inside." In more robust economic times, many key processes were left pretty much on their own, subject to very blunt macromeasures of success/failure. This situation is changing.

In today's environment, informed executives not only want to (and are obligated fiduciarily) to be able to look under the hood to make sure things are running right, they are increasingly looking for some form of external certification that attests that everything is copacetic. Line-of-business executives are scrambling to create comparative benchmarks wherein they can demonstrate to peer executives, boards of directors, investors, suppliers, customers, and regulators that "we are doing things *right!*"—that substantive and undisputable year-on-year improvements are being generated.

## Role of Business Analytics in Innovation

The scope and scale of the analytics inside the enterprise has undergone/ is undergoing a significant transformation. The next step is for business analytics to become an active and significant contributor to the new product/new service design process. For this to occur, an order-of-magnitude improvement in creative problem-solving/innovation practices is required in many organizations. In prospecting for weak signals that matter, in trying to shield the enterprise from disruptive innovations and/or take advantage of them, Clayton Christensen[34] suggests that senior management must:

- Deeply understand current usage.
- Test hypotheses about what usage behavior(s) will change.
- Test hypotheses about how usage behavior will change.
- Test hypotheses around what behaviors will stay the same.
- Examine which product/service dimensions are underserved.
- Examine which product/service dimensions are overserved.

Business analytics is the tool set that lets you do all this.

Every analyst has enormous creativity and problem-solving capacity. Unfortunately, it is frequently pointed at the wrong kinds of problems. Three kinds of problems exist:

1. **Alpha problems.** New, never-before-experienced issues requiring experts
2. **Beta problems.** Problems that have kind of/sort of been solved before that require pattern recognition skills
3. **Gamma problems.** Reasonably routine problems requiring matching a problem to an appropriate and preidentified problem-solving rule

History shows us that, over time, issues that formerly could be dealt with only by high-end, high-price, alpha problem solvers evolve into problems that can be handled quite competently by less expert pattern recognizers or rank-and-file rules-based operators. Much of the work of traditional business analytics has migrated from open-ended problem solving to pattern recognition and rule-based activities. Alpha problem-solving analysts need to work on alpha problems. For that reason, it is incredibly important to understand the kind of problem you are trying to solve.

I conducted a series of workshops across the United States on the topic of innovation. In those sessions, we asked executives: "Are you innovative?" Typically 75 to 80 percent responded, "Yes, I am innovative!" I asked that same set of executives: "Is your organization innovative?" Typically only 20 to 25 percent answered, "Yes." Human beings are—or can be—impressively adaptable and creative, yet most appear to work for companies that stifle such urges.

We all know that organizations are not very good at innovation. The opportunity for business analytics and analysts is that organizations want to become good at innovation.

The former chief innovation officer at Chicago-based Wrigley explained that "at the end of the day, every business looks for two things: Protect my business and Grow my business. Innovation is all about both of these."[35] Innovation is not a "weird" thing or a "special" thing. It is a natural part of *every* business's day-to-day activity. During the dot-com era, the mainstream innovation agenda and high ground (at least as far as the media was concerned) was highjacked by a bunch of work-as-play boutique consultants who insisted that creativity could be unleashed only by bringing crayons, toys, and building blocks to an enterprise. With a little more analysis and a lot less Romper Room, the companies they consulted with might still be alive today.

Innovation is real work requiring real data and analysis. Sideline observers mistake the first part of the innovation process—the ideation phase—for the entire process. If you create only ideas, you are doing little more than generating information pollution. Ideation is just the tip of the value iceberg. If you were a global consumer electronics company focused on the wireless/mobility market, you might have 30,000 to 35,000 engineers working for you. At any given point in time you can grab them in the hallway, ask them what their ideas are, and they would shoot 10 at you. These could be patents. They could be product extensions. The first phase of an innovation process might focus on grinding down to determine the *real* ideas that have the market potential really to become something.

Michael Schrage suggests that organizations organize 5×5 "X" teams: Give five people five days to come up with five experiments. The budget for each experiment cannot exceed $5,000. The time of trial of the experiment cannot exceed five weeks, and you have to show a business case demonstrating that scaling these experiments would generate an impact of $5 million in savings or growth.

A big part of successful innovation involves migrating people out of the mode of thinking up a science fair project. High-yield innovation involves a much more end-to-end, customer-focused (i.e., what would a customer want?) mind-set. Is there a business model behind this idea that we could we take to market? Successful innovators create a rigorous funnel with discipline across several different areas:

- Technology
- Financial impact of an opportunity
- Execution risk—is it real, could it become something?
- Strategic relevance

In the commercialization phase, teams figure out how to prototype these things and get them into pilot projects with different opportunities/customers.

## Innovation Requires Process

Overwhelmingly, the data indicates that companies doing really well at innovation have a process for innovation. They have a structure. Innovation is not something that just happens. You have to understand what the business issues are and try to innovate around them.

Senior management at one of the largest organizations in the world felt it needed to try a centralized approach. These managers recognized that innovation insights existed out in the businesses. Believing that they needed an organization at the center that could facilitate the conversion of ideas into money, they set up a Global Innovation Services Group to catalyze innovation across the organization. This group is designed to help would-be innovators get traction for their ideas. It is a small group—not much bureaucracy, a manager, and maybe three staff people. There is an innovation specialist, an innovation technologist, and an innovation evangelist.

The group exists to bring the power of business analytics to the rich-but-as-yet-unoptimized idea pipeline.

## Notes

1. According to Nassim Nicholas Taleb, *The Black Swan: The Impact of the Highly Improbable* (New York: Random House, 2007), a black swan is an event with three attributes: (1) It is an outlier, as it lies outside the realm of regular expectations, because nothing in the past can convincingly point to its possibility; (2) it carries an extreme impact; and (3) in spite of its outlier status, human nature makes us concoct explanations for its occurrence after the fact, making it explainable and predictable. Taleb summarizes the three attributes: rarity, extreme impact, and retrospectively explained.

2. Quoted in Stephen Kern, *A Cultural History of Causality: Science, Murder Novels, and Systems of Thought* (Princeton, NJ: Princeton University Press, 2004).

3. Andrew F. Krepinevich, *Seven Deadly Scenarios: A Military Futurist Explores War in the 21st Century* (New York: Bantam, 2009), 2.

4. Ibid.

5. Jackie Fenn and Mark Raskino, *Mastering The Hype Cycle: How to Choose the Right Innovation at the Right Time* (Boston: Harvard Business Press, 2008).

6. Gary L. Neilson, Karla L. Martin, and Elizabeth Powers, "The Secrets to Successful Strategy Execution," *Harvard Business Review* (June 2008), web version.

7. Harold L. Sirkin, James W. Hemerling, and Arindam K. Bhattacharya, *GLOBALITY: Competing with Everyone From Everywhere For Everything* (New York: Business Plus, 2008).

8. Personal interview with author Spring, 2009.

9. Lowell Bryan, Jane Fraser, Jeremy Oppenheim, and Wilhelm Rall, *Race for the World: Strategies to Build a Great Global Firm* (Cambridge, MA: Harvard University Press, 1999).

10. Stephanie Clifford, "Cable Companies Target Commercials to Audience," *New York Times*, March 4, 2009.

11. Clayton M. Christensen, Scott D. Anthony, Gerald Berstell, and Denise Nitterhouse, "Finding the Right Job for Your Product," *MIT Sloan Management Review*, April 1, 2007, web version.

12. David Weinberger, *Everything Is Miscellaneous: The Power of the New Digital Disorder* (New York: Henry Holt, 2007).

13. David Brooks, "The Odyssey Years," *New York Times*, October 9, 2007.

14. Adam Greenfield, *Everyware: The Dawning Age of Ubiquitous Computing* (Berkeley, CA: Peachpit Press, 2006), 81.

15. A.G. Lafley and Ram Charan, *The Game-Changer: How You Can Drive Revenue and Profit Growth with Innovation* (New York: Random House, 2008), 1.

16. Clive Humby and Terry Hunt with Tim Phillips, *Scoring Points: How Tesco Is Winning Customer Loyalty* (London: Kogan Page, 2004), 3.

17. Richard H. Thaler and Cass R. Sunstein, *Nudge: Improving Decisions about Health, Wealth, and Happiness* (New Haven, CT: Yale University Press, 2008), 2.

18. Barry Jaruzelski, Kevin Dehoff, and Rakesh Bordia, "Money Isn't Everything," *Strategy & Business* (Winter 2005), web version.

19. Nancy F. Koehn, *Brand New: How Entrepreneurs Earned Consumers' Trust from Wedgwood to Dell* (Boston: Harvard Business School Press, 2001), 140.

20. Clair Cain Miller, "Another Voice Warns of An Innovation Slowdown," *New York Times*, September 1, 2008.

21. Morton Meyers, *Happy Accidents: Serendipity in Modern Medical Breakthroughs* (New York: Arcade Publishing, 2007), 18.

22. James Burke, *Connections* (New York: Simon & Schuster, 2007).

23. Conversation with author at the *India Today* Conclave Conference [New Delhi 13 MAR 2007].

24. Jane Jacobs, *The Death and Life of Great American Cities* (New York: Random House, 1993).

25. Dr. Harry Shum, who oversees Microsoft Research Asia from the Haidian District in Beijing (170 scientists), comments, "Microsoft began to realize we

can't find all the talented people in the U.S. Nowhere in this universe has a higher concentration of I.Q. power." See Chris Buckley, "Let a Thousand Ideas Flower: China Is a New Hotbed of Research," *New York Times*, September 13, 2004.

26. Top 30 Innovations of the last 30 years, available at www.pbs.org/nbr/site/features/special/top-30-innovations_home. See also: http://knowledge.wharton.upenn.edu/article.cfm?articleid52163:

    1. Internet, broadband, World Wide Web (browser and html)
    2. PC/laptop computers
    3. Mobile phones
    4. E-mail
    5. DNA testing and sequencing/human genome mapping
    6. Magnetic resonance imaging (MRI)
    7. Microprocessors
    8. Fiber optics
    9. Office software (spreadsheets, word processors)
    10. Noninvasive laser/robotic surgery (laparoscopy)
    11. Open source software and services (e.g., Linux, Wikipedia)
    12. Light emitting diodes (LEDs)
    13. Liquid crystal display (LCD)
    14. Global positioning systems (GPS)
    15. Online shopping/ecommerce/auctions (e.g., eBay)
    16. Media file compression (jpeg, mpeg, mp3)
    17. Microfinance
    18. Photovoltaic solar energy
    19. Large-scale wind turbines
    20. Social networking via the Internet
    21. Graphic user interface (GUI)
    22. Digital photography/videography
    23. Radio-frequency identification (RFID) and applications (e.g., EZ Pass)
    24. Genetically modified plants
    25. Biofuels
    26. Bar codes and scanners
    27. Automated teller machines (ATMs)
    28. Stents
    29. SRAM [static random access memory—a type of semiconductor memory] flash memory
    30. Antiretroviral treatment for AIDS

27. Rob Walker, *Buying In: The Secret Dialogue Between What We Buy and Who We Are* (New York: Random House, 2008), 59.

28. Vincent Vinikas, *Soft Soap, Hard Sell: American Hygiene in an Age of Advertisement* (Ames: Iowa State Press, 1992).

29. The Value Studio is a collaborative workshop convened quarterly by the IT Leadership Academy at Florida State College at Jacksonville. The author serves as the master of ceremonies. Colonel Curtis Carver delivered the keynote speech at Value Studio 14 in Jacksonville, FL, 18 February 2009.

30. Michael Schrage speaking at the CIO 100 Symposium & Awards Ceremony, August 25, 2008.

31. Ian Ayres, *Super Crunchers: Why Thinking-by-Numbers Is the New Way to Be Smart* (New York: Bantam Books, 2007), 41.

32. C. K. Prahalad and M. S. Krishnan, *The New Age of Innovation: Driving Cocreated Value through Global Networks* (New York: McGraw-Hill, 2008), 84.

33. Conversation with author at Value Studio program [Spring 2006].

34. Clayton M. Christensen, Mark W. Johnson, and Darrell K. Rigby, "Foundations for Growth: How to Identify and Build Disruptive New Businesses," *Sloan Management Review* (Spring 2002), web version.

35. Panel discussion, "A Fireside Chat on Innovation," CIO Executive Summit, Chicago, IL, October 10, 2005.

# Chapter 8

# Where Is All This Going?

**W**hen I was working with the World Bank, my colleagues helped me to understand that "world opinion is the second superpower." There is enormous power in first understanding and then reshaping mental models. The aphorism "Seeing is believing" is actually misexpressed. Experience proves that humans tend to have trouble "seeing" things that they don't already believe. Billions, maybe trillions, of dollars and multiple Nobel Prizes have accrued to those who understand the complex interaction of belief systems and real-world decision making. *The New Know* posits a nascent era of informed and augmented decision making.

## A New Kind of World

*Every day*, there is more to know, more ways to know, and heightened expectations on the parts of customers, citizens, investors, and regulators that you will do something efficacious with what you know.[1]

*Everywhere* you look, work, politics, society, science, technology, and even art are defined by growing complexity. "When your manager in Boise, Idaho, uses a Japanese corporate satellite to run CAD/CAM units in Argentina, the way the London accountants say the Taiwan headquarters wants, using software uplink live from Sydney," you begin to get a feel for the complexity of the world we live in.[2] Complexity is part of the DNA of modern existence. It cannot be avoided. It cannot be escaped. It should not be feared or hidden. It must be embraced, and the best way of doing that is with business analytics.

If you think about the world we live in today—I mean really think about it—you will conclude that we are at a hinge of history, complexity-wise. Decisions that once were made over months, weeks, and days now must be made in a matter of hours, minutes, or seconds. Our world is speeding up. Organizational objectives used to be straightforward and immediately understandable; now they involve complex trade-offs. Uncertainty is increasing. Strategies that were recalibrated annually now require monthly, weekly, and sometimes daily reexamination and adjustment. Unaugmented human cognition is not enough. The requirements we now face outstrip the decision-making infrastructure many organizations have in place. In the IBM *2008 CEO Study*, researchers discovered that while 83 percent of chief executives expect substantial change, only 61 percent feel confident in their ability to manage that change.[3] In the future, we are going to have to think very hard about how we think very hard. The cognitive infrastructure in many enterprises is on the verge of collapse.

The volume of digital data, the variety of information, and the velocity of decision making now required are transforming business analytics from a nice-to-have competency to a must-have requirement. A tipping point has been reached regarding "smart" resource allocation. Analytics can now address a larger set of problems.

Truth be told, many key decisions in many organizations are made without the benefit of balanced business analytics: data appropriately collected, appropriately calibrated, appropriately analyzed, and appropriately integrated into the decision-making process.

At the 2008 Gartner Business Intelligence Summit (February 5-7, 2008) held in Amsterdam, The Netherlands, the center-stage analysts probably thought that they would shock the audience with their prediction that "by 2012, more than 35% of global 5000 companies will regularly fail to make critical decisions because they don't have access to timely information and the analysis to do so."[4] In 2009, the global financial system came close to collapsing because financial service executives *did not know* what was going on in their businesses.

## A New Kind of Decision Making

Time and time again I come back to the base reality that what we have to know—what society and the workplace says/thinks we have to know—has expanded past the point of what an unaugmented individual mind can know. How we bridge the need-to-know/capacity-to-know gap is via the technologies and practices of business analytics (including statistics, operations research, data mining, and forecasting).

There is a biological analog to this data overload problem. Earlier I mentioned that the five human senses process more than 11 million pieces of information every moment. This is more than a win-a-prize-on-a-game-show fun factoid. Timothy Wilson, a psychology professor at the University of Virginia, contends that this size chunk of data is just too much information for the human conscious mind to handle. Our nonconscious brain filters out most of the data, presenting to our conscious mind what years of evolution have told us is what we must know. One of the messages of the New Know is that you and your organization will have to put in place the analytical tools that let you expeditiously analyze and efficaciously act on all the information available to you.

Decision making and decision-making skills are increasingly coming under the microscope. Analytical decision making has become a sought-after core competency of high-performance organizations. The faculties at business schools around the world and alpha practitioners of strategy consulting are gradually coming to a consensus that adopting a capabilities-driven strategy may be the new secret sauce.[5] "Capabilities-driven strategy" is an expensive way of saying what your company is good at. Your organization is going to have to be good at analytics.

When consumer packaged goods giants such as Procter & Gamble and Unilever have game-changing discussions with large retailers such as Walmart around the big idea of "how do we operate as if we were one company?" the data that drives that conversation, the frameworks that precipitated having this conversation in the first place emerge from the informed and improved practice of business analytics. Analytics has migrated far beyond mere reporting. Optimization applications have migrated to the point where they can support change and not prevent it. Sophisticated decision support systems are now delivered in weeks, not years.

The hinge of history has opened on a new era of complexity. Executives need to realize that we no longer live in a world where we can get away with seat-of-the-pants inductive reasoning alone. Gone are the smooth curves and nice regular cycles that were thought (erroneously) to describe the world of the past. The world has become a much messier place. And it is getting messier all the time.

Think about the future decision-making environment. Ray Kurzweil, entrepreneur and futurist, sees the pace of information growth and knowledge expansion accelerating to a point when one day, at the outer edge of some readers' lifetimes, "when scientists become a million times more intelligent and operate a million times faster, an hour would result in a century of progress" in today's terms.[6] Are the decision-making processes we have in place today going to be able to keep up with that kind of world?

In the future, leaders will make decisions based on a review of scenarios with explicitly weighted probabilities. Executive decision making skills will be subject to the same type of rigorous statistical analysis that professional baseball players experience. Think managerial baseball cards. Future technology investments will be scrutinized as to whether they enable decision superiority.

Decision making is very much top of mind. The 2008 American presidential election was all about decision making and decision-making styles. President Bush's memoir is tentatively titled *Decision Points*. Robert B. Barnett, the Washington lawyer who negotiated the deal with the publisher on Mr. Bush's behalf, stated the book will cover Mr. Bush's decisions relating to September 11, the invasions of Afghanistan and Iraq, and the government's response to Hurricane Katrina. Decision making is now one of the things people look at.

# We Now *Know* Better

Scott Kirsner, author of *Inventing the Movies*, covers the innovation and venture capital beat for the *Boston Globe*. He is a great community builder and does a brilliant job moderating conversations with big-dog thought leaders. At a Future Forward event, he interviewed Harvard Business School professor and author Clayton Christensen.[7] In this particular interview, Christensen talked about how practice, knowledge, and widely held conceptions of causality changes over time. Here the good professor was talking about methods of quality control as they existed 30 years ago. He recalled being introduced to the statistical process control chart. In the early days of the quality movement, manufacturers would make a product and measure a critical performance parameter. Performance was plotted on the chart. There was an upper and lower control limit. As long as the performance parameter was inside those limits, you shipped the product. If it was outside, you rejected it. While there was always a target you were manufacturing toward, you rarely hit the target. There was always a scatter of points. Intrinsic randomness in manufacturing processes was the accepted explanation for why you could not hit the target every time. Christensen remembers that most quality control processes that existed up to the 1970s focused on how to deal with this randomness. Six sigma and the quality method changed all this by saying "There is no randomness." Every time you make something different from what you intended to make, there is actually a cause for that unexpected mutation. It just appeared to be random because you did not know what caused it. Six sigma and the quality movement brought tools to the workplace that enabled manufacturers to understand all the other factors that affect their ability to do things exactly right every time. Once we understood the factors that affected the process, and once we could control those factors, manufacturing became a science, and not an art. Business analytics is on the cusp of doing for decision making what six sigma did for the quality movement.

Executives no longer have to guess. Centuries of art, literature, and myth have glorified decisive leadership. There is something powerfully human in the act of deliberately choosing a path; of self-consciously weighing options, imagining potential outcomes, and arriving at a choice. I hope this will remain true forever. However, what constitutes good and great decision making has changed. A lot of what history books refer to as heroic leadership was, in fact, luck.

A battle has been raging for quite some time over which mode of decision making is best, gut instinct or analytical. This is the wrong way to look at the problem.

> Sometimes we need to reason through our options and carefully analyze the possibilities. And sometimes we need to listen to our emotions. . . . The crucial skill, scientists are now saying, is the ability to think about your own thinking . . . the willingness to engage in introspection, to cultivate what Philip Tetlock, a psychologist at the University of California, Berkeley, calls "the art of self-overhearing."[8]

## A New Kind of Skill Set

At the Toronto Artscape conference, keynote speaker Alan Webber challenged the assembled multinational luminaries:

> From Toronto to Tokyo, from Copenhagen to Chicago, from San Paulo to San Francisco—in virtually every major city in every industrialized country in the world—leaders of business, government, and not-for-profits are preoccupied with the same fundamental question: What do we need to do to compete successfully in the economy of the future?[9]

I believe the answer is business analytics.

Business analytics—statistics, forecasting, data mining, and operations research—has a long, proud, and essentially unappreciated history. Our species has been solving important and complex problems using quantitative methods for a long time. The discipline is evolving from one dominated by "old masters"—practitioners who pioneered and perfected a particular style of quantitative problem solving—to one led by charismatic tribal elders—seasoned executives who recognize that a blend of quantitative tools and techniques, a blend of classic approaches and new experiments, and a nuanced feel for organizational dynamics is now in order.

The best analysts are constantly measuring themselves against the best problem solvers of the past. We learn from our ancestors and move forward. Great analysts bring many styles of quantitative problem solving to bear on the problems facing organizations today.

Sadly, the experts who built the first-generation decision-support cathedrals are, for the most part, no longer with us. I am hoping that historians undertake to study the world in which they lived and the techniques they perfected. A new breed of twenty-first-century problem solvers using an expanded skill set and tool kit is taking the stage.

As we move to a more fact-based mode of decision making, we are going to have to upgrade the skills we bring to data collection. The aerospace and defense industries have long been pioneers in the business analytics space. They had to be. They were living in a monstrously complex world long before most of the rest of us (think of the logistics associated with D-Day and all the moving parts associated with the Apollo moon mission). Speaking with many tribal elders in this field, I discovered a broad and general concern that numerous jobs in this industry require advanced multifaceted analytical skill sets that many of the employees in the industry do not have. Historically the educational system—particularly in the field of science and technology—produced a special type of engineer, a special type of quantitative problem solver—one who might have trouble migrating to different types of problem-solving environments.

Futurists agree that education needs to prepare students for a multithreaded career. Future career success will accrue to those successful at working betwixt and between the boundaries of discrete disciplines. Most Baby Boomers were trained in one profession, one discipline, one career. Most have been rewarded for their expertise in that one area. And yet, increasingly, the future that is emerging will require cross-disciplinary thinking, the ability to work across categories and at the boundaries of expertise.

Managers will need to know what their people know, paying particular attention to individuals who have won the skills trifecta: business savvy, technology savvy, and analytically inclined. The knowledge gap (i.e., what people don't know but need to know about the business, the technology, or the analytic options/techniques available) can be spanned many ways. But it must be spanned.

The good news is that access to knowledge is changing. The time associated with retooling a personal competence set has been significantly reduced. Take, for example, the work going on at the newly formed Singularity University in Moffett Field, CA.[10] A group of visionaries, recognizing the critical role that biotechnology and bioinformatics, nanotechnology, future studies and forecasting, finance and entrepreneurship, and artificial intelligence, robotics, and cognitive computing will play in the future are creating a series of 10-week, 10-day, and 3-day courses. Singularity University's three-phase program starts with a series of plenary lectures in which students take the same coursework and learn basic principles about the 10 disciplines the institute covers. The second phase consists of a deeper investigation into one of the disciplines; in the third phase, the entire student body collaborates on a team project. Success with business analytics requires crossing boundaries (as they encourage at Singularity University). Analysts need to cross the disciplinary boundaries of analytics—statistics, forecasting, operations research and data mining. They also have to work across departmental boundaries.

Every discipline in every organization is going to have to come to grips with using and understanding the output of higher-end models, even the sales force. A very senior executive at a very well-known global technology company recently told a group of academics that "salespeople and mathematics do not go together." Despite this, or perhaps because of this, this enterprise embarked on a very significant business analytics exercise designed to materially improve sales force productivity.

## A New Customer Knowledge

The New Know is ushering in a Golden Age of Customer Knowledge. Looking at sales databases, it is now possible to ascertain a given customer's long-term value—its expected benefits to a company—after taking into account the expected costs of maintaining a relationship with a customer over an extended period of time.

Business 101 tells us there are two mistakes we should not make: spending money on customers we should not spend money on and not spending money on customers we should spend money on. To a statistician, these errors are called false positives and false negatives.

Respected academic researchers have determined that roughly a quarter of all customers are misclassified, falsely positive or negative. A company that makes misguided marketing decisions one out of every four times could gain considerably by reconsidering its targets in a more sophisticated way.[11] The researchers surfaced two fascinating insights. The first they called the 20–55 rule: Of the actual top 20 percent of future customers, roughly 55 percent will be misclassified as poor or average customers and thus will not receive special treatment. This false negative rate was strikingly consistent across different models and data sets, ranging from 51 to 55 percent. They dubbed the other rule the 80–15 rule: Of the actual bottom 80 percent of future customers, roughly 15 percent will be misclassified and will receive special treatment.

Organizations need to be able to identify new sales prospects quickly, easily and at low cost. Sales bosses need to ensure that the sales force is selling the best products (i.e., highest margin) to the best customers (i.e., most likely to buy). Every commercial organization on the planet today needs a base business analytics capability that assists in identifying new sales opportunities at existing customer accounts as well as non-customer ("whitespace") companies. The days of seat-of-the-pants, wing-and-a-prayer sales force management are over. Business analytics enables you—actually almost forces you to reinvent your organization's sales process.

Sales force productivity is a big issue in good economic times and bad. Analytics-based solutions can make significant contributions. These analytic solutions emerge from rigorously defined data models that often integrate all relevant data into a common database. Choices of the data to be included in data models are driven both by end-user requirements as well as the need for relevant inputs to analytical models. New Know analytics blends the best of human AND machine decision making. All businesses need to predict the probability of purchase behavior and estimate the realistic revenue opportunity. Analytic insights need to be delivered expeditiously to frontline decision makers—sales representatives and sales executives.

## Experiments, Mistakes and Questions

The next economy will belong to those who can make the best mistakes in the most appropriate (e.g., modeled and risk-adjusted) environment and learn the most important lessons from them. As we learned in Chapter 7, it has never been cheaper or easier to conduct business experiments. Microsoft could not enjoy the market share and margins it does without its strategic deployment of beta versions of software. A killer issue facing information technology professionals is that they are not allowed to make mistakes. Disciplines that are not allowed to make mistakes cannot grow. The expression is "trial and error," not "trial and success," because learning happens when we make mistakes.

Two vertical markets today competing fiercely on analytics are pharmaceuticals and oil and gas. Both industries historically have experienced failure rates (e.g., the percentage of time that a drug discovery does not pan out or the percentage of time they do not find oil) in the 10 to 50 percent range. These industries are using business analytics to help them fail better. That is to say, they want to fail faster, earlier, cheaper, and *smarter*.

Enlightenment thinkers understood that human reason is fallible. They understood that reason is more than just rational thought; it is also a process of trial and error, the ability to learn from past mistakes. The Enlightenment cannot be fully appreciated without a strong awareness of just how frail human reason is.[12]

Nicholas Taleb, author of the very provocative *Black Swan*, argues that the ability to ask what-if questions defines and sustains us. He quotes Daniel Dennett, the American philosopher who goes so far as to state that the ability to ask "what if" questions is an evolutionary advantage:

What is the most potent use of our brain? It is precisely the ability to project conjectures into the future and play the counterfactual game—"If I punch him in the nose, then he will punch me back right away, or worse, call his lawyer in New York." One of the advantages of doing so is that we can let our conjectures die in our stead. Used correctly and in place of more visceral reactions, the ability to project effectively frees us from immediate, first-order natural selection—as opposed to more primitive organisms that were vulnerable to death. In a way, projecting allows us to cheat evolution: it now takes place in our head, as a series of projections and counterfactual scenarios. . . . For Dennett, our brains are "anticipation machines"; for him the human mind and consciousness are emerging properties, those properties necessary for our accelerated development.[13]

## A New Kind of Leadership through Analytics

There appears to be a bit of a cultural disconnect between the type of leader the media celebrates and the type of leadership that works. John Kotter, a professor at the Harvard Business School, has studied the actions of people who run organizations for over 30 years. On page 1 of his book *John P. Kotter on What Leaders Really Do*, he informs readers that "most organizations today lack the leadership they need."[14]

As the world changes, so too must styles and modes of leadership. In the sales environment, in the past, senior management would hand down sales targets to sales management who would try to meet them by placing more feet on the street (i.e., hiring more salespeople) and hoping the increased biomass would save the day. In today's world, sales targets don't just happen—they are financially engineered with sophisticated analytics and collaboratively allocated to the sales force. Sales bosses use sophisticated analytics to target potential new high-performance new sales resources *and* collect data, perform analyses, engage processes, and redraw/recalibrate the boundaries of markets and increase a sales force's productivity.[15]

In thinking about New Know management decision making, I recall the classic tale of a hungry donkey torn between two haystacks of identical size at opposite sides of the barn. The donkey stands in the middle of the barn between the two haystacks, not knowing which to select. Hours go by, but it still can't make up its mind. Unable to decide, the donkey eventually dies of starvation. The French logician and philosopher Jean Buridan's commentaries on Aristotle's theory of action were the impetus of this story, known as Buridan's ass.

There are *consequences of not deciding* and implications accruing when we decide (i.e., move early with imperfect information or wait for better information). In the New Know, not only will leaders have to decide, leaders will have to decide when to decide and how to decide. Perhaps ironically, one of the fastest-growing areas in analytics is helping organizations decide when to make decisions. The message in the New Know is that there is more to think about.

The future is going to be messy. We may not have all the answers, but let us hope we have at least asked all the pertinent questions. In discussions about the future of analytically informed leadership, I inevitably bump into this question: "Do leaders start to look like cubicle monkeys?" Again there is this tragic misconception that "real leaders don't do math." This is changing. Analysts don't look like analysts anymore. At the 2009 INFORMs Conference on Operations Research Practice titled "Applying Science to the Art of Business," the analytics team from award-winning fast-fashion retailer Zara could easily have been mistaken for a rock-and-roll band or male models. Analysts and analytics are a lot different today. Analytics will be on the front lines.

George Washington's officers were under orders to "have a white paper in their hats to be distinguished by," a custom that endured in the United States from the banks of the Delaware to the coast of Normandy, where officers and noncoms had white stripes painted on the back of their helmets. It was a sign for the men to follow their leaders and a signal to the officers that they were to lead from the front.[16] The leaders at the front will be the most informed. The leaders who are informed are the ones people will follow.

In a complex world, the role of the leader is not to provide answers but to make sure the right questions are being asked. Austria's leading quantum physicist, Anton Zeilinger, points out that in his field, the question you ask determines the outcome of your experiment. Leif Edvinsson, the world's first professor of intellectual capital, is pioneering a new field, quizzics, which is the art of asking the right question, the right way.

## Analytical Infrastructure

After World War II, the U.S. government saw the building of highways, bridges, and dams as vital to national security and economic development. The results were spectacularly successful as measured by growth in postwar job creation, income levels, and gross domestic product.

We stand at a hinge of history. We need to rebuild our analytical infrastructure. Organizations are now slogging through that most awkward of in-between moments similar to when the stable was empty but not yet rebuilt into a garage.

In a letter dated November 17, 1944, President Franklin Delano Roosevelt requested that Dr. Vannevar Bush, director of the Office of Scientific Research and Development,[17] make recommendations regarding how the United States might best structure its public and private resources to take full advantage of the promise of science. Roosevelt was convinced that "[n]ew frontiers of the mind are before us, and if they are pioneered with the same vision, boldness, and drive with which we have waged this war we can create a fuller and more fruitful employment and a fuller and more fruitful life."[18]

Bush's report, *Science: The Endless Frontier*, was released publicly in 1945. It generated front-page headlines in the *New York Times* and is considered one of the most impactful policy documents ever issued. Bush essentially laid out a blueprint for a new era of science, specifying in broad brushstrokes what we wanted to know and the institutions whereby we might come to know what we wanted to know. Such ex ante institutional planning has not really happened in the business analytics world—yet. It is my hope that, after reading this book, you will be motivated to draft your own version of *Science: The Endless Frontier* that sets forth the blueprint for investments necessary to rebuild your organization's analytical infrastructure.

# Notes

1. "In 2011, the amount of digital information produced in the year should equal nearly 1,800 exabytes, or 10 times that produced in 2006," according to market research firm IDC. The rising costs to manage these increasing data volumes combined with new regulations and emerging data types are causing organizations to struggle with traditional approaches to information management. IDC white paper, *The Diverse and Exploding Digital Universe* (March 2008).

2. James Burke (author of *Connections*) in his introduction to Peter J. Denning, ed., *Talking Back to the Machine: Computers and Human Aspiration* (New York: Copernicus, 1997), xxiii.

3. IBM *2008 CEO Study, Enterprise of the Future* www.ibm.com/ibm/ideasfromibm/us/ceo/20080505/index.shtml

4. Gartner Business Intelligence Summit, Amsterdam, The Netherlands, February 5–7, 2008. Jeff Kelly, SearchDataManagement.com, March 10, 2009.

5. Robert Weisman, "Working to Strengths Is Survival Strategy: Narrow Focus May Help Firms Stay Agile," *Boston Globe*, December 7, 2008.

6. Published on KurzweilAI.net March 7, 2001 see: www.kurzweilai.net/articles/art0134.html?printable=1

7. Author notes from interview conducted at Future Forward meeting in Portsmouth, NH (October 2004). www.futureforward.com.

8. Jonah Lehrer, "The Next Decider: The Election Isn't Just a Referendum on Ideology. It's a Contest between Two Modes of Thinking," *Boston Globe*, October 5, 2008.

9. Alan Webber, Toronto Artscape conference [September 30, 2005].

10. http://singularity.org

11. Edward Malthouse and Robert Blattberg, "Can We Predict Customer Lifetime Value?" *Journal of Interactive Marketing* 19, no. 1 (2005): 2–16.

12. Lee Harris, *The Suicide of Reason: Radical Islam's Threat to the Enlightenment* (New York: Basic Books, 2008).

13. Nassim Nicholas Taleb, *The Black Swan: The Impact of the Highly Improbable* (New York: Random House, 2007), 189.

14. John P. Kotter, *John P. Kotter on What Leaders Really Do: A Harvard Business Review Book* (Boston: Harvard Business School Press, 1999).

15. D. Ledingham, M. Kovac, and H. Simon, "The New Science of Sales Force Productivity," *Harvard Business Review* (September 2006): 124–133.

16. David McCullough, *1776* (New York: Simon & Schuster, 2006).

17. This is the organization that coordinated the activities of some 6,000 leading American scientists in the application of science to warfare.

18. www.nsf.gov/about/history/nsf50/vbush1945_roosevelt_letter.jsp

# The New Know

## *A Few Afterwordish Thoughts*

### Alan Webber

When my dear friend and techno-mentor Thornton May called to ask me to write an afterword for his book, I immediately said yes. Over the last 20 years, I've learned that going where Thornton goes, reading what Thornton reads, listening to what Thornton says—in short, saying yes to Thornton's propositions—is a wise policy. By doing so, you will always meet fascinating people, encounter fresh thinking, explore new territory, discover important insights, and learn things you never even knew you were interested in. In other words, you will be introduced to the future—a place where Thornton dwells and the rest of us occasionally get to visit.

Knowing all this, I said a resounding yes to Thornton's question.

Then I retreated into asking Thornton a question: What is business analytics? Is it a new arena of management thinking that combines contemporary business theory with ancient Greek philosophy? An emerging field that crosses Peter Drucker and Plato, Jim Collins and Aristotle?

I honestly didn't know. As is usually the case with Thornton, I didn't know where he was taking me—I just knew that I would be glad to have made the trip.

If you have read this book, as I now have, you'll know that you and I were both right to trust our time and our minds to Thornton's care. The usual rules apply for time spent with Thornton: It's a cross between a meeting of the Mensa Club and the Comedy Club.

*What do we all need to learn? What do we bring back with us from this inspired and inspiring visit to the future?*

The world is changing. In many respects it already has changed. In most respects even the changes that we think we can see and understand we only dimly perceive and vaguely comprehend. And today's disruptions are prologue for what comes next. And then what comes after that. We are all discovering that the old rules of business—of work and of life—are often ill suited for the new challenges that we face today and the unimaginable developments we'll find in the future.

The world is changing, and while the requirements remain the same, the techniques, tactics, and tools are also changing. We're learning to cope with business moving at the speed of thought, work fueled by the power of knowledge.

We're learning to deal with information that is both instantaneous and permanent—at the same time.

We're learning to work with organizations that are unit-of-one size and global—at the same time.

We're learning to make decisions based on too much information and too little information—at the same time.

We're struggling to adapt to insatiable customer demands and unspoken customer desires—at the same time.

We're having to keep our existing operations running, growing, prospering and to change them deeply, restlessly, permanently—at the same time.

People are more important than ever and so is technology—at the same time.

Making money is essential and an inadequate scorecard—at the same time.

You have to be fast and agile at the same time that you are smart and cautious. You can't succeed by being all things to all people, and you can succeed only by knowing who you are in the first place.

You have to remember all this and leave time, room, energy, and curiosity to learn whatever and whenever the next big idea—or unending stream of small ideas—comes along next.

It turns out that this is what business analytics is all about—this and more.

It turns out that we are all like Neo at the end of the film *The Matrix*: Our eyes are finally open, allowing us to see the streams of data that comprise, define, compose, and create reality—and see reality as it is for the first time.

So the answer to the question, what is business analytics is this:

The work of business analytics is to understand change.

The work of business analytics is to understand the customer.

The work of business analytics is "choice architecture"—organizing context within which people can make better decisions.

The work of business analytics is the work of innovation—knowing where to look, what questions to ask, what the answers mean.

The work of business analytics is sensemaking—separating the signal from the noise, recognizing patterns that may be obscured by the trivia of transactions or buried in the morass of dailyness.

The work of business analytics is detecting weak signals—spotting trends before they arrive, sighting the future while still standing in the present.

The work of business analytics is to cut through complexity—recognizing that simplicity is the new currency.

The work of business analytics is to bridge the gap between the need to know/capacity to know, producing the kinds of useful, actionable information that allows organizations to focus on what matters and convert choice to action.

The work of business analytics is knowing when to decide and how to decide—to support, promote, and enable leadership that works.

That is the text of Thornton's excellent presentation—and it's a text that deserves attention and discussion and adoption.

But in addition to those points, Thornton's analysis has two key subtexts that need to be made explicit. First, while Thornton's book is all about the growing value and increasing importance of data, this is a book that is not about technology. It is about people. Technology by itself is never enough. It's always necessary and never sufficient. And so Thornton consistently comes back to the fundamental duality of work and success in a time of great change: People need technology, technology needs people. We're moving from an either/or past to a both/and future.

The second underlying insight about business analytics goes to the structure and operation of every organization, every business, every institution: We desperately need integrative thinking. If we're going to have any shot at creating a future that works, at solving pressing problems in business and in society, at generating new opportunities and more hopeful possibilities, we need to learn to link as we think.

Today problems are still pigeonholed in obsolete categories. Companies are still organized around functions that have little or no relationship to how work gets done—or what real customers experience. It's as if we are still trying to cram reality into the ranks and files of a checkerboard, oblivious to the fact that reality has exploded into an endless variety of shape-shifting dimensions. We talk endlessly about "thinking outside the box"—mindlessly ignoring the simple fact that the only box we're inside of is the one we create in our own minds.

To solve old problems, we need to create new connections. To imagine new possibilities, we need to work across—or erase—old boundaries. To meet our own potential, we have to embrace new ambiguities. To achieve real success, we have to be willing to let go of old and obsolete ways of thinking, working, and communicating. We need new capabilities, new skills, new rules. Most important, we need to combine what we know and what we can know in new hybrids, ways of working that run across the vertical and horizontal boundaries that are the vestigial remains of the age of railroads and the structure of the Prussian army.

What's exciting about the notion of business analytics is not the name—no, certainly not the name.

What's exciting about it is the idea, the capability, the message. It's the idea of seeing the world with fresh eyes; the capability of transforming how the organization gets its work done, how it makes decisions and nurtures innovation; and it's the message: We have met the future—and now it's up to us. There's real work to be done.

# Index